Mohawk Saint

Catherine Tekakwitha and the Jesuits

Allan Greer

OXFORD
UNIVERSITY PRESS

OXFORD
UNIVERSITY PRESS

Oxford University Press, Inc., publishes works that further
Oxford University's objective of excellence
in research, scholarship, and education.

Oxford   New York
Auckland   Cape Town   Dar es Salaam   Hong Kong   Karachi
Kuala Lumpur   Madrid   Melbourne   Mexico City   Nairobi
New Delhi   Shanghai   Taipei   Toronto

With offices in
Argentina   Austria   Brazil   Chile   Czech Republic   France   Greece
Guatemala   Hungary   Italy   Japan   Poland   Portugal   Singapore
South Korea   Switzerland   Thailand   Turkey   Ukraine   Vietnam

Published by Oxford University Press, Inc.
198 Madison Avenue, New York, New York 10016

www.oup.com

First issued as an Oxford University Press paperback, 2006

Oxford is a registered trademark of Oxford University Press

Library of Congress Cataloging-in-Publication Data
Greer, Allan.
Mohawk Saint : Catherine Tekakwitha and the Jesuits / Allan Greer.
p.   cm.
Includes bibliographical references and index.
ISBN-13 978-0-19-517487-8; 978-0-19-530934-8 (pbk.)

1. Tekakwitha, Kateri, 1656–1680.   2. Mohawk women—Biography.
3. Mohawk Indians—Religion.   4. Women saints—New York (State)—Biography.
5. Chauchetiáre, Claude, 1645–1709.   6. Jesuits—Missions—New York (State)—History.   I. Title.
E99.M8T4583 2005
282'.092—dc22   2003069774
[B]

Printed in the United States of America
on acid-free paper

To Brenda, with love

Preface

WHAT DREW ME TO THE "MOHAWK VIRGIN," CATHERINE TEKAKWITHA, WAS THE desire to learn more about the native experience of contact and colonization. Historians are well acquainted with the cataclysms that engulfed the Americas and their indigenous peoples following Columbus's voyages: the bloody conquests, the devastating epidemics, the advent of wonderful new tools and weapons that could lead to commercial dependence, the introduction of a strange religion, Christianity. But how did these vast, impersonal processes play out at the level of specific, individual lives? Surely generalizations about colonial war, disease, economic upheaval, and religious change can provide only an imperfect sense of what it was like to live through these unpredictable upheavals. I was hoping to gain a better understanding of the larger processes of colonization by taking as my subject not "Indians," not even "Iroquois" or "Mohawks," but a particular native person.

Until now, the history of Native Americans of the colonial period has been written largely in terms of faceless collectivities: "the Arawaks" greet Columbus on the shores of Hispaniola, the "Narragansetts" suffer defeat in Metacom's War, a faction of "the Mohawks" aligns itself with the French and accepts Catholicism, and so on. The names of a few native leaders such as Powhatan, Pontiac, and Moctezuma are familiar enough, but the flattened portraits that emerge from European source materials provide hardly a hint of how these individuals—much less the millions of Indians who were not recognized as leaders—thought and felt. And as is always the case in history, the evidence, such as it is, tends to focus on men and male concerns. Hence my interest in Catherine Tekakwitha, a Mohawk woman of the early colonial period whose short life happens to be more fully and richly documented than that of any other indigenous person of North or South America in the colonial period.

After she died in 1680, two French Jesuits became convinced that the young woman they had known merely as one of several pious converts was, in fact, and quite uniquely, a saint. First Claude Chauchetière, and then later his colleague Pierre Cholenec, felt called upon by God to bear witness to this extraordinary phenomenon. Each of them gathered information about her, and over the years, each drafted long texts recounting her life and enumerating her inspiring virtues; after decades of false starts and revisions, one of Cholenec's biographies was finally published in 1717. The finished product and the handwritten drafts, complete with all the shifting emphases, minor inconsistencies, and occasional contradictions that one would expect from two different observers structuring and reshaping fading memories, constitute a uniquely rich trove of source material. It opens the possibility of reconstructing an early colonial native life and of personalizing one of the great events of world history, the encounter of European and indigenous American cultures.

Though the sources on Tekakwitha are incomparable, they are certainly not transparent. The Jesuits were writing hagiography, not history. Their texts had a sacred quality; composing them was an act of devotion, and the truths they meant to communicate were religious truths about the triumph of life over death and about God's intervention in human affairs. Historical truth was a secondary consideration. Hagiographers tend to lift their subject up out of history in order to place her in a celestial realm along with other saints, but my job was to bring Tekakwitha down from heaven, resituating her in the historical context of colonial North America. Since it was apparent that little could be said confidently about Tekakwitha without a fairly thorough examination of the conventions and traditions of the ancient Christian genre of hagiography, I found myself in the unaccustomed role of literary critic, attempting to analyze, critique, and decode enigmatic texts. I suppose it was not an entirely novel assignment, since no historical source is ever truly innocent or transparent. Still, hagiography is a special case, and so I turned to the literature on "sacred biography" in classical times, when the cult of the saints first emerged, in the Middle Ages when hagiography flourished, and in the early modern period when the printing press and the advent of new scholarly techniques gave it a fresh lease on life. Even a brief survey of that field was enough to suggest that the Tekakwitha texts stood out as an intriguingly unusual colonial variant in the grand tradition of hagiography.[1]

While close-up history of this sort implies a willingness to grapple with tricky source materials, it also involves more than the usual attention to the historical and cultural context in which the documents were created and in which their subjects lived. Accordingly, my research also led me into the anthropological and ethnohistorical literature on the Mohawks and the other five Iroquois nations of the seventeenth century. In recent years, researchers have used missionary writings and archaeological excavations, interpreted in the light of anthropological theory, to enrich our understanding of the history of the Five Nations during that crucial century, and I have borrowed extensively from their work in order to develop a vantage point independent of that of the hagiographers, Chauchetière and Cholenec, and also to flesh out the portrait of Tekakwitha for modern readers. At the same time, I hope my detailed study of this one life will contribute to ongoing discussions of the Iroquois experience of colonization. Dependent upon the prior achievements of more broadly framed research, this microstudy of a single Iroquois is meant to complement, and occasionally to challenge, prevailing views of Iroquois history, particularly on the subject of conversion to Christianity.

The sources on Catherine Tekakwitha led me not only into the seventeenth-century world of the Mohawks (my original destination) and into the textual realm of hagiography (inevitably for anyone who works with saints' lives) but also into the Counter-Reformation France of Tekakwitha's Jesuit biographers. One of the two, Claude Chauchetière, was clearly the prime instigator in the movement to recognize the Iroquois woman as a saint. His complex and vivid personality bubbles forth from all his missionary writings, including those dedicated to Tekakwitha, and he left a substantial autobiographical text to boot. To a historian dependent upon the willingness of the dead-and-buried to confide their thoughts and feelings to paper, and to one who shared Chauchetière's fascination with native North America, the lure of this Jesuit was irresistible.[2] And so I found myself recounting the life of the European missionary alongside that of the North American native who became the central focus of his existence.

When historians consider the Christian missions to the Indian peoples of colonial America, they often proceed as though the missionaries were readily understandable. Catholic writers of an earlier generation portrayed them— and particularly the Jesuits—as heroic soldiers of Christ. Protestant or secular chroniclers traditionally took a somewhat different view: without approving of the content of the evangelists' message, they could still admire their efforts to bring civilization into the dark wilderness. Until the second half of the twentieth century, there was minimal interest in the native societies as anything more than a backdrop for an essentially European story. Historiographically, the situation changed dramatically in recent decades as researchers adopted a more critical attitude toward Jesuit writings about Indians and, combining these sources with archaeological and ethnographic evidence, developed a sympathetic portrait of the rich and vibrant native cultures that confronted missionaries in the seventeenth century.[3] As understanding of what were once disparaged as "pagan" ways grew, the concomitant tendency was to view the Jesuits and other Christian missionaries as a malevolent force.[4] From hero to antihero, the image of the Jesuit was turned upside down, but it was not fundamentally altered. As in the traditional pro-missionary account, the missionary still seemed to be the embodiment of Christian European civilization; he (and it) was a fully integrated subject, certain about his aims, and supremely confident in their ultimate triumph. And historians—with perhaps a guilty sense of connection to an ancestral version of invading Western civilization—seemed to think they understood the Jesuits.

My encounter with Claude Chauchetière led me to question all these assumptions. Looking closely at his childhood and education in France, his momentous decision to volunteer for overseas service in Canada, his difficult early years as a missionary, and his later career as the biographer and promoter of Catherine Tekakwitha, I was increasingly struck by what a strange and mysterious creature this man was. His motives were rarely obvious or even fully coherent; his sense of missionary purpose could be quite uncertain; his attitude toward Indians was variable and contradictory. The better I got to know Chauchetière, the less confident I felt about characterizing him, or the enterprise of which he formed a part, in any simple way. Phrases such as "the Jesuits tended to believe that . . ." and "Jesuit practice was to . . ." do appear in the pages that follow; these might be read, charitably, as shorthand for more complicated observations ("among the contending elements of Jesuit belief, the one that was most visible and prominent in the current context was . . ."), though I suppose they might also be taken as signs of the limits of my own ability to avoid simplification.

My point is that it is much harder than we usually care to admit for scholars of the twentieth and twenty-first century to understand either Iroquois or European people of the seventeenth century. When I refer to Claude Chauchetière as "strange and mysterious," my use of these terms merely registers the distance that separates the mentality of his milieu from my own secular, turn-of-the-millennium outlook. Such a symptom of "the shock of the old" suggests a need to approach missionaries with the kind of sympathetic ethnographic imagination that ethnohistorians try to bring to their studies of Native American cultures of the past. If historians need, in some measure, to make themselves into anthropologists to study the Indians of an earlier age, they must do something similar in examining the Europeans who contacted them.

From Tekakwitha to the manuscripts that recounted her story to the Jesuit who wrote these texts, my inquiries moved me in the direction of a dual biography. Accordingly, this book tells the story of two intersecting lives: a woman and a man coming from distant quarters of the globe who met in a bark-covered longhouse on the St. Lawrence. In organization, it is only partly biographical, however. From the particulars of Tekakwitha's and Claude's personal experiences, the book goes on to examine in broader terms some of the themes that emerge from the story of their encounter. Death, spiritual practices, the body, illness and healing, sexuality, and the boundaries of the self are the main subjects of the chapters that follow. In each case, I have tried to combine Iroquois and French perspectives. Though difference—the great cultural gulf separating natives and newcomers—will be readily apparent, convergent tendencies are just as notable. In spite of the missionary sources' tendency to exaggerate difference, natives and French had a good

deal of common, or at least commensurable, ground in their religious beliefs, medical practices, ceremonies, and customs.

Mine is hardly the first book devoted to Catherine Tekakwitha. Over the past
three centuries her biography has been recounted in at least three hundred
books, published in more than twenty languages.[5] Most of these, needless to
say, are Catholic devotional works based, sometimes quite loosely, on the
original accounts of Chauchetière and his Jesuit colleague, Pierre Cholenec.
Latterly, brief profiles of the Mohawk saint have appeared in scholarly works
of history, most notably in Nancy Shoemaker's frequently cited article, "Kateri
Tekakwitha's Tortuous Path to Sainthood."[6] The Shoemaker article remains
an excellent introduction to Tekakwitha's life narrative and its implications
for our understanding of native women's response to Christianity, but given
the limited scope of the author's research and her lack of access to the original French sources, it should not stand as the last word on the subject.[7]

Since the name "Kateri Tekakwitha" has come up, I should add a word about
my own title and my decision to refer to the central character as "Catherine
Tekakwitha." Iroquois people of the seventeenth century might have more than
one name in succession as they passed through the stages of life from infancy
to old age. There is no indication of what she was called as a young child, but
when Jesuits first met her during her teen years, she had a name they usually
rendered as "Tegakouita." It was hard for them to choose between k and g
because the Mohawk sound they wished to reproduce falls somewhere
between those two letters as pronounced in French (or English). When English speakers developed their written version of her name, they inserted the
letter w as a more efficient means of reproducing the sound that the French
rendered as "oui," and so we end up with "Tekakwitha" (still a very rough
approximation of the Mohawk, which sounds more like "Degagwitah,"
with the accent on the penultimate syllable).[8] Baptized at the age of nine-
teen in memory of Catherine of Siena, she became "Catherine" as well as
"Tekakwitha," and the hagiographic narratives that were published in the
two centuries following her death invariably referred to her as "Catherine
Tekakwitha" or "Catherine Tegakouita." "Catherine" pronounced in French,
but with a Mohawk accent, comes out as a sound that an English-speaking
listener might write as "Kateri," and that is exactly how that version of
the name entered the record a little more than a century ago. It first
appeared in a biography portraying Tekakwitha as a true "child of the forest" untouched by "civilization"; the white American writer, Ellen Walworth,
rechristened her heroine to give her a purer, more "authentically Indian"
identity (see epilogue). Since "Kateri Tekakwitha" was born in an atmosphere
of fin de siècle primitivism, I prefer to call her "Catherine."

Acknowledgments

HISTORIANS ALWAYS DEPEND ON THE HELP AND SUPPORT OF OTHERS—COLLEAGUES, students, archivists and librarians, funding agencies, friends, and family—but as I brought this book to completion, I was struck more forcefully than ever before by the truth of that commonplace observation. I welcome this opportunity to acknowledge, with heartfelt gratitude, some of the debts I incurred over the years of research and writing.

Let me begin by mentioning some especially helpful archivists: Robert Toupin, S.J., of the Archives de la société de Jésus, Canada français; Patricia Birkett of the National Archives of Canada; Johanne Lefebvre of the archives of the diocese of St. Jean-sur-Richelieu, Quebec; and Marie-Pierre Cariou, archivist of the city of Landernau, France. I benefited also from the assistance of the knowledgeable staffs of the Robarts Library, Toronto; the University Library, Cambridge; and the Newberry Library, Chicago. Financial assistance from the Social Sciences and Humanities Research Council of Canada, as well as a Connaught Fellowship from the University of Toronto, allowed me to travel abroad in pursuit of source materials. A succession of graduate student assistants played an invaluable role in tracking down additional documentation: Carolyn Podruchny, Giovanni Pizzorusso, Todd Webb, Nora Jaffary, Edwin Bezzina, Lynn Berry, Michelle Leung, and Gwen Rice.

In my efforts to gain a better understanding of Tekakwitha's achievements as a craft worker, I came to appreciate the expertise of ethnographers and museum curators specializing in native material culture. Ruth B. Phillips of the University of British Columbia Museum of Anthropology and Trudy Nicks of the Royal Ontario Museum helped me get my bearings in this (for me) unfamiliar field, while Carl Benn of the Toronto Historical Board instructed me on aspects of Iroquois costume. The artifact collections and curatorial knowledge I encountered in Europe were a revelation. Jonathan King of the North American Ethnology section of the British Museum and Laura Peers of the Pitt Rivers Museum, Oxford, were both of immeasurable assistance, as was Christian Feest, at the University of Frankfurt, who opened his files to me and patiently explained the mysteries of twining and false embroidery.

Among the experts in a variety of other fields who were kind enough to answer my questions, I would like to mention Dauril Alden, Marie-Aimée Cliche, Isabelle Cochelin, Alain Croix, Brian Deer, Denys Delâge, Carlos Fausto, Serge Gagnon, Gretchen Green, George Hamell, Paula Holmes, Asunción Lavrin, Ann Little, Antonio Rubial Garcia, Father James Powell, Dean Snow, Sister Eva Solomon, Matthieu Sossoyan, John Steckley, William Taylor, Laurier Turgeon, and Roy Wright. I am grateful to Evan Haefli for bringing the Joseph Kellogg manuscript to my attention, and to Anne Scheuerman, who provided the cover photograph.

Most of the book was written in the idyllic environment of Clare Hall, Cambridge, where I was fortunate enough to spend a year as a visiting fellow. I also benefited greatly from a stint at the Newberry Library, Chicago. Grateful as I am to these institutions, I cannot neglect to mention the stimulation and support I have received over the years from my colleagues at the University of Toronto, both in the Department of History and at University College.

Several people read the manuscript, in whole or in part, and gave me the benefit of their criticisms and suggestions. I would like to single out Catherine Desbarats, who gave the work a thorough and insightful reading. My thanks go also to Jodi Bilinkoff, Mark Philips, Mariana Valverde, and Michael Wayne. I have profited greatly from the intellectual companionship and encouragement of these friends, as well as that of Sean Hawkins, Ken Mills, and Natalie Davis. I wish also to acknowledge the assistance of Brian Deer, former director of the Kahnawake Cultural Centre, who kindly went over the manuscript and saved me from some potentially embarrassing errors. Of course, responsibility for the book remains mine.

I benefited from discussing my research on different occasions with audiences at York University, University of Toronto, McGill University, University of Virginia, St. Lawrence University, Université de Montréal, University of Alberta, the Shelby Cullom Davis Center for Historical Studies at Princeton University, the Forum on European Expansion and Global Interaction, Sixteenth Century Studies Conference, the British Association for Early American History, the Omohundro Institute for Early American History and Culture, and the Museo Roca, Buenos Aires.

I am immensely grateful for the encouragement and wise counsel I have received throughout the publishing process from Susan Ferber of Oxford University Press. Jennifer Kowing expertly guided the book through the production process.

Above all, I want to thank Brenda Gainer for inspiring and sustaining me.

Contents

Mohawk Saint

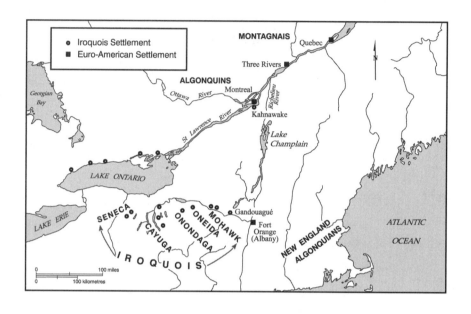

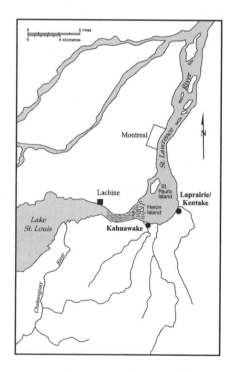

1

Beautiful

Death

HE CAME TO VISIT HER EVERY DAY, AS SHE LAY WAITING TO DIE.

It was the spring of 1680, during the Catholic season of Lent, and Catherine was scarcely able to rise from her mat on the floor of the bark-covered longhouse. Much of the time she was alone with her illness, lying close to a smoldering fire; at her side were a carved wooden dish with her day's supply of corn porridge and some water in a bark bowl. Only a handful of women, children, and old people remained in this Christian Iroquois village on the banks of the St. Lawrence, and during the day they were busy outdoors gathering firewood or preparing the ground for spring planting. Most of the men and many of the women were still many days' journey to the north or the west, at their hunting camps along the Ottawa and its tributaries. They would return for Easter, laden with beaver skins and other furs to discharge their debts with the French merchants of Montreal. Then there would be solemn church services and jubilant feasting, but now Kahnawake (or Sault St. Louis, as the French called it) was generally quiet.

Catherine, also known by her Mohawk name, Tekakwitha, was about twenty-four years old at the time of her death. She came from a village on the Mohawk River, at the eastern extremity of the Iroquois country in what is now New York State. A childhood bout of smallpox had left her frail and sickly, and her health had not been enhanced by the punishing habits of ascetic penance she acquired in her twenties. After accepting Christian baptism and then, in 1677, joining in the migration from her native land north to the Jesuit-sponsored mission settlement of Kahnawake/Sault St. Louis, she joined a group of Christian Iroquois women who renounced sex and marriage, while disciplining their bodies with fasting, flagellation, and deliberate exposure to the pain of fire and the discomfort of cold. Life tended to be precarious for all Indian people in this "contact period" of wars and epidemics; adding voluntary hardship to the mix only ensured that Catherine would become one of the multitude who died young. Beginning in February, she had been laid low by "a slow fever and a severe pain in the stomach, accompanied by frequent vomiting"; by early April, there seemed no hope of recovery.[1]

Her one regular visitor in the daytime was Father Claude Chauchetière. This thirty-four-year-old Jesuit from Poitiers had been in Canada for three years, and so he knew enough of her language to communicate with Catherine. Claude and Catherine had come to Kahnawake at about the same time and were hardly strangers, but until now they had not been well acquainted. Missionaries and native converts generally led separate lives at Kahnawake; moreover, Chauchetière had not baptized Catherine or served as her confessor; Pierre Cholenec, a Breton priest only slightly older and more experienced than Claude, claimed that honor. As the junior missionary at Kahnawake, Chauchetière was expected to visit the sick and dying Indians, encouraging them to stay true to their baptism at this critical stage, warning them not to turn in desperation to pagan "jugglers" (shamans), watching for the moment when they would have to be brought to the church for the last rites.

Claude's attentions to the sick woman were more than perfunctory. He felt drawn to her and came more often and stayed longer than he needed to. Catherine always seemed glad to see him, the priest later reported. Listening to his words or joining him in prayer, she never uttered a word of complaint about her condition. Sometimes he came trailing a band of children, and she would watch with interest as he showed them pictures he had drawn to illustrate scenes from the life of Jesus or depictions of the terrors of hell. Chauchetière's writings make it clear that these encounters were much more important to him, the ministering priest, than they were to her.

What was it about the young "sauvagesse" that fascinated him? It was nothing she said or did during these visits, for he never bothered to record her words, emphasizing instead the sighs and heartfelt looks that marked her silent prayers. Until recently, she had been an obscure and retiring member of the community, one of many Iroquois women devoted to extremes of prayer and penance. But shortly before Catherine's final illness, Father Cholenec had pronounced her "the most fervent" of all, and in a confidential letter to his superiors he reported that a mysterious light surrounded her when she flagellated herself.[2] French and Iroquois Christians were beginning to believe that the shy and homely Catherine possessed special spiritual powers, and Chauchetière found confirmation of this in the tranquil composure with which she faced pain and death.

Claude appears to have been drawn to Catherine's cabin by some inner need that made him susceptible to her aura of holiness. We tend to imagine the Jesuits of New France as determined men of integrated personalities and unshakable confidence in themselves and their divinely ordained mission, but Claude Chauchetière hardly corresponded to that description, least of all in the spring of 1680, when his self-confidence reached an all-time low. Since coming to Canada, fired with evangelizing idealism, he had experienced the greatest difficulty coming to terms with the realities of life as an Indian missionary. The passage of time only seemed to increase his trouble and anguish. For a year, he had been struggling with "a great inner affliction" that brought him to the edge of despair, but as Chauchetière came to understand things in retrospect, the encounter with Catherine transformed him completely.[3] Something in the dying woman's serenity began to affect the distracted and self-absorbed Jesuit, lifting him from the depths of gloomy doubt.

That was not the way it was supposed to be. He was the colonizer speaking to the colonized; it was man to woman, priest to layperson, educated to illiterate, healthy to sick, civilized to savage: every aspect of their encounter urged the Jesuit to see Catherine as his inferior. However exemplary her behavior since conversion, she remained what missionaries liked to call "a child in the faith," still dangerously close to nature and to the sin-drenched environment of the New World. When Jesuits of the seventeenth century held up the innocent and guileless Indian as a reproach to the sophisticated sinners of Europe, their rhetorical strategy depended on a generally shared assumption that Christianity was absolutely true, indigenous beliefs false. The ideals of urban life, civic order, and refined manners that had been valued in Europe since classical times were thought to apply universally to all humanity. These attitudes ran deep in Chauchetière's culture and in his mental makeup. His raison d'être as a missionary, not to mention that of the entire colonial enterprise of which he was a part, depended on a basic hierarchy: religiously and culturally, natives of the Americas needed the help, guidance, and leadership of Christians from Europe.

Eventually, Claude Chauchetière would come to see Catherine as his spiritual superior and view his encounter with her as a transformative moment, but as he sat in her longhouse, he would have appeared to a casual observer simply as one more Jesuit hovering at the side of an Indian sickbed, soon to be an Indian deathbed. A living Jesuit and a dying native: it was one instance among countless similar ones enacted in wigwams and longhouses across eastern North America in the seventeenth century.[4]

Death is a prominent theme in the history of the Jesuit mission to the Indians of New France. Leaders of the Society of Jesus originally conceived of the venture into North America as one bringing peace, happiness, and eternal life to the poor natives, yet missionary writings from Canada soon came to be suffused with a morbid sensibility. Of course, as good Christians, all Jesuits were trained in memento mori, the practice of meditating on the fragility and the short span of human life in order to counteract the natural tendency to be caught up in the trivial vanities of the world. But here in war-torn, disease-racked America, they faced death everywhere they turned, not just as an imaginative device for meditation but as a terrible corporeal reality: sick, wounded and dying Indians (the moribund Other they had come to save) confronted them at every turn, while stories of martyred Jesuits (reminders of the vulnerability of the bodily self) horrified and fascinated them. Epidemics and violent conflict, the common accompaniments of colonization, were never far away as the missionaries moved with the expanding French commercial and imperial penetration up the St. Lawrence and into the Great Lakes and the Mississippi. "No doubt we carried misery with us," Father Jérôme Lalemant admitted, "since, wherever we set foot, either death or disease followed us."[5]

Passing through once-thriving native villages suddenly transformed into sick wards and charnel houses, the missionaries were desperate to baptize the dying.[6] They sometimes tried to cure the ill, distributing sugar, raisins, and other medicinal substances, but their motives were frankly strategic, a matter of gaining the Indians' confidence and beating the devil-worshiping shamans at their own game. What really mattered was the harvest of souls. Every gravely ill Indian was, to a Jesuit, the prize in a contest with the highest possible stakes: either she would die outside the church and suffer eternal torment, or she would confess her sins, enter the fold, and live forever in perfect happiness. Because they knew from experience that healthy converts often strayed from the Christian path after they had been baptized, an outcome more deplorable than simple refusal of baptism, the Jesuits took special satisfaction in baptizing the moribund. Early in the history of the New France mission, Jean de Brébeuf spoke of feelings that would be echoed by other seventeenth-century Jesuits: "The joy that one feels when he has baptized an Indian who dies soon afterwards, and flies directly to Heaven to become an angel, certainly is a joy that surpasses anything that can be imagined. . . . One would like to have the suffering of ten thousand tempests that he might help save one soul, since Jesus Christ for one soul would have willingly shed all his precious blood."[7]

If dying adults were especially prized, dying infants were even more so, for unlike their pagan parents, they were too young to have sinned. "This is the most certain fruit that we gather in this country," wrote a Jesuit among the unconverted Iroquois, "where it is desirable that the children should die before obtaining the use of their reason."[8] Sick babies exercised an irresistible attraction over these missionaries, who sought them out wherever they went. However, the non-Christian parents of Tekakwitha's homeland were determined to keep them at bay. Unlike the Hurons, who were evangelized a generation earlier, the Iroquois did not necessarily believe that baptism caused death, but they did have the feeling that the missionaries wished to steal their children's souls. Perhaps they could sense something of the attitude of men who could write a sentence containing the chilling phrase "It is desirable that the children should die." From the Jesuit point of view, this parental resistance was a challenge to be overcome by stealth and ingenuity. Watching for the moment when an infant was left unattended, they sometimes managed a surreptitious christening. When the adults began mounting a round-the-clock guard to keep him at bay, Father Jean de Lamberville took to carrying a bit of wet sponge hidden up his sleeve. He sat with one anxious family through an entire day and evening waiting for his opportunity; then, when the adults were discussing the little boy's fever, trying to assess his prospects for recovery, the missionary darted out his hand to feel the patient's brow, muttering some incomprehensible Latin words under his breath as he did so. To explain the child's wet head, "I said, in retiring, that he suffered from a very burning fever, and that he was all in a sweat." Knowing the child was close to death and that his soul would soon be with Christ, Lamberville smiled inwardly at this hard-won victory.[9]

In reviewing the achievements of the Iroquois missions for 1679, the Relation of that year reported that "they have passed into heaven more than 200 souls of sick children and adults, all dying after baptism."[10] Of course the Jesuits were anxious to baptize healthy people, too, laying the foundations for a native Catholic society on earth, as well as populating heaven through direct deposit. But whenever we are tempted to regard these missionaries simply as agents of European cultural assimilation, we should remind ourselves that they tended to evaluate their success in very different terms.

The death of the Indian is one major theme of Jesuit writings from New France; the death of the missionary—actual, anticipated, feared, and desired—is another. Even before Father Isaac Jogues became the first Jesuit martyr when the Mohawks killed him in 1646, the *Jesuit Relations* were dwelling on the dangers of life in a war-torn land among, to them, "barbarous" peoples. Canada became known as a land of "crosses" where natives were resistant to the gospel message and where missionaries had to live with continual hardship and the ever-present danger of bloody, flaming, painful death. This was its attraction to the mystically inclined: an opportunity to renounce the self and participate in the suffering of Christ. Early in the history of the New France mission, in 1633, Father Paul Le Jeune made this comment when reporting on the murder of a Frenchman by an Algonquin: "This shows you how unsafe our lives are among these Barbarians; but we find therein exceeding consolation, which relieves us from all fear; it is that dying at the hands of these Barbarians, whose salvation we come to seek, is in some degree following the example of our good Master, who was put to death by those to whom he came to bring life."[11] Sometime before he was burned, tortured, and executed by the conquering Iroquois, Jean de Brébeuf meditated on death in his private journal: "I perceive in myself a great desire to die, that I may enjoy God; I turn with all my heart from all created things, which must be left behind at death; my heart is at rest in God alone."[12]

The historian Philippe Ariès has argued that European Christianity of this early modern period, in its Protestant as well as in its Catholic version, developed a new attitude toward death and dying. Whereas the Christian culture of the Middle Ages embraced life and the flesh, held death in horror, and concentrated on helping the dying prepare for the loss of life and all its pleasures, the new sensibility was characterized by the pervasive presence of death in life: "Death is now an intrinsic part of the fragile and empty existence of things, whereas in the Middle Ages death came from the outside."[13] Ariès purveys a somber view of this somber period, suggesting that religious writers feared life and bodily existence more than death and that their melancholy constantly threatened to take them over the precipice and into existential nothingness.[14] Certainly Jean de Brébeuf knew the temptation of despair of a sort that makes death seem a relief. Claude Chauchetière, too, experienced times of desolation when his life felt meaningless and alienated from God. Both Jesuits found a way out of their inner torment through death: in Chauchetière's case, the death of a Mohawk woman brought deliverance; for Brébeuf it was his own martyr's death.

Martyrdom staged a comeback in the sixteenth and seventeenth centuries as the struggle against Protestantism and the missionary thrust into Asia and America placed Catholics in situations where they might be killed by hostile unbelievers.[15] As a schoolboy at the Jesuit college of Poitiers, Claude had read and heard about the horrible/beautiful ends of Brébeuf and his four colleagues, put to death in the wars of the 1640s by Iroquois, still wholly unconverted at the time. Presumably, he would have echoed Marie de l'Incarnation's exclamation when news of Isaac Jogues's death reached her convent in Quebec City: "Oh, how sweet it is to die for Jesus Christ!"[16] To be a martyr was to be a saint. It meant joining the pantheon of heroes whose physical and spiritual strength had been equal to the cruel persecutions inflicted on the primitive church; it also meant reenacting the Passion of Christ, thereby participating in it. Jean de Brébeuf's long, hard, and frustrating career among the Hurons ended with every trace of futility erased for, in retrospect, the martyr's life was utterly meaningful.[17]

Tales of martyrdom and sainthood point up the reverse side of the Jesuits' death obsession, for missionary hagiography is filled with the promise of resurrection; focused on death, it also revolves around the imaginative denial of death. To write of the killing of a martyr was to illustrate the immortality of the soul, as well as the fragility of the flesh. And, of course, even the "ordinary" deaths of baptized native babies were seen as a prelude to eternal life. The French Jesuits concentrated on all these signs of ultimate triumph partly because their experience in New France produced such meager results in the real world. Catherine and her fellow converts at Kahnawake were the exception to the rule: so many Indians rejected Christianity or else accepted it only on death's door, that the number of native Christians remained fairly small through most of the seventeenth century. Certainly, the fruits of the Canadian mission seemed disappointing after the massive conversions that had accompanied earlier Jesuit missions to India, Brazil, and Paraguay.[18] Hence the apocalyptic tone that creeps into so many of the Jesuit *Relations* of the midcentury decades, as frustrated missionaries look forward to the ultimate victory of Catholic Christianity in a great North American conflagration.[19]

When old-world diseases such as smallpox raged through unprotected indigenous populations like flames through a dry forest, it must have seemed to the victims that the world was indeed coming to an end.[20] Smallpox was first communicated to the Mohawks by Dutch traders in 1634,[21] and the resulting scenes of carnage probably resembled this one reported from the upper Connecticut Valley, where the epidemic struck about the same time:

> Those Indeans . . . fell sick of the small poxe, and dyed most miserably; for a sorer disease cannot befall them. . . . They fall into a lamentable condition, as they lye on their hard matts, the poxe breaking and mattering, and running one into another, their skin cleaving (by reason therof) to the matts they lye on; when they turne them, a whole side will flea of at once, (as it were,) and they will be all of a gore blood, most fearfull to behold; and then being very sore, what with could [cold] and other distempers, they dye like rotten sheep. The condition of this people was so lamentable, and they fell downe so generally of this diseas, as they were (in the end) not able to help on[e] another; no, not to make a fire, nor to fetch a little water to drinke, nor any to burie the dead.[22]

Socially as well as immunologically unprepared for the viral onslaught, Mohawks and other native peoples were devastated by the primary and secondary effects of illness. Many died simply because there was no one healthy to take care of them. When so many were laid low, it became impossible to maintain supplies of food, water, and fuel, and many traditional healing practices such as the use of fasts and sweat lodges only served to spread the contagion faster.[23] It is estimated that at least half, and likely as much as three-quarters, of the Mohawk population perished in that one terrible visitation from smallpox; and more epidemics were on the way—none quite as devastating as that initial blow, but many of them severe by any other standard. In addition to deadly outbreaks of measles and influenza, the Five

Nations were hit once again by a serious smallpox epidemic in 1661–63; this one carried off about a thousand people, Tekakwitha's mother among them. "The smallpox, which is the Americans' plague, has wrought sad havoc in their villages and has carried off many men, besides great numbers of women and children; and, as a result, their villages are nearly deserted, and their fields only half tilled," reported the *Jesuit Relations* for 1662–63.[24] Western Iroquois villages that had escaped the 1634 epidemic were badly affected, but so too were the Mohawks, the children of the survivors of the first on-slaught facing another bout of the dreaded virus.

The Iroquois culture in which Tekakwitha grew up was, in its own way, as obsessed with death as that of early modern Europe, but whereas Euro-pean Christians worried particularly about the death of the self, the oblit-eration of the subject's life, and the impending judgment that would decide his eternal fate, the Iroquois were more concerned about the effects of death on the bereaved survivors. Jesuits marveled at the composure with which Iroquois and other natives faced death. The old and sick, for all their love of life and their willingness to do whatever they could to regain their health, would accept their own mortality when hope of recovery was gone. If a man felt his time had come, "He first announces his approaching death to his relatives, has his friends assemble and feasts them as his farewell to them; he himself furnishes them reasons for consolation in the impending loss. With the same composure as a man preparing for a little voyage, he has himself washed, greased, painted and packed up alive in the position which he is to assume in his tomb."[25] Claude Chauchetière praised the Catholic converts of Kahnawake for their Christian resignation at the point of death, interpreting their tranquillity as a sign they were predestined for heaven,[26] but their seemingly pious behavior was really no different from that of any "pagan" Iroquois.

Unlike the Hurons, the Mohawks did not assemble the bodily remains of an entire nation in a great ossuary; however, they did celebrate a version of the Feast of the Dead at which all the recently deceased would be collec-tively honored. Iroquoian peoples seem to have had different beliefs about the fate of an individual human spirit after death, and outside observers such as the Jesuits struggled to describe these in the alien, Christian-influenced vocabulary of European languages. "Ghosts" lingered near corpses for a few days, according to one anthropologist; they sometimes appeared to people and frightened them, but they soon departed for good.[27] The missionary-ethnographer Joseph-François Lafitau notes that souls were thought to travel westward along the Milky Way until they reach "*Eskennanne*, or the Country of Ancestors," where they lived forever, beyond contact with living human-ity. Lafitau suggests that each person actually has two "souls," one of which stays with the material remains until the Feast of the Dead.[28] Iroquoian peoples lamented the passing of loved ones all the more bitterly in that they recognized as a sad reality something the Catholic missionaries could never accept: once the dead are gone, they are gone completely and forever.

While the Iroquois expected the dying to display self-control, their expectations for grief-stricken survivors were just the opposite. They believed that the death of a spouse or a parent or a local leader could unleash a torrent of grief so overwhelming that, if not properly dealt with, it was capable of driving people insane. The Iroquois saw health and welfare as dependent on moderation and balance; grief over the loss of another upset that balance, threatening literally to unhinge the mourner.

They told stories of a bereaved father, Hiawatha, an Onondaga headman who lived in the distant past at a time of turmoil and strife before the Mohawk, Oneida, Onondaga, Cayuga, and Seneca nations joined together in the Great Peace of the Iroquois League.[29] He had seven daughters whom he loved dearly, but they all died, one by one, victims of the spells of a sorcerer employed by a hostile political faction within his village. The effects on this normally self-restrained man were dramatic: "The grief of Hayonwhatha was terrible. He threw himself about as if tortured and yielding to the pain. No one came near him so awful was his sorrow. Nothing would console him and his mind was shadowed with the thoughts of his heavy sorrow."[30] Because no one at Onondaga comforted him, he wandered away from his home, aimlessly traveling through the forest. One day, he came upon a lake where thousands of ducks floated on the water. He shot some with his bow before the rest of the birds took flight, carrying the lake off with them and leaving dry land for Hiawatha to walk on. Traversing the lake bed, he noticed small shells, some black, some white, and an impulse told him to gather up the shells and carry them in a leather pouch. That evening, he arranged the shells on strings and hung the strings on a pole, sensing that somehow they held the key to his eventual recovery. "Men boast what they would do in extremity but they do not do what they say. If I should see anyone in deep grief I would remove these shell strings from the pole and console them. The strings would become words and lift away the darkness with which they are covered. Moreover what I say I would surely do."[31]

Long wandering eventually brought Hiawatha to the land of the Flint People (Mohawks). Nearing a village, he decided to camp in an abandoned hut beside a cornfield. In an encounter at the edge of the woods, the Mohawks invited him to accept their hospitality, and so he came, still heedless and distracted, to live once more in a human community. In the same Mohawk village dwelt Deganawidah, a mysterious figure whose message of peace had until then fallen on deaf ears. Since the two had always been fated to meet, Deganawidah instantly recognized Hiawatha and knew just what his "younger brother" needed. "Dwell here with me," he said. "I will represent your sorrow to the people here dwelling." Taking some of Hiawatha's threaded shells and adding more of his own making, Deganawidah formed four bundles with a total of thirteen strings of wampum. Then he took them up, one by one, and used each string to guide his speeches of consolation as Hiawatha sat opposite him, gradually shedding the burden of grief that had oppressed him so severely. When he had finished, Deganawidah handed him the bundles of wampum so that they could be used ever after to neutralize anger and grief in the interests of establishing peace through the land. "In the future they shall be used in this way: They shall be held in the hand to remind the speaker of each part of his address, and as each part is finished a string shall be given to the bereaved chief (Royaneh) on the other side of the fire. Then shall the Royaneh hand them back one by one as he addresses a reply; it then can be said, 'I have now become even with you.'"[32]

With Hiawatha's grief now purged, he and Deganawidah set off on their joint mission to tame the wild sorcerer Tadadaho and to bring together the Senecas, Cayugas, Oneidas, Mohawks, and Onondagas in a great league of peace. Their epic formed the founding myth of the Confederacy of the Five Nations, a constitution in the form of a story. Through the centuries, a ceremony of condolence recalling the primal encounter of the two heroes and featuring soothing speeches prompted by patterned wampum strings formed the central ritual affirming and maintaining Iroquois unity. When the Iroquois negotiated peace treaties with former enemies, they usually phrased their overtures in the language of mourning and condolence. Thus it can be said that their strategies for coping with what in our terms might be considered the "personal" distress of bereavement structured Iroquoian approaches to social life, politics, and even diplomacy.[33]

When Tekakwitha's parents died, there would have been wailing and lamentation, women relatives particularly acting out their grief by cutting their hair, throwing themselves on the ground, lacerating their skin, and rolling in ashes and dirt. Her whole clan, probably the Turtle clan of the Mohawks, would have been cast down with sorrow, together with the Bear clan who formed, along with the Turtles, one moiety of Mohawk society. It would have been up to the people of the Wolf clan—an entire moiety to themselves among the Mohawks—to act the part of the "clear-minded ones," taking responsibility for organizing the condolence ritual and pronouncing the healing words that would bring the others back to normality. Quite possibly, the epidemic then raging through Iroquoia nullified these ceremonies, but the cultural ideal called for an encounter in the longhouse, with the two moieties facing one another across a hearth, a speaker on one side using wampum to prompt the speeches of condolence needed to soothe the grief of the other side.

Iroquois mourning practices were a reflection of Iroquois conceptions of the human subject. Whereas Claude Chauchetière came from a culture where death was construed as an individual drama, albeit one that concerned a person defined to a significant degree by relations with others, the Iroquois tended to draw wider boundaries around the human self. For example, when Tekakwitha's mother died in the mid-1660s, many others were personally injured. Her death would have been felt as an amputation to her immediate family and to the Turtle clan as a whole; less directly and therefore less painfully, it represented a loss to the village of Gandaouagué, to the Mohawk nation, and to the Iroquois League. Tekakwitha no doubt suffered the greatest pain in being deprived of a mother's love and support, but hundreds of other men, women, and children would have felt implicated in this weakening of the strength of the Turtles. A name, an identity, a vital element in a larger human and spiritual entity was missing, and it left a gaping hole until such time as a living replacement was found, the lost personage "requickened," and the completeness of the clan restored. Perhaps a girl of the Turtle clan, one who was lucky enough to have survived the epidemic of the early 1660s, had reached puberty about the right time, gone into seclusion with other girls of her age, and experienced the sort of dreams that marked the passage into adult status. If so, she might have taken on aspects of the dead woman's identity. But what if no one was available, or what if—an all too common situation, surely, at this time of soaring mortality—there was only a handful of teenage initiates to replace hundreds of deceased Iroquois? Then the only solution to the gnawing sense of loss lay in war and the integration of enemy captives into the diminished clan.

Aggressive impulses, born of bereavement but deflected outside the village and the league, together with an imperative need to secure human replacements to maintain the spiritual strength of lineages, gave rise to what Daniel Richter calls the "Mourning War Complex."[34] Though men did the fighting, it was often women who instigated the campaigns. Women formed the nucleus of any Iroquoian clan, and because it was they who felt any reduction of the clan's strength most directly, they tended to be the ones urging warriors to mount expeditions. Revenge was one motive for war, for every loss in battle called out for blood vengeance against the nation responsible, but Iroquois warfare was also a response to bereavement more generally, including that occasioned by death through disease. Thus, according to Richter, neighboring peoples bore the brunt of Iroquois grief, transformed into violent rage. Capturing alien people was the object of every campaign, a successful military expedition being one that avoided casualties and brought live captives back to the village. Frightened, brutalized prisoners would then be ritually adopted into clans that were still mourning the loss of members who had never been replaced. Some captives were then really integrated into the society, taking on the name and resuscitating the social identity of a deceased Iroquois (this is exactly how Tekakwitha's mother, born an Algonquin, had become Mohawk), while others were put

to death amid terrible tortures. Either way, concretely or symbolically, the
dead had been replaced, the clan had recovered its strength, and the passions
provoked by grief had been calmed.

The tragic Mohawk history of illness and death was written all over Catherine's
face for Claude Chauchetière to study as he maintained his vigil. Her pock-
marked skin and squinting eyes told of the awful smallpox years of the 1660s,
when she took ill at about the age of six. She survived the disease but never
fully recovered her health, and for the rest of her life she remained weak in
body, impaired in vision, and disfigured by scars. Though smallpox tends
to hit children more severely than adults, in her family it was the parents
who succumbed: her mother definitely died in the epidemic, and her father may have as well (he is scarcely mentioned in the accounts of her life).
Europeans would have called her an "orphan," but the sentimental connotations of that term would be misleading in an Iroquois setting where lines
of kinship and dependence were less narrowly focused and where biological fathers were less important than maternal uncles. Even so, the girl must
have been deeply injured, emotionally as well as physically, by the sudden
shock delivered to her small world, while all around her, Iroquois society
felt the trauma of successive upheavals.

Not that Claude Chauchetière's youth had been protected from the pain
of bereavement. His mother had passed away when he was nine, and at
age sixteen he lost his father.[35] This was in 1662, just about the time of
Tekakwitha's illness and bereavement, and a time of famine and disease
through most of France. It was a classic "subsistence crisis" of the ancien
régime, where harvest failure and food shortage led to malnutrition, population movement, and the spread of deadly diseases through the weakened
bodies of economic refugees.[36] The spreading wave of destitution and hunger
at the beginning of Louis XIV's reign brought hordes of famished peasants
flooding into cities such as Chauchetière's hometown, Poitiers. In the month
of February alone, twelve hundred rural refugees streamed through the city
gates. Though efforts were made to keep out newcomers and to relieve the
hunger of the homeless beggars crowding Poitiers's lanes and squares, sani-
tary conditions inevitably collapsed and unnamed fevers spread through the
squalid encampments, then lapped over into the fashionable residences
occupied by the likes of the lawyer Jehan Chauchetière.[37] The list of casualties therefore included a handful of the rich as well as hordes of the poor.

Many years later, at the age of fifty, Claude Chauchetière recalled his feelings at the time of his father's death in a long letter to his brother. The letter
told the story of his life; it was a confession or spiritual autobiography of
the sort that religious people of the time often wrote as testimony to the

workings of Providence in their own lives. Whereas his biography of Catherine, true to Iroquoian patterns of kinship, focuses on her mother's death and neglects her father, his account of his own childhood centers on his father's death, making no mention of his mother. This should in no sense be taken to indicate that his mother meant nothing to him; he may well have felt her loss deeply, even if her death did not strike him in retrospect as a crucial element in God's plan for him. Jehan's death, on the other hand, appeared to be fraught with significance, partly, perhaps, because it left the boy entirely parentless, partly because it occurred at a decisive moment in his educational and professional development; but surely it loomed large also because of the prime role his society bestowed upon fathers as the pinnacle of domestic authority, the custodians of family fortunes, the progenitors of life itself.

The mature Claude recalled vividly the feelings of the adolescent Claude, the sense of loss and abandonment on finding himself an orphan. This being a spiritual document, he also remembered the religious conversion that bereavement provoked:

> It was an hour after my father had given us his blessing and then died.
> I threw myself on my bed, devastated to find myself an orphan, but I
> said to God, "I put myself in your hands, do with me as you please."
> I experienced a marvelous interior transformation, the first of many
> that would follow. My acceptance into the company [i.e., the Jesuits]
> is one result of this blessing that God poured over me at that time.[38]

Devotion to his father, submission to the will of God, and a vocation to enter the Society of Jesus are all rolled up together in this one short passage. The first in a series of personal and religious crises that punctuate Claude's account of his life, the one initiated by Jehan Chauchetière's death constitutes one of the turning points—the death of Catherine forms another—in the personal narrative he constructed out of half a century of experience.

In spite of what was said earlier about the general tendency for European Christian culture of the period to focus on the death of the self, Claude Chauchetière's autobiography reminds us that the French, like the Iroquois, also experienced death collectively, with ritual practices of mourning involving the family and the wider public. Jehan Chauchetière was fortunate enough to have died in circumstances that allowed him to bestow his blessing, hours before he expired, on the three sons gathered round his bedside. Presumably he confessed his sins and received the last rites at about that time, and so left the world in the prescribed manner, amid ceremonies implicating the church as well as his nearest kin. His son would then have acted out his grief, both publicly in mourning attire and a curtailed social life, and privately as described in the letter to his brother (though this distinction is somewhat misleading, since his "private" feelings were inseparably

connected to his religious conversion and his decision to become a Jesuit).
In form, Jehan's had been a "good death" that, as Claude came to interpret
events, had played its part in the providential scheme of his own existence.

Catholic France in the early modern centuries was much taken with the
image of the good death. Attention focused also on elaborate deathbed
scenes, overblown versions of the good death, depicted in paintings and
publications that featured a prominent and exemplary figure, such as a
monarch, a bishop, or a saint, expiring in the midst of crowds of tearful
retainers, his eyes raised to heaven, a look of pious resignation on his coun-
tenance. The setting was normally one of Baroque splendor, the mood both
sentimental and spectacular. This was "beautiful death," an idealized image
of an event that was at once intensely personal and, because it centered on
an eminent personage, dramatically public.[39] Though the edifying deaths
of humble individuals of exceptional piety were occasionally celebrated, it
was unheard of for a "beautiful death" scene to be written with an American "savage" in the central role. Yet that was just what Claude Chauchetière
was about to do.

Holy Week came late in 1680, and so it was mid-April when the hunting
parties, counting off the days on the notched sticks they carried with them,
returned to Kahnawake in preparation for Easter.[40] Catherine sunk lower
and lower, and when it appeared that she would not last more than a few
hours, fellow villagers gathered around her, together with a few French
settlers who had been drawn by the young woman's reputation for holiness. Chauchetière was joined by Pierre Cholenec, who took charge at the
end, administering the last rites and later delivering the eulogy. The two
Jesuits each penned eyewitness accounts of the death scene, and, in spite of
a common tendency to emphasize their own clerical ministrations, each
provides ample indications that this was primarily an Indian affair.

During the last two days, her "dear companion" Marie-Thérèse Tegaiaguenta, the young Oneida widow who had shared her devotions and penances, was almost constantly at Catherine's side. Another, younger, woman
also visited the cabin after having gone to the woods to do penance and
pray for Catherine's salvation. Catherine seemed to have some mysterious
special knowledge of this visitor's secrets. She had words of advice and
encouragement for each of the women, some of which the Jesuits managed
to overhear: "Take courage, despise the words of those who have no faith";[41]
"Be assured that you are pleasing in the sight of God and that I shall help
you when I am with Him";[42] "Never give up mortification."[43] On the afternoon of Thursday, April 17, she died at last in the arms of Marie-Thérèse.
"Catherine's face was turned toward heaven. Her companion embraced her

with one hand, supporting her neck with the other, and listening with attention to the last words of the dying Catherine." Chauchetière heard her say, "I will love you in heaven," and then, with scarcely a murmur, "she died as if she were falling asleep."[44]

Soon after, people noticed a transformation in her appearance. Father Cholenec was amazed: "This face, so marked and swarthy, suddenly changed about a quarter of an hour after her death, and became in a moment so beautiful and so white that I observed it immediately (for I was praying beside her) and cried out. . . . I admit openly that the first thought that came to me was that Catherine at that moment might have entered into heaven, reflecting in her chaste body a small ray of the glory of which her soul had taken possession."[45] Chauchetière said nothing of whiteness in his account of this incident, but he did insist that the Tekakwitha's face "appeared more beautiful than it had been when living."[46] With this momentous death, both Jesuits implied, God had removed the marks of disease, suffering, and racial inferiority, transforming the Mohawk woman into a radiant corpse exuding a saintly aura.

Indians and missionaries had a hand in marking this as an extraordinary death, and it is impossible to tell, on the basis of the Jesuit writings, whether the impulse to venerate Catherine came from one quarter more than from the other. Once they were sure that she was no longer alive, the Iroquois present began "to regard her body as a precious relic," kissing her hands and treating all her personal possessions as sacred objects. Several people kept watch through the night; the next day, Good Friday, mourning began in earnest.

At the mission chapel, Pierre Cholenec tried to preach a sermon on the Passion of Christ, but he was stopped repeatedly by eruptions of lamentation. As he noted, "I think that never was seen so piteous a spectacle, or rather, one so devout and touching, for suddenly everyone began to burst forth with such loud cries and sobs that it was necessary to let them weep for quite a long time." He naturally interpreted the behavior of his native listeners in Christian terms, but there was something very Iroquoian about the reaction to Tekakwitha's death. "That same day," Cholenec continues, "and for eight days running, such excessive penances were performed in the settlement that it would be difficult for greater to be done by the most austere penitents in the world."[47] Was this Christian penance performed in remembrance of the Crucifixion of Jesus and the death of a local ascetic, or was it traditional Iroquoian grieving practice, or was it some combination of the two? And what brought the period of self-abasement to an end when eight days had elapsed? The Jesuit says nothing on that score, leaving open the distinct possibility that a Mohawk condolence ceremony—not a church matter and therefore something the missionary would have passed over in discreet silence if he indeed was aware of it—intervened to calm the mourners' grief and bring their outburst to a conclusion.

The French had a different way of honoring the departed. A Canadian settler who came to pay his respects was moved to contribute a pine coffin so that Tekakwitha could be buried in the European fashion. But where would her body be interred? On this point, a dispute broke out between the two resident Jesuits. "After her death Father Chauchetière did all he could to persuade me to have her buried in the church," wrote Cholenec, "but to avoid such an unusual thing, I had a grave made in the cemetery." Burial in any church was an honor reserved to the elites of Catholic Europe; to accord such a distinction to a "mere Indian" would indeed be "unusual." But the enthusiastic Claude Chauchetière was already beginning to believe that he had witnessed the death of a saint. Cholenec, more conventional in his general attitude toward natives, was generally more cautious, well aware that what looked like signs of divine favor could just as easily be tricks of the Devil. In time, however, he would come round to the view that Catherine was one of God's chosen. Meanwhile, it would be up to Claude to confirm his own intuition, convince his Jesuit colleagues, and then proclaim to the world that a savage woman of the Mohawk nation was in fact a saint.

During her last months on earth, a feeling had been abroad at Kahnawake that Catherine was specially blessed, but only now that she was dead could the missionary begin to think of her as a saint. For Catholics, saints were the dead who had triumphed over death. Since entering the Christian tradition in the late fourth century, the cult of the saints had taken on a number of attributes. Long before the rise of the papacy and the institution of canonization, believers began venerating fallen religious heroes—martyrs originally, but later bishops, hermits and other exemplary figures—whose tombs became holy shrines and whose bodily remains were treasured. The saint was the living Christian's friend in heaven, a reassuring human visage to the "towering order of the universe," and an intercessor who could help secure favors from an otherwise remote God. However, at the core of the Catholic cult of saints was an "imaginative dialectic" in which death was simultaneously confronted and denied.[48]

How could Claude verify his sense that Catherine was one of the select few who had never truly died, even though their bodies had perished? Certainty would only come after the passage of years, but his faith was sustained initially by a series of mysterious visitations in which Catherine appeared to him and to others. Significantly, the first visions came to the two Iroquois women who had been closest to Tekakwitha: the clan mother Anastasia Tegonhatsiongo, her mentor; and her beloved companion, Marie-Thérèse Tegaiaguenta. Late one night shortly after the death, when she was still in deep mourning and passing sleepless nights lamenting the loss of her "daughter," old Anastasia looked up to see Tekakwitha herself kneeling at the foot of her sleeping mat and holding a wooden cross that shone like the sun. Around the same time, Marie-Thérèse was awakened before dawn one morning by someone knocking on the outside of the longhouse wall, next to where she lay. "Are you asleep?" asked a familiar voice. "I've come to say good-bye; I'm on my way to heaven." She rose and went outside to investigate; there was nothing to see, but she could hear a distant voice calling, "Adieu, adieu, go tell the father that I'm going to heaven."[49] There was a friendly quality to these visitations, though Anastasia and Marie-Thérèse both admitted they found their spectral encounters frightening. Significantly, they occurred right after the death, which would accord with Iroquoian traditions about the souls of the dead lingering near their bodies for a few days.[50]

Not long after that, it was Chauchetière's turn to receive a visitation. Catherine had been dead six days by that time, and he was praying for guidance at her grave, as he had been doing on a regular basis since the funeral. On this first occasion he saw her not in a familiar and personal setting but in a vision of Baroque splendor; for two hours he gazed upon her "surrounded in glory with a majestic bearing, her face lifted toward heaven as if in ecstasy."[51] Whereas the two native women had been visited by a friend taking her leave, Claude saw a mystic saint already removed from the social setting of her life and lodged in heaven.

In the months that followed, Claude experienced more apparitions. Some transmitted cryptic instructions, as when Catherine appeared to him as a rising sun and he heard a voice intoning words from the Book of Exodus: "Inspice et fac secundum exemplar" (Examine and make from it a copy). Obediently, he painted an oil portrait of Catherine—the one that still hangs in the church at Kahnawake—showing her with a crucifix in her hand, as she had appeared to Anastasia, with the mission chapel in the background.[52]

Some of Chauchetière's visions of Catherine were accompanied by what seemed to be prophetic images, as when he saw "a church turned on its side." When lightning struck an oak tree close by the chapel four months after her death, he wondered whether the event had somehow been foreshadowed by the mysterious image. Three years later, the chapel was actually destroyed by a violent tornado. Just to make this foretold disaster all the more meaningful, it happened that Claude and two other Jesuits were inside the building when the tornado struck; all escaped from the rubble unscathed. Comparing notes, they discovered that each of them had prayed to Tekakwitha earlier in the day.[53]

Signs of this sort were just what Claude was looking for to confirm his impressions about Catherine. He began recording these wondrous occurrences in a little notebook, "in order to keep an accurate record and to determine what came from God and what did not,"[54] along with biographical data on Catherine's life gleaned from interviews with Anastasia, Marie-Thérèse, and Pierre Cholenec. Clearly he was making an effort to subject his desire to believe to the discipline of reason and evidence. As he began to

Claude Chauchetière, oil portrait of Catherine Tekakwitha. Chauchetière drew
many portraits of Tekakwitha, but this is the only one that survives. Her costume, combining European and Iroquois elements, corresponds to textual
descriptions. The setting, however, bears no real resemblance to Kahnawake.
Catherine seems to float over a pastoral landscape with a large church as its most
prominent feature. Unlike the images that proliferated in later centuries, pictures
which invariably place Tekakwitha in a woodland setting, Chauchetière presents
his subject as a saint rather than a creature of nature. Photograph courtesy of
Anne M. Sheuerman.

Claude Chauchetière, *Thunder Strikes Next to the Chapel*. A pen-and-ink drawing, one of Chauchetière's illustrations for his manuscript history of the Sault St. Louis mission. In August 1680, lightning struck an oak tree standing beside the mission chapel, but the building was unscathed. Chauchetière was inclined to attribute this happy outcome to the protection of the recently deceased Tekakwitha. The missionary-artist himself must be one of the frightened figures in the foreground, but which one? © Archives départementales de la Gironde, H Jésuites.

assemble these fragmentary materials on the life, death, and postmortem miracles of a holy woman, his career as hagiographer had been launched. The "little notebook" was hardly a *vita sanctorum*, but even so Claude tended to treat this initial assemblage of rough notes almost as if it were a sacred object. He would leave it tucked between the pages of a great volume of the *Lives of the Saints*, and when visitors happened to pick it up and leaf through its pages, he sometimes reacted as though this casual manifestation of interest were divinely ordained.[55]

It was an intimidating step, moving from the role of witness to an exemplary death to that of hagiographer. Not that he needed to worry about the propriety of writing in the hagiographic mode about a religious heroine who had never been recognized by church authorities, much less canonized. "Sacred biographies" of uncanonized saints proliferated in Catholic Europe at the time, and the countryside teemed with local cults revolving around holy figures who filled essentially saintly functions.[56] Indeed, this broad and uncontrolled culture of saintliness was a precondition of the church's authorized cult of saints, for it alone could generate new candidates for canonization and provide the evidence of miracles required by the Vatican. Only with canonization could altars be dedicated to a saint, and only then could she enter into the church's calendar of required celebrations. But unofficial figures could still be venerated and prayed to, and as long as they were not directly called "saints," their life stories could be narrated as though they were saints. What made Father Chauchetière hesitate to dedicate a hagiography to Catherine Tekakwitha was not her uncanonized status; it was the fact that she was an Indian.

While Claude Chauchetière was preparing his sacred biography, Pierre Cholenec was also writing about Catherine's life and death, but in a different vein. In the aftermath of her funeral, he wrote confidentially to the Jesuit superior in Quebec enumerating her virtues and describing the wonderful effects they were continuing to produce among the Christian Iroquois.[57] But Cholenec seemed still to regard Catherine as a "pious savage," her profile corresponding to that of many exemplary converts mentioned in the missionary annals of North and South America. The *Jesuit Relations* for 1667–68 contains a typical pious Indian story under the title "Precious and Admirable Death of a Savage Girl 14 Years Old" and tells of a child who had taken a vow of perpetual chastity. Her piety was rewarded with visions of the Virgin Mary; occasionally, she could even catch the scent of paradise wafting on the night air. She died young, and, in a classic sign of saintliness, her corpse was found to be intact when the tomb was opened nine months later.[58] Though they contained hagiographic elements, these stories of native piety remained sketchy and incomplete—in this case the "savage girl" was not even named—unlike a fully developed saint's life. No one preserved relics, no one organized a healing cult, and no one wrote a full-scale sacred biography. That may be because, in all the American fields of Catholic evangelizing, Indians tended to be regarded primarily as the *objects* of apostolic attention: thus there was a tendency for their spiritual achievements to be credited, so to speak, to the missionary's account. In missionary writings, the pious Indian usually appeared as an actor in someone else's drama.

A colonial version of Christian hagiography had emerged by the seventeenth century in the lands colonized by the Catholic empires of Spain, Portugal, and France, but until Chauchetière's time, colonial hagiography consisted almost entirely of stories of *European* religious heroism acted out in an overseas environment portrayed as essentially hostile to Christianity. Jean de Brébeuf and the other martyrs of New France, Mexico, and Paraguay, killed by Indians thought to be actuated by hatred of the faith, were the subject of numerous hagiographic texts; others told of the courage of missionary nuns who exiled themselves from the security of Europe in a dangerous and forbidding land.[59] Indians are never absent from these inspiring narratives of the New World. Whether kneeling to accept baptism, thrusting firebrands at the suffering body of the martyr, or accepting the healing ministrations of the hospital nun, the native plays a crucial role in every drama of colonial saintliness. It is a supporting role, however, and not an accidentally secondary one; rather, Indians are cast as enabling figures because of basic features of the narrative logic of colonial hagiography. Thus a "pious savage" story belonged to a different genre than a "colonial saint" story, and the central figures of each would have resided in separate regions of Pierre Cholenec's mental universe.

Claude Chauchetière's impulse to proclaim Catherine as a saint, to bury her in the church and publish her remarkable life story, ran up against Cholenec's sense of ontological propriety. The two Jesuits seem to have been in general agreement that God had singled Catherine out in some way, but the younger man's tendency to treat her as a candidate for sainthood seemed to Cholenec a category mistake: "savages" and "saints" belonged to different contexts, and Cholenec had difficulty bringing the two concepts together. Claude soon discovered that other Jesuits, including the superior of the New France missions, were no more encouraging than his colleague. He seemed to feel the combined wisdom of his religious order, not to mention the weight of his entire culture, bearing down against his convictions about Catherine and reinforcing his own inner uncertainties. Sometimes he wondered whether the visions and apparent prophecies were tricks of the Devil,[60] and he asked God to give him clearer proof that he was right about her.

That confirmation, the miraculous cures that would provide Chauchetière with the reassurance he sought, as well as the process by which he molded the raw data of Catherine's life story into a religiously meaningful hagiographic text, will be examined later. For now, suffice it to say that he did complete a biography sometime between 1685 and 1695. After coming

Grégoire Huret, *Blessed Deaths of Several Fathers of the Society of Jesus*. This frequently reproduced and widely circulated engraving was published as an illustration in François Du Creux's *The History of Canada or New France* (1664). It brings together, in a single scene, the martyrdoms of six Jesuits and two lay servants. The most prominent figures are Isaac Jogues, kneeling in the bottom left, and Jean de Brébeuf, standing at the torture stake on the right. An Algonquin Catholic convert, Joseph Onahare, is barely visible in the top right. The Jesuits were visibly unsure whether or not to include a "savage" in this tableau of spiritual heroes; they simply erased this marginal figure in later versions of the picture. Photograph courtesy University of Toronto.

round to the idea that Catherine merited a full sacred biography, Pierre Cholenec followed suit with his own version of the life about 1696; a later, revised version by Cholenec finally appeared in print in 1717. In addition to these three successive hagiographies, there were several other fragmentary texts by one or the other of the two Jesuits who knew her best.[61] Together, these writings constitute an unparalleled body of source material, a double window looking into the Iroquois Christian world of Catherine Tekakwitha, their central subject, but also, when viewed from a different vantage point, into the world of the French Jesuits who penned them.

→ 2 ←

Gandaouagué:
A Mohawk
Childhood

On a bluff overlooking the Mohawk River in northern New York stood a collection of longhouses enclosed in a protective palisade—the village of Gandaouagué—and it was here that Tekakwitha was born in or about the year 1656. To that place her Algonquin-born mother had been dragged, bewildered and in mortal terror, by a Mohawk war party that had captured her near Three Rivers, midway between Montreal and Quebec on the St. Lawrence. Her mother is not named in the Jesuit accounts, nor are the time and exact circumstances of her capture known, but Chauchetière and Cholenec both insist that she was a devout, baptized Catholic.

The Mohawks and the Algonquins had been enemies for as long as anyone could remember, and from about 1640, their conflict seemed to intensify. The Mohawks were very much in the ascendancy, thanks partly to the firearms they procured from the Dutch traders at Fort Orange (Albany); driven on, through this time of upheaval and deadly epidemics, by the imperatives of the Mourning War complex, they pressed their advantage against the Algonquins and their Montagnais and French allies. Except during the brief periods of truce, raiding parties set off for the north, hoping to encounter a band hunting and fishing along one of the rivers that ran down to the St. Lawrence from the northern interior of what is now the province of Quebec. To read in the pages of the *Jesuit Relations* of the harrowing fate that awaited victims of these raids is to understand why they inspired mortal terror. Two Algonquin women escaped from Mohawk captivity in 1642, and the ordeal they later recounted to a Jesuit father was probably similar, in its broad outlines, to what Tekakwitha's mother went through a few years later.

Camped by a northern stream, the Algonquins had felt secure from attack, but the Mohawks managed to track them down and secretly surrounded their encampment in the night.

> Those tigers entered their cabin, arms in hand, and seized them, some by the hair and others about the body. Some, wakened by the noise, tried to mount a defense, but they were quickly slaughtered. The battle was soon over as the Iroquois found everyone paralyzed either with sleep or with fear. They bound them with strong cords, men, women and children, and within an hour, they were masters of their lives, their meager fortunes and their cabins.

The Mohawks conducted the captives to their own country, killing those who could not keep up with the forced march. Three women were carrying small babies, which slowed them down, and so the captors tore the infants from their grasp, roasted them over an open fire, and ate the cooked flesh before the eyes of the mothers. On reaching their destination at one of the Mohawk towns, the remaining prisoners were beaten and slashed by the people assembled there; some fingers were hacked off. They were tied to scaffolds and burned, "with torches and firebrands." Women and children took a leading part in the torture: "The smallest among them applied these [firebrands] to the soles of the feet of the unfortunates, through openings in the scaffold, while the others applied them to their thighs and sides." Many were killed amid even more severe tortures, but others were eventually spared. "I learn that they killed only the men and the more aged women, sparing about thirty of the younger ones in order that they might dwell in their country, and marry as if they had been born there."[1]

The women who told this story to the Jesuits would not have understood all the rituals surrounding their ordeal, but other sources suggest that all the captives, including those who were killed, would have been adopted into a Mohawk clan. Torturers would have addressed them as "uncle" or "sister" as they wielded the firebrand in a ceremony that vented grief as it reinforced a depleted population and replenished the spiritual strength of Mohawk lineages through the incorporation of living members and dying enemy warriors.

One can only begin to imagine what this experience would have been like for Tekakwitha's mother: the sense of utter powerlessness and complete vulnerability as she watched those closest to her injured, humiliated, and killed; her own physical pain and the anguish of knowing she might die at any minute. Once the determination was made that the Algonquin woman would be integrated into a Mohawk clan, however, the demeanor of her tormentors would have changed abruptly, and she would be cared for with the greatest kindness. At that stage, most captives would be pathetically grateful and desperately anxious to fit in and please their new kinsfolk. This cruel system of assimilating outsiders did not work perfectly in every case (two Algonquin women did escape in 1642), but it proved a highly effective mechanism for breaking down and reconfiguring personal identities in the interests of bolstering the Iroquois population.[2]

And so it was that, through war, brutality, and loving-kindness, Tekakwitha's mother became a Mohawk. At some point she married a Mohawk man and by so doing confirmed and solidified her new status. Thousands of others of diverse origin—Algonquin, Montagnais, Mahican, French, Sokoki, Abenaki—shared her fate. This influx of newcomers, combined with the mortality effects of wars and epidemics, had produced a massive turnover in the Mohawk population by the time Tekakwitha came into the world. With death and forced adoptions continuing through the second half of the seventeenth century, assimilated former enemies probably outnumbered "old-stock Iroquois." (Of course the term "old-stock," redolent of European fetishes about bloodlines, has limited meaning in an Iroquois context where personal identities were not so strictly determined by biological descent.)

The mixing of peoples through war, migration, fusion, and fission was by no means unprecedented in native North America, though it seems to have proceeded at an accelerated pace in the colonial period, particularly at the edges of European empire. In the Southeast, the Creek and Cherokee nations arose as conquering coalitions that absorbed the remnants of shattered tribes, while the Five Nations played a similar role in the Northeast.[3] A bellicose response to the opportunities and challenges presented by rapidly shifting conditions gave the Iroquois a regional ascendancy and kept them from melting away under the heat of infectious disease and imperialist pressure. Though their population declined somewhat from the peaks of the early seventeenth century, the influx of captives worked to reinforce the human and spiritual webs of kinship and to stave off demographic collapse.

Ideally, there was no real distinction between native-born Mohawks and war adoptees, once the latter had proved themselves. Former enemies frequently rose to positions of leadership in seventeenth-century Iroquois society. Yet assimilation could never be total, especially when the proportion of newcomers rose as high as it did in the middle decades of the century. Inevitably, tension and conflict developed within these multiethnic communities, dissension that sometimes deepened beyond the ability of consensus-oriented Iroquois politics to contain it. Schisms then ensued, with whole portions of a village or a nation splitting off and migrating to a new location.[4]

Of all the villages across the Iroquois lands, Tekakwitha's was probably the most ethnically diverse. The Mohawks were the easternmost of the Five

Nations, and she was born in the farthest east of the three Mohawk settlements. It was, by virtue of its location, the most exposed to attack from
enemies in New England and Canada, and it was also the first stopping place
for Mohawk war parties returning with prisoners. Quite likely, the majority of adults she knew as a girl would have arrived the same way her mother
had, as captives torn from a distant land.

When Tekakwitha was two or three years old, the entire settlement moved
three kilometers westward to a new site where the soil was fertile and ample
supplies of wood were close at hand.[5] Though solidly anchored in a given
region, Iroquoian villages generally relocated after ten to twenty years at a
given spot. Dwindling supplies of fuel and declining crop yields, the inevitable result of intensive cultivation, signaled the need to select a new site
somewhere in the vicinity. After the village council had made its decision,
men would begin the work of opening up a clearing in the forest and constructing dwelling places in its midst. Women would then visit the new
location to scrape up topsoil and form it into mounds; then they would plant
maize, squash, and beans in the rich earth of the hillocks. When all was in
readiness, the entire community would ferry their possessions to the new
village and settle in.

The new village was known as Gandaouagué, a name that Europeans rendered in various ways: "Caughnawaga," "Kaghnuwage," "Cahaniaga." The
name, or a version of it, stuck to the human community through a series of
subsequent relocations, and a cognate name, possibly a different version of
the same name, was applied to the breakaway Catholic village of Kahnawake
to which Tekakwitha and many of her fellow villagers would later move.
Gandaouagué occupied this particular location from 1659 to 1666, and it
was here that the smallpox epidemic struck in 1661—63, depriving the six-
year-old Tekakwitha of her health, her mother, her brother, and possibly
her father. The population by then was only a fraction of the two thousand
that archaeologists propose as the upper limit for an Iroquois village of the
period.[6]

Standing as it did at the eastern extremity of the Mohawk territory, Gan-
daouagué was something of a commercial, as well as a military, outpost.
Close at hand was the Dutch settlement of Fort Orange, taken over by the
English and renamed Albany in 1664. The biographies make mention of
Tekakwitha's uncle visiting Fort Orange as though it were a frequent occur-
rence. Iroquois traded furs to the Dutch and took away a variety of European products, as well as wampum beads that the traders had procured from
Indian manufacturers on Long Island. By various means, including the influx of war booty, goods of French and English origin also wound up at
Gandaouagué. Archaeologists working at the site unearthed many European
objects, including iron knives and axes, musket parts, glass beads, and rolled
copper, alongside bone, pottery, and other items of indigenous origin.[7]

Because most items made by seventeenth-century Mohawks were composed of materials, such as wood and leather, that would have decomposed over the years, archaeological research has a bias in favor of European products, and so we need to balance archaeological with historical evidence and remember that bows, moccasins, and bark vessels likely outnumbered guns, buckles, and copper pots.

Along with these useful objects, excavations at the original Gandaouagué site also unearthed charred palisade posts, reminders of the village's violent end in 1666. After years of offensive operations against enemies to the north, the tables had suddenly turned when the Algonquin-Montagnais-French alliance was reinforced with the arrival of a force of a thousand soldiers from France, and the Mohawks found themselves on the defensive. The other four Iroquois nations had already made peace by 1666 when a French army set out to invade the Mohawk homeland. Gandaouagué was the first settlement in their path, but they found it empty. Tekakwitha's people, forewarned of the attack and knowing they would be no match for their powerful adversaries, had taken refuge in the forest. The invaders looted the village, then burned it to the ground and destroyed all the crops in the fields. It was a setback, though not a terrible calamity—the Jesuits make no mention of the event in their biographies of Tekakwitha—and the villagers were able to rebuilt Gandaouagué at a new site on the opposite (north) bank of the Mohawk.[8] The eastern Mohawk village remained there from 1666 until 1693, long after Tekakwitha had moved away to the St. Lawrence.

A brief written description of this last incarnation of Gandaouagué survives from 1677, the year Tekakwitha left for Canada. An emissary sent by the British governor of New York to visit the Iroquois settlements reported, "Cahaniage [i.e., Gandaouagué] is double stockadoed round has four ports about four foott wide a piece, contayns about 24 houses, & is situate upon ye edge of an hill, about a bow shott from ye river side."[9] The presence of a reinforced palisade—it would have been constructed of tree trunks planted in the earth, side by side, to form two concentric circles—shows how concerned the inhabitants of Gandaouagué were about military security after being burned out by the French in 1667 and closely besieged by the New England Algonquians in 1669. The "houses" within this defensive perimeter would have been classic Iroquoian longhouses, made of bark over a timber frame.

Samuel de Champlain penned the classic description of the Iroquoian longhouse; he was talking about the buildings he observed among the Hurons early in the seventeenth century, but the Mohawks of Gandaouagué occupied essentially similar "cabins":

Their cabins are in the shape of tunnels or arbors, and are covered with the bark of trees. They are from twenty-five to thirty fathoms long,

more or less, and six wide, having a passage-way through the middle
from ten to twelve feet wide, which extends from one end to the other.
On the sides there is a kind of bench, four feet high, where they sleep
in summer, in order to avoid the annoyance of the fleas, of which there
were great numbers. In winter they sleep on the ground on mats near
the fire, so as to be warmer than they would be on the platform. They
lay up a stock of dry wood, with which they fill their cabins, to burn
in winter. At the extremity of the cabins there is a space, where they
preserve their Indian corn, which they put into great casks made of
the bark of trees and placed in the middle of their encampment. They
have pieces of wood suspended, on which they put their clothes, provisions, and other things, for fear of the mice, of which there are great
numbers. In one of these cabins there may be twelve fires, and twenty-
four families. It smokes excessively, from which it follows that many
receive serious injury to the eyes, so that they lose their sight towards
the close of life. There is no window nor any opening, except that in
the upper part of their cabins for the smoke to escape.[10]

Couples and their offspring ("families," in Champlain's terms) had their
own designated spaces to sleep within the building, but most aspects of
existence—notably eating, cooking, child rearing—were carried on in a
broader setting not limited to a single nuclear family. In some respects, the
fifty or so people (numbers varied greatly) inhabiting a longhouse might
be considered a "family," for it was occupied by women, together with their
husbands and children, who claimed a common ancestry through the female line.

Archaeologists have dug up even more artifacts of European and Euro-
American origin at this, Tekakwitha's third, village and the place where she
passed her teen years: gun parts, mouth harps, a French coin, bells, pewter
spoons, lead shot, iron awls, thimbles, and nails.[11] More and more, it would
seem (though the rather unsystematic excavations provide no certain indica-
tors), the people of Gandaouagué were procuring foreign tools and materials
and putting them to use. Even during Tekakwitha's eleven-year residence here,
exotic objects made of brass and iron were ceasing to be rarities as they, along
with imported fabrics, foods, and alcoholic beverages, worked their way into
the fiber of Mohawk life. And if they were consuming imported goods, the
Mohawks must have been reorienting their economy in order to pay for those
purchases. Mostly this meant trapping furs, procuring them from neighbors,
or capturing them in war. According to some historians, the drive to gain
control of salable furs even affected Iroquois war and diplomacy.[12] At the root
of these changes was the European presence on the shores of North America,
a presence that was growing rapidly and transforming the conditions of
existence for all the Iroquois peoples.

It is apparent that Tekakwitha grew up in an environment of flux and hybridity as Mohawk society, close to the edge of European empire, but not under its yoke, felt the powerful effects of colonization. The Mohawks were defeated by the French in 1666, but they were never conquered or subjugated. Were they nevertheless "assimilated"? When they took up guns, iron pots, and Christianity, did they, in some measure, cease to be Mohawk and start to become Europeanized?

In the past, historians might have tried to sum up the process of colonization in just these terms. Exposure to European technology and to the civilization of the newcomers more generally had the effect, it was suggested, of undermining or destroying "traditional Iroquois culture" while beginning the process of "assimilating" natives to European culture. More recently, however, we have come to realize just how misleading these terms and the assumptions that underlie them are. Native cultures were not fixed and timeless edifices, ready to crumble on first exposure to Europe's transatlantic thrust. Rather, they were historically evolving societies that had known centuries of change, not to mention periodic upheavals—the most significant one we know of in the case of the Iroquois being the adoption of agriculture around A.D. 1000—long before the time of Columbus. As in the past, Mohawks of the seventeenth century adopted products, ideas, and techniques from the outside world; they adopted human beings from neighboring nations, too; and the technology, like the people, was integrated into their society. Inevitably their culture changed in the process, but it was neither eradicated nor replaced by a foreign culture.

There is no denying the fact that the Mohawks of Tekakwitha's day lived through major crises and that their customs and outlook were profoundly affected by the colonial presence. But, then, Europeans in America were also transformed through contact with native societies. Our understanding of these processes is badly skewed if we think in terms of a zero-sum "contest of cultures," with Indian civilization falling victim to a triumphant Euro-American culture. The language of "layering" and "interpenetration" or, to borrow Natalie Davis's vocabulary, the "braiding" of cultures, better serves us. [13] With a renewed conceptual apparatus of this sort, we can hope to come to terms with the continuity of Mohawk and Iroquois culture through all the shocks and ruptures of the seventeenth and subsequent centuries and down to the present day.

As a child, the Jesuits relate, Catherine was shy, retiring, and good-natured. "A certain natural modesty, which is the guardian of chastity," led her to shun social gatherings. Because the smallpox had left her eyes sensitive to light, she wore a blanket over her head, partially obscuring her "ugly" face.

Furthermore, she was an "orphan" entrusted to the care of relatives who were indifferent to her welfare and happiness.[14]

The pathetic image of Catherine as a lonely, neglected orphan became a fundamental theme of twentieth-century iterations of her story, but Chauchetière's and Cholenec's original biographies were not sentimental in this way. Since hagiography is a catalog of virtues as much as it is a narrative of events, their aim was partly to highlight their subject's modesty, a particularly feminine attribute related, as Chauchetière states explicitly, to the prime virtue of chastity. But there was another reason to stress Catherine's isolation, one that will be discussed at greater length later: the Jesuits needed to demonstrate to European readers how an unbaptized girl living among "pagan savages" could possibly have the makings of a future Catholic saint. Chauchetière addresses this issue head-on in an early chapter: "She was a heaven, covered by the darkness of paganism, but a heaven indeed, because she was very far removed from the corruption of the savages. She was gentle, patient, chaste, innocent, and behaved like a well-bred French child."[15]

Was Tekakwitha really a lonely outcast? The idea seems implausible in light of the almost universal report of European observers to the effect that Iroquoian peoples cherished their children, and not just their direct genetic offspring: "The Indians are greatly attached to their children," wrote a French officer well acquainted with the Mohawks, "especially the girls, whom they regard as the principal support of their families."[16] Indeed, the Jesuits themselves give contradictory evidence on this point. Claude Chauchetière's brief account of Tekakwitha's childhood refers repeatedly, though vaguely, to "aunts" and "relatives" and "those who cared for her," revealing that the girl remained a dependent member of the longhouse into which she had been born. It is not clear what her precise relation might have been to these "aunts," for kinship terms resisted translation; her mother was a captive and thus not likely to have had any biological sisters at Gandaouagué, and any sisters of her father probably would not have lived in Tekakwitha's household. Presumably the girl was cared for by the women of her longhouse, all of them relatives (by adoption) of her mother, and all of them to be addressed in terms that Europeans might render as either "aunt" or "mother." What does seem clear, reading against the grain of the hagiography, is that the death of her "blood relations" (to use European vocabulary foreign to the Iroquois) left her still within the bosom of a larger family with dozens of women to feed her, teach her craft skills, tell her stories, and arrange marital matches for her. The members of this family, sheltering under the poles and bark of the longhouse, drew some of their sense of identity from that structure and from the collectivity that it symbolized.

Each Mohawk longhouse belonged to one of three clans—Turtle, Wolf, or Bear—and was thus connected, through extended lines of kinship, with other longhouses scattered through the Mohawk villages and, beyond that, across the lands of the Oneida, Onondaga, Cayuga, and Seneca. The Jesuits never say which clan Tekakwitha belonged to, leaving that crucial constituent of her identity a mystery, but the chances are good that she was a Turtle. Clans were fairly evenly distributed within a given village through most of the Five Nations, but Mohawk clans tended to cluster in a particular village, and in Gandaouagué the Turtles predominated. Clans were central to Mohawk society in a number of ways: through the rules of exogamy, they determined who an individual could marry; they provided the framework for the condolence ceremony, as well as for the adoption of captives and the installation of chiefs; they provided a sense of connection and solidarity joining people across the Five Nations. On the one hand, they seemed to divide Iroquois society; on the other hand, they functioned to bind it together more closely, for clan lineages ran across other social and geographic divisions, uniting longhouses scattered across the lands of the Five Nations under the emblem of the Wolf or the Bear or the Turtle. Moreover, within a given village or nation, the different clans came together in rituals such as the condolence ceremony to act out relations of reciprocity and mutual support. Whereas the political structures of the Five Nations were entrusted to men, clans were primarily associated with women, the central figures in all matters pertaining to kin and lineage. Nor were clans exclusively human institutions. Their animal emblems suggested affiliation to the creatures of nature and to the unseen world of spirits.

Even in the absence of concrete details on so many aspects of Tekakwitha's childhood, it does seem clear that she was not as isolated as the hagiographers imply. Her sense of herself could hardly have been separate from the complex web of relations that connected her with others. This motherless child was an integral member of her longhouse, and from that longhouse, lines of clan affiliation and political alliance radiated outward through the Mohawk nation and the Iroquois League, as well as through the sphere of animals and tutelary spirits. How could Tekakwitha have understood herself as a self-contained individual when her personal identity had been constituted in relation to others, as one node in an interconnected web?[17]

Tekakwitha may well have been a quiet and thoughtful child who loved solitude, just as the Jesuits claimed, but growing up in a Mohawk village she would not have had many opportunities to be alone. Depending on the time of day and the season of the year, the longhouse and the village precincts tended to be a place of dense human interaction. Children played together in noisy groups, the boys usually separating from the girls, and both pursuing a combination of organized sports and unstructured play. Among the Hurons, a people culturally similar to the Mohawks, the French missionary Gabriel Sagard was plagued by mischievous pranks, all the more infuriating because he knew he would never be allowed to strike a child in this Iroquoian setting. Though not a good sport, Sagard was a keen observer of Huron child's play, which clearly combined amusement with preparation for adult roles.

> Just as the little boys have their special training and teach one another to shoot with the bow as soon as they begin to walk, so also the little girls, whenever they begin to put one foot in front of the other, have a little stick put into their hands to train them and teach them early to pound corn, and when they are grown somewhat they also play various little games with their companions, and in the course of these small frolics they are trained quietly to perform trifling and petty household duties.[18]

Claude Chauchetière provides a fairly detailed account of Tekakwitha's apprenticeship in the duties and skills of a Mohawk woman. It corresponds roughly with Sagard's description, though the tone is rather more serious; the conventions of the hagiographic genre require Chauchetière to highlight his subject's virtues of industry and obedience rather than dwelling on any fun and companionship.

"Catherine's job was to help her mother [presumably one of the women of the longhouse] carry small loads of wood, to put fuel on the fire when her mother told her to, and to fetch water when the people in her cabin [i.e., longhouse] needed it."[19] At the different locations occupied by Gandaouagué, there were springs on the hillsides leading down to the river valley; like other children from the village, Tekakwitha would have only had to go a few hundred paces at the most to fill her square bark pail with fresh water for the longhouse. Gathering firewood was a more demanding occupation, one that kept Mohawk women, as well as their children, busy, especially during the spring months. Usually, they collected deadfalls and dry branches—relatively smokeless fuel ready for immediate use—from the stricken forest surrounding their cornfields. Here the men of the village had previously "girdled" the trees, killing them by cutting a deep notch all around the base.[20] After all the easily gathered material had been used up, women would chop limbs from the lifeless standing trees; this could be a hazardous procedure: in her twenties, Tekakwitha was once knocked unconscious when struck on the head by a branch of a falling tree.[21] Women trudging homeward, their backs bent under the weight of their bundles of fuel, were a common sight in the vicinity of an Iroquois settlement. When supplies of firewood within easy walking distance of the village were exhausted, it was time to think about relocating the community.[22]

While helping with basic fetching chores, young Tekakwitha was gradually acquiring fine handicrafts skills:

> People who knew her at a young age say that she was clever and skillful, especially with her hands, making everything that little Indian girls

make. To judge by the objects that I saw her make, I would say that she did very delicate work with porcupine quills and moose hair. She made the straps which the Indian women and girls use to carry wood. She also made the belts that the elders use in conducting the affairs of the nation; these are composed of beads. Another occupation of the Indian women is sewing, which they learned from captives living among them or from the wives of Christians from Europe. She also knew how to make a kind of ribbon that the Indians make from eel skin or from strong bark. She prepared these skins or barks and she made them red by applying the color with sturgeon glue which the Iroquois make very good use of. She knew even more than the [other] Iroquois girls, for she made excellent baskets and boxes, as well as the buckets that the Indians use to ladle water. With such skills she was never idle: sometimes she made a mortar for pounding corn, sometimes she prepared bark for weaving mats, sometimes she set up the poles on which corn was stored. This is to say nothing of her daily tasks sustaining the lives of others: grinding corn, making soup and Indian bread, filling the plates to feed all and sundry. And though she was infirm, she was always the first to work.[23]

This passage, based partly on Chauchetière's direct observation, partly on a procedure of reading back from the objects he knew Tekakwitha made to the childhood apprenticeship he did not witness, merits unpacking, for it constitutes an exceptionally full catalog of Iroquois women's work in this period.

Claude begins with decorative work he had definitely seen her busy with: "very delicate work with porcupine quills and moose hair." Decorations made with colored quills and moose hair were the pride of native women from almost all the nations of the northern forest, almost everywhere porcupines and moose were found and, thanks to trade, far beyond that range. Tekakwitha would have used these materials to embellish moose hide moccasins, as well as the long deerskin shirts Iroquois men and women commonly wore and the leather pouches they carried.[24] When working with porcupine quills, she would have to cut the ends off to form hollow tubes (minus the dangerous barbs). With vegetable dyes, charcoal, and earth, she could color them black, blue or, more likely, various shades of red and yellow, ready to form contrasting patterns. Flattening the tubes was a matter of holding one end in the teeth while running a thumbnail down the length of the shaft. Since the quills were attached by folding the two ends over parallel threads on the hide, she had to outline her pattern in sinew. Sketching the lines with a bone marker—perhaps a horseshoe motif on the instep of moccasins, or a square shape on a leather pouch—she would then punch a series of holes with an awl; next, stiffening her deer sinew with saliva, she could push the fiber through the holes and create a framework on which the looped-over quills would hang. No needle was required for this operation; in fact, no imported tools or materials were used in quillwork. With threads on the outer surface now describing the area to be decorated, Tekakwitha had to insert the two ends of each quill under adjacent sinews to create the finished pattern, covering the structural underpinnings in the process.

With colored moose hair, Tekakwitha learned to create patterns of tracery finer than what could be accomplished with porcupine quills. Bundles of hair went together in loops, which she then stitched to the hide with sinew threads. The loops and swirls, sometimes creating a floral pattern, contrasted with the thicker, more solid areas of quillwork. The latter had a ribbed texture that made it look almost like beadwork. Together, the quill and moose hair combination allowed Indian women to develop an infinite variety of styles to decorate clothes and other personal objects. Through long hours of practice, Tekakwitha emerged into adulthood as one of the masters of this quintessentially North American art.

"She made the straps which the Indian women and girls use to carry wood." The burden strap (Gus-ha'-ah) was in fact used for transporting all sorts of loads: fuel for the longhouse fires, but also supplies to be carried on long overland journeys; Chauchetière's drawing of early Iroquois visitors to Montreal shows just such a device in use (see p. 94). It consisted of a long strap, three or four inches wide at the middle, where it passed across the bearer's forehead, and tapering at the ends, where it was attached to the burden. With a burden strap distributing the weight over the back, head, and arms, a Mohawk woman could carry substantial loads. Fashioned from stout nettle stock or from the fibrous inner bark of the basswood, the Gus-ha'-ah was more than just a useful tool; decorated with quillwork and moose hair, it became a work of art, one which made a strong aesthetic impression on the famous nineteenth-century ethnologist Lewis Henry Morgan. "Of all their fabrics," he observed, "there is no one, perhaps, which surpasses the porcupine-quill burden-strap, in skill of manufacture, richness of material, or beauty of workmanship."[25]

Young Tekakwitha had to learn to prepare her bark or nettle fibers, then stretch the longest ones out in parallel lines. In the middle section, the wide part that would rest on her forehead, she bound these warp strings with weft fibers using a technique known as "twining."[26] A more laborious process than weaving, twining involves two weft threads that must be threaded individually, above and below the stationary warp fibers; between each warp thread, the two wefts are given a twist. We must visualize Tekakwitha, slowly threading and knotting her way along the nettle stock as a durable burden strap of the proper shape gradually emerged. Crafting a plain utilitarian object out of these materials would have been an impressive enough achievement,

Burden strap (*Gus-ha'-ah*), which usually was made from bark or nettle fiber and decorated with quillwork or colored moose hair. "She made the harnesses which the Indian women and girls use to carry wood." Lewis H. Morgan, *League of the Ho-de-no-sau-nee or Iroquois* (Rochester, N.Y.: Sage and Brother, 1851), 365. Reproduction courtesy University of Toronto Digital Studio.

but Tekakwitha's work was colorfully embellished. If she wished to decorate the *Gus-ha'-ah* with colored quills, she then had to slip them under and over the weft fibers on the outside surface of the strap, with the ends of the quills all carefully concealed so that an undulating, quill-sheathed surface was all that appeared to the eye. Moose hair decoration, the technique Tekakwitha most likely favored, was even more difficult to execute, since it required the weft strings to be decorated during the twining process itself. As she brought a string around to the front, she would wrap a coil of colored moose hair around it just where it would show on the front surface; then that fiber would pass to the back, where it was left unembellished, and its mate would come forward and receive its moose hair coating. This process, known technically as "false embroidery," produces a finely decorated surface on one side, with no trace of color or stitching on the other side.

"She also made the belts that the elders use in conducting the affairs of the nation." With this sentence, Chauchetière signals one of the ways that Tekakwitha's female sphere of craft work intersected with the world of politics and diplomacy, supposedly the exclusive preserve of men in Iroquois society. When leading men gave important speeches to conclude agreements, they would hold in their hand a strip of beadwork with white and dark beads forming patterns, sometimes featuring stylized human or animal figures. The pattern corresponded to the substance of the oration, and when the speaker had finished, he presented the belt to the opposite party. It functioned as a record of the proceedings, as a symbol of their significance, and as a gift of intrinsic value that cemented relations between human groups. Ever since Dekanawideh used strings of shell beads to soothe Hiawatha's grief, the presentation of beadwork, or "wampum," had also been central

to Iroquois condolence ceremonies. Indeed, ritual condolence, the mainte-
nance of political partnerships, and the establishment of diplomatic links
were all intimately connected aspects of the culture of the Five Nations in
the seventeenth century, and though the "elders" were the conspicuous
actors, they depended on the cooperation and skill of girls and women like
Tekakwitha to create the essential tools of politics and diplomacy.

Iroquois beadwork developed rapidly in the seventeenth century. Shell
materials had long been imported from the distant Atlantic coast through
indigenous trading systems, but the quantities were limited, and so ceremonial wampum usually took the form of single strings of variegated beads
along a deer sinew. But the advent of the Dutch, Europe's most active
entrepreneurs, revolutionized the wampum trade. During Tekakwitha's
mother's day, Dutch traders encouraged the Montauk of Long Island to
manufacture drilled shell fragments for sale; aided by metal tools, the latter
managed to increase their output enormously, with the result that the Dutch
were able to ship massive quantities to their Mohawk customers upriver.
Barrel-shaped pieces of whelk shell provided a white color, while similarly
shaped fragments of quahog shell gave a black or purple bead. Iroquois
women quickly responded to this newfound abundance, producing wider
and longer wampum belts with more elaborate configurations. This is one
of the many instances in which colonial trade, far from destroying indigenous arts and crafts, provoked a native renaissance.[27]

Wampum beads had a large enough caliber that they could be threaded
without the use of a needle. Traditional single-strand strings were fairly
simple to make by anyone with a hand steady enough to poke a deer sinew
through one bead after another, but the wide patterned belts that had become common by Tekakwitha's time demanded skill and patience. Most
likely, she employed a bow loom consisting of a bent stick that supplied
tension to six or seven, or as many as twenty, parallel strings of sinew, held
apart by perforated wooden or leather spacers at either end. The girl learned
to set up the warp on her loom so that it looked like a hunter's bow with
multiple strings, to run her weft sinew over one warp thread, through a
bead, under the next warp, and so on to the end of a row, then back again
through all the beads but crossing the warp under and over in the opposite
way. The white and dark beads, hundreds or even thousands of them, would
be fixed in place as the belt gradually emerged and the profoundly meaningful figures took shape.[28]

Even as the industrialization of shell bead production vastly expanded the
flow of wampum-making materials into the Mohawk villages, European
beads, mostly glass beads of all sizes, from tiny "grains" to large cat's-eyes,
and tinted with all sorts of colors, were also flooding the Iroquois country.
These gaudy imported products were not found acceptable for ceremonial
purposes, but Iroquois women did buy them for ordinary decoration.[29]

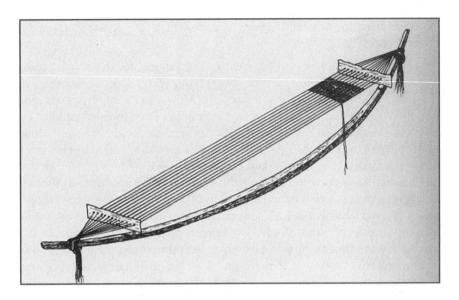

Bow loom used to weave wampum belts. William C. Orchard *The Technique of Porcupine-Quill Decoration among the North American Indians* (New York: Museum of the American Indian, 1916), 107. Reproduction courtesy University of Toronto Digital Studio.

Tekakwitha wore strings of glass beads in her hair, and no doubt—though Chauchetière makes no explicit reference to this—she used them to decorate clothing, as well as pipes, tomahawks, and other objects.

"Another occupation of the Indian women is sewing, which they learned from captives living among them or from the wives of Christians from Europe." In fact, Indian women sewed garments of buckskin long before they ever saw Europeans; Chauchetière might more accurately have stated that techniques changed greatly with contact, though imported cloth and steel needles were probably more important than Christian instruction. Tekakwitha's grandmothers would have fashioned long, loose-fitting skin shirts, joining the pieces together with sinew in much the same way as the western Canadian natives observed by an early nineteenth-century fur trader:

> In sewing leather, instead of thread, they make use of the sinews of animals. When this substance is some moistened, they separate a fiber, and by running their finger along between it and the main sinew, they part it to a sufficient length. The sinews of the caribou [or deer] may be made as fine and even, as fine thread. These fibers, when thus separated, they twist at one end between their fingers, which gives them a sharp stiff point, when they are dry. They use awls, which they

obtain from us, or an instrument of bone which they construct themselves, in sewing.[30]

Tekakwitha surely knew how to wield awl and sinew, for that sewing technique was still used in her lifetime for working with hides, for example, in
the manufacture of moccasins and shirts. But Mohawk clothing styles changed
rapidly over the brief span of years separating her Gandaouagué childhood,
when she seems to have worn mostly leather garments, and her young adulthood at Kahnawake, when woolen cloth was common and garments were
often sewn with steel needles and imported thread.

Chauchetière's drawings of the Kahnawake people show women dressed
in leggings with a cloth skirt and blouse; in cold weather they wrapped themselves in a wool blanket, which sometimes formed a hood. Tekakwitha usually kept her head under the hood to protect her sensitive eyes from the
sun. Men wore similar shirts and leggings, but they covered their lower body
with a breechclout. Many, though not all, of the materials were European,
but the cut and styles were still distinctively Iroquoian. So, too, were the
decorative touches: fringes, beadwork, and painted leather.[31] Mohawks of
the time were dressing differently than their ancestors not because native
people wanted to look like Europeans but because new materials and techniques were coming to America and expanding the range of design possibilities. Seated on her mat, bow loom at her side, wool broadcloth, needle,
and thread in her lap, Tekakwitha was perpetuating ancient Iroquois traditions even as she seized the opportunity to use Dutch or French goods to
make durable, attractive clothes.

"She also knew how to make a kind of ribbon that the Indians make from
eel skin or from strong bark. She prepared these skins or barks and she made
them red by applying the color with sturgeon glue which the Iroquois make
very good use of." The "ribbon" Chauchetière refers to here is a characteristic
Iroquoian hair adornment. More than simply a device to tie hair at one point,
it was arranged in a coil to encase the hair at the back of the neck. A later
Kahnawake missionary, Joseph-François Lafitau, describes the style in these
terms:

> Most of the women of the Indian tribes braid their hair and let it hang.
> The Iroquois and Huron women part it on both sides of the head and
> pull it all back or in as close as they can. They then gather up the hair
> that is hanging down and comb into it crushed bark of slippery elm
> which serves to hold it. After coiling it up so that it does not fall any
> farther down than the small of the back, they cover it with a prepared
> eel skin dipped in a very brilliant vermilion. Their beauty consists prin-
> cipally in this.[32]

The Mohawks caught eels in fish weirs built in the shallows of their river:
two lines of rocks piled up in a V shape with a narrow opening leading to

Huron woman pulverizing corn with implements similar to those used by all Iroquoian peoples of the time, including the Mohawks. "Sometimes she made a mortar for pounding corn . . ." H. P. Biggar, ed., *The Works of Samuel de Champlain*, 6 vols. (Toronto: Champlain Society, 1922–36), vol. 3, plate 6. Reproduction courtesy University of Toronto digital studio.

a basket-weave trap at the downriver apex. Since fishing was a favorite activity of elderly men who stayed in the village when other men were away on war or trade expeditions, Tekakwitha likely obtained her eel skins from some older man of the longhouse. She then painted the skins red, using either pulverized earth of the right hue or else the juice of certain plants. To make the coloring stick to the surface, she mixed it with a clear, viscous substance derived from sturgeon roe that had been mashed, strained, and turned into "glue."[33]

"She made excellent baskets and boxes, as well as the buckets that the Indians use to ladle water." Iroquois baskets were soft containers made not by weaving canes but by twining pliable roots or basswood bark fibers. Mohawks relied more on various-sized vessels constructed of solid bark to store their foods and carry water. From the inner bark of the red elm, Iroquois women formed large containers—Lafitau refers to "great casks, in tun shape, five to six feet high"—for storing charred corn, beans, dried fruit, and other staple foods. They also made small bowls or dippers by bending the wet bark and stitching it to a rim made of a green hickory splint bent into a circle.[34] When they could obtain birch bark, which was abundant along the St. Lawrence near Kahnawake, they found it much easier to work with. After her move to the north, Tekakwitha became adept at crafting birch bark into bowls, buckets, and boxes, stitching joints with spruce roots, and then sealing them with pitch if the vessel was to hold liquids. She may also have decorated them with patterns where she scraped off portions of the white outer bark to reveal a contrasting dark layer.[35]

"Sometimes she prepared bark for weaving mats." There were many mats in an Iroquois longhouse; people sat on them, slept on them, and, in winter, hung them at the entrance to keep out the cold. Sometimes they were woven from reeds or cornhusks, but Chauchetière saw Tekakwitha preparing bark fibers for this purpose. Another Kahnawake missionary described the process: "They strip from this bark [basswood] what is most delicate and nearest the thready body; they shred it into ribbons with their finger nails, ret and macerate these in the water as people used to do for hemp and linen."[36]

These crafts that Tekakwitha learned as a child growing up in Gandaouagué were skills that almost all Mohawk girls acquired at the time. Was she more proficient or more productive than the others—perhaps as a result of physical handicaps that sometimes prevented her from participating in other activities—or was Chauchetière simply drawing selective attention to pursuits that Europeans admired in women? "Industry," after all, was a religious virtue, and moralists of the time praised women, including upper-class ladies, whose hands were constantly busy producing useful and attractive objects. The Jesuit gives rather summary treatment to other duties the girl became accustomed to, duties that in a home like the one Claude grew up in would have been left to female servants. The growing, storage, and preparation of food loomed large in the life of any Mohawk woman, especially at certain seasons of the year, and Tekakwitha surely devoted at least as much time to helping to ensure that the people of the longhouse were all well fed and that fuel was always on hand for the fires as she did manufacturing clothes and boxes. Yet Chauchetière mentions this only in a brief passage: "her daily tasks sustaining the lives of others: grinding corn, making soup and Indian bread, filling the plates to feed all and sundry."

Corn (maize) was the central element of the Iroquois diet and the most important of the "Three Sisters," the trinity of corn, beans, and squash. Different varieties of corn were grown and they could be prepared in various ways. Sometimes the kernels were charred and then pulverized with a large mortar and pestle. If young Tekakwitha really made a mortar, as Chauchetière suggests she did, she may have had help, as this was a hard, tedious job. In the standing stump of an oak log, a deep depression had to be hollowed out by alternately burning and scraping the hard wood. The pestle was carved from a longer piece until it took the form of an elongated dumbbell. One of the girl's daily tasks was then to place charred corn in the depression and pound it into meal with blows from the pestle. The meal might be used to bake unleavened bread, but more commonly, Tekakwitha would boil it to make a thick soup or porridge, sometimes flavored with some meat or herbs. The French referred to this dish by its Algonquin name, *sagamité*. Compared with her foremothers, who had to boil their water in wood or pottery vessels by dropping in heated rocks from the fireplace, Tekakwitha had a relatively easy task cooking with imported copper or iron pots.[37]

Members of the longhouse did not necessarily eat together at a collective meal, and visitors arriving at any time of the day could expect to be offered a serving from the pot simmering by the fire. Women and girls brought the food in a bark dish. Writing for a French audience, Chauchetière somehow gives the impression that Tekakwitha played the part of the selfless and humble servant, fetching meals for the men of her household. Yet her dispensing duties could be interpreted quite differently. Among the Mohawks, food was under the control of women, and so the gesture of serving may well have contained an element of asserting female power over male appetites.[38]

Almost everything to do with food and subsistence was the exclusive province of Iroquois women, from the planting of crops through harvest and storage to the grinding of grain and the preparation of meals. The agricultural and the female were so intimately associated that Iroquoian languages contained expressions that united a feminine subject and an agricultural action in a single word: "She plants," "She weeds," "She stirs up the earth." Myth and ritual gave further expression of this deeply embedded association. A Seneca creation story told of corn springing from the breasts of the Earth Mother after she gave birth to the twins who originated the human race.[39] Male shamans attempting to cure illness sometimes wore cornhusk masks with female features because corn and women were symbolically associated as the sustainers of life.[40]

In listing the pursuits that displayed Tekakwitha's industrious virtues, Chauchetière emphasizes domestic tasks that European readers would recognize as feminine, but at other points in his biography he makes it clear that she also participated in agricultural pursuits. Between April and September, field work kept Mohawk women busy and away from the longhouse for long hours every day. In describing her first encounter with a missionary, when Tekakwitha was about eighteen and confined to her bed by a foot injury, the Jesuit remarks that it was unusual in the planting season (for men, the time of the spring hunt) to find anyone about the longhouse in midday. "As it was spring everyone in the house was going out to work their fields. Catherine had been several times, for she was not in the habit of staying in the cabin doing nothing while the others worked."[41] Poor health and occasional injuries may have kept Tekakwitha at home more than other girls, but when agricultural tasks were pressing, she would normally be out in the fields with the others.

Although each individual was assigned her own tract of land, most of the labor was performed collectively. The girls and women formed themselves into work parties and, under the supervision of a respected senior matron, together would take on the succession of seasonal tasks from planting to harvest.[42] Singing and chatting together lightened the burden of otherwise tedious jobs; according to Chauchetière, Tekakwitha was a cheerful companion on such occasions, though he hastens to add that she never indulged in the malicious gossip that so often marred the proceedings. The work group also had a sacred and ceremonial function, especially important at planting time when it seemed vital to persuade spiritual forces to aid rather than frustrate human efforts to ensure a bountiful crop.

Every spring, the women of Gandaouagué would prepare the soil, using digging sticks to scrape the earth together in low hills about a meter in diameter. Then, carrying their seeds in a small basket attached at the waist so that their hands were free, they would plant the corn, along with beans and squash. The "Three Sisters," complementary elements of a balanced diet, also grew well together as the bean tendrils climbed the growing corn stalks, and the squash spread along the ground, discouraging weeds.[43] The planting ceremony held about this time involved music and dancing, as well as a prayer of thanksgiving for past support and a somewhat obliquely phrased request for timely rains and other conditions favoring bountiful crops. Smoke wafting upward from burning tobacco would take these words up to the heavens.[44] As the crops matured, the Mohawks held further ceremonies of thanksgiving and propitiation; in a general way, these rites probably resembled the Corn Sprouting Ceremony, the Corn Testing Ceremony, and the Green Corn Ceremony celebrated by Iroquois people in modern times, but there is no definite information on seventeenth-century practices.[45] It does appear that, although the Iroquois were naturally anxious about their crops, their invocations of supernatural cooperation had none of the desperate quality that characterized supplications on the part of people in the arid Southwest, always on the edge of oblivion if the rains failed.[46]

In summer, Tekakwitha would be recruited to join the women and girls going to weed the fields. There were also expeditions to gather strawberries and other wild fruits. Finally, the corn, beans, and squash would be reaped in the fall and brought back to the village for husking and drying—more group tasks—and stored in the longhouses.

If there was a degree of monotony even to such a varied seasonal work routine, it was relieved by the festivals that intervened at different times through the year. Some feasts were eat-all affairs for men only, but most

rituals involved both sexes. Transactions with the sacred and sociable enjoyment tended to merge in these specially designated times, marked off from
the mundane world of everyday life. Chauchetière insists that Tekakwitha
was too shy to attend feasts, tinged as they were in his eyes with pagan
spirituality, but even if she did keep to the background, it strains credulity
to suggest that she was utterly uninvolved in festivities that periodically filled
the longhouse, indeed, the entire village. Elsewhere in the biography, Claude
notes that, on moving to Kahnawake and being asked to reflect on the sins
she may have committed during her previous life in the midst of "paganism," Catherine replied simply that "she had always done as she had seen
others do among the Iroquois."[47]

People reserved their best finery for festivals, grooming themselves carefully, both to enhance their personal reputation by appearing to best advantage and to contribute to the splendor of the occasion. The Jesuits sometimes
denounced this "vanity" as a specifically female failing (though Iroquois
men seem to have been just as concerned about their appearance) in the
same terms they used to criticize women's styles in Europe. And when she
looked back over her essentially spotless preconversion life among the
Mohawks, the mature, Christian Catherine could find only one sin with
which to reproach herself, that of letting the women of her longhouse beau-
tify her:

> The natural inclination which girls have to appear attractive makes them
> put great value on bodily ornaments. For this reason, Indian girls of
> seven or eight are foolishly fond of beadwork. The mothers, who are
> even more foolish, sometimes spend long hours combing and dress-
> ing the hair of their daughters. They go to great trouble to have their
> ears pierced, beginning when the girl is still in the cradle. They paint
> their faces and they cover themselves with beadwork, especially when
> they are supposed to go dancing.

These women tried to train her in "vanity," hoping, says Chauchetière, to
attract a mate for her at an early age, but "the little Tekakwitha had a natural
indifference for these things," just as she had a natural aversion to marriage.[48]
"Indifferent" she may have been, at least in comparison to the girls most
fanatically devoted to self-adornment, but she did take the trouble to master the intricacies of beadwork, quillwork, and dyeing, and she was wearing strings of beads in her hair and around her neck when she first came to
Kahnawake.[49]

Thoughts turned to betrothal and marriage when a girl reached the age
of twelve or thirteen, but Tekakwitha would have none of it:

> When she attained the age of marriage, they [the women of her house]
> tried to trick her. They brought a young man into the cabin and told

him to sit down next to her; and when he was seated they told Catherine
to give him some sagamité, intending by this means to marry her and
make her go with him as her husband. Whereupon, Catherine left the
cabin and went to hide in the fields. They tried to get her to return but
this girl kept herself hidden behind a bin of corn.[50]

This vividly recounted scene, reconstructed from an older woman's testimony many years after the event, gives a wonderful glimpse of Iroquois
marital customs, even as the Jesuit's hagiographic agenda distorts the sense
of the proceedings.

From other ethnographic sources, we know that clan matrons did engage
in matchmaking and sometimes pressured teenage girls to comply with their
arrangements, so there was nothing unusual in Tekakwitha's experience.
Catholic readers in Europe would be reminded of the heroic struggles of saints
like Catherine of Siena to preserve their virginity in the face of parental
attempts to force them into marriage, but marriage was something quite
different among the Mohawks than it was in fourteenth-century Italy or
seventeenth-century France. Iroquois girls were free to reject overtures of the
sort described here, exactly as Tekakwitha did. And what if she had fallen for
the "trick" and offered the boy some food? They would then have been considered "married," but only in a highly provisional way; there would not necessarily be any sex, possibly not for years, until both parties were ready for it;
and if Tekakwitha found her mate was not to her liking, she would have no
difficulty dissolving the relationship. Besides giving a misleading impression
of what was at stake in the marital ceremony he so accurately describes,
Chauchetière also misconstrues the motives of the clan mothers who orches-
trated it. His text implies that their aim was hostile, that they wanted to rid
themselves of the ugly orphan, but if proceedings had gone according to plan,
they would, as the modern cliché puts it, "gain a son rather than lose a daughter." Marriage would not have detached Tekakwitha from the longhouse;
rather, it would have brought her "husband" into its orbit. He would probably continue to sleep in his mother's house for a time, but as he developed
skills as a hunter, the game he brought back would belong to Tekakwitha's
longhouse; that fact alone, rather than any desire to be rid of the girl, would
explain why she was hounded by matchmakers.[51]

Focused as they were on the battle between matrimony and virginity,
the Jesuit biographers made no mention of another event that would have
preceded Tekakwitha's brush with marriage. To have been considered ready
for marriage, the girl must have reached puberty, a truly momentous stage
in any female Iroquois life. At the first sign of menses, she would have been
hustled away from the longhouse and placed in a secluded hut, for menstrual blood was considered a potent and dangerous substance capable of
contaminating cooking fires, making people ill, and spoiling the effects of

medicine. Every month thereafter, she would have to retire to the menstrual hut. Meanwhile, she faced an extended initiation ceremony that marked her transition from childhood and her adoption of a new and distinct adult identity.[52] Joseph-François Lafitau provides the following, somewhat generic, account of initiation customs, one clearly shaped by his experience as a missionary among the Iroquois of Kahnawake:

> The Huron, Iroquois and Algonquian tribes also have their initiations which they still celebrate. All that I know about them is that they are begun at the age of puberty; that they [the initiates] retreat into the woods, the youths under an elder or a shaman's direction, the young girls under a matron's. During this time, they fast very strictly; and, as long as their fast lasts, they blacken their faces, the tops of their shoulders and their chests. In particular, they pay careful attention to their dreams and report them exactly to those in charge of them. The latter examine, with scrupulous care, their pupils' conduct and confer often with the ancients about what concerns them or happens to them, to determine what they should take for their Oiaron or Manitou on whom the future happiness of their life must depend. They also draw conclusions to determine for what these initiates ought to be fitted in the future, so that the test is a sort of vocational one.[53]

Whatever precise form her initiation took—and, as Lafitau freely admits, he did not actually observe the ceremony (none of the male, European writers who wrote on the Iroquois would ever be allowed in on the secret)—much was at stake for Tekakwitha as she joined other girls in a quest for supernatural guidance, a quest that was at once collective and intensely personal.

War and the effects of war had to be a central fact in Tekakwitha's childhood. For the first ten years of her life, raiding parties from Gandaouagué and from other Iroquois villages would have been seen departing on a regular basis, and those that returned successfully would have had captives to run the gauntlet at the entrance to the village. Chauchetière insists that Catherine was repelled by torture, even before she converted to Christianity: "She never had the savage woman's spirit of cruelty; she could not bear to see anyone harmed, not even a slave [i.e., captive], and she thought it a sin to watch a man being burned."[54] But how could she have avoided the spectacle of prisoner torture and execution? It was a fact of Iroquois life, a formative experience that surely played a part in shaping the program of ascetic penance she developed as an adult and a Christian.

Of course, torture and killing were also a feature of life in seventeenth-century France, and in this case, cruelty was not necessarily connected with war. Public executions featuring hanging, burning, and various forms of bodily mutilation form a prominent and recurrent motif in the diary of a merchant who lived in Poitiers when Claude Chauchetière was growing up.[55] The young Jesuit-in-training may well have been part of the crowd of ten thousand spectators who gathered in the market square in 1665 to watch a condemned murderer broken on the wheel, an exceedingly painful ordeal.[56] Thus, the French boy and the Mohawk girl both knew about, and probably witnessed, scenes of cruel death. But these basically similar events had quite different meanings in their respective cultures. In early modern Europe, the criminal was an insider to be turned into an outsider, a deviant member of the body politic who had to be brutalized, destroyed, and expelled. Among the Iroquois, the tortured body always belonged to an outsider in the process of being turned into an insider, an alien enemy who was ritually incorporated into an Iroquois lineage to replenish its spiritual strength before he or she was physically destroyed. Except for witches, who were secretly executed without torture, Iroquoian people could never legitimately kill or injure their own.

For the first ten years of her life, Tekakwitha would have known war itself only indirectly as the exploit of Iroquois men in distant locations, but Gandaouagué itself suddenly became the theater of conflict in 1666 when the French invaded. The girl would have been among those who took refuge in the woods and then returned to a scene of smoldering devastation. Less than three years after Gandaouagué had been rebuilt, it was attacked once again. The Mohawks had by then made peace with their northern neighbors but continued to be embroiled with a coalition of Mahicans and New England Indians, formidably armed thanks to their trade with the English. On August 18, 1669, a large force of these allies besieged Gandaouagué, firing through the log palisade and threatening for a time to overwhelm the defenders. The Mohawks counterattacked, however and, led by a man named Kryn, drove the enemy away, then returned to Gandaouagué with ten prisoners for torture.[57] Four years later, Kryn would lead a large party of Mohawks to the new Christian settlement of Kahnawake, but it was this military campaign that established his reputation as a man of consequence.

Meanwhile, the military invasion of the French had been followed by a missionary invasion. When peace was established in 1667, the Mohawks, like the other Five Nations, agreed to admit Jesuits to their villages. Accordingly, Fathers Jacques Frémin, Jean Pierron, and Jacques Bruyas accompanied the negotiators home from Montreal, traveling in the Iroquois canoes south along Lake Champlain and Lake George, then proceeding on by land, presumably along the same trail by which Tekakwitha's mother had been conducted to Gandaouagué two decades earlier.

And so we proceeded in company and, by short marches, came to within three-quarters of a league of their principal town, called Gandaouagué. . . . We were received there with the customary ceremonies and with all possible honors. We were conducted to the cabin of the foremost captain, where all the people crowded in to look at us, quite delighted to see among them such peaceable Frenchmen, when the French had appeared there not long before as though in a fury, putting everything to the torch.

The warmth of the Mohawk welcome was due partly to the foreign origin of much of the population and its prior exposure to Catholic teachings. That, in itself, was no guarantee of a positive attitude toward Christianity, however; many of the missionaries' staunchest opponents were former captives who had opposed the Jesuits twenty years earlier when they were still Hurons. It was also an expression of the unanimous Mohawk desire to placate the French and establish good relations. The Jesuits tended to be seen, in this context, as representatives of a pro-Iroquois faction within French Canada. From the Mohawk point of view, the missionaries were ambassadors, but also hostages, whose lives ensured that the French governor would honor his commitment to peace.[58]

After an auspicious start, the trio of Jesuits soon experienced the same frustrations as so many of their predecessors had among the Hurons and other Indians. They learned that politeness, hospitality, and genuine curiosity about the French religion did not lead to the kind of conversions they hoped for. People listened attentively to the Jesuits' speeches; they built a chapel and came to pray; they even, in one desperate attempt to propitiate an angry missionary who threatened to unleash a French attack, burned the turtle rattles of their shamans;[59] but very few Mohawks went all the way. "In eight months I have baptized only fifty-three persons," reported Father Pierron in 1669, adding this crucial clarification: "nearly all of whom have gone to Heaven."[60] Setting out to convert living nations, the missionaries were finding once again that their only assured harvest of souls was among the dead and the dying.

But where was Tekakwitha? The recently reconstructed Gandaouagué was the first stop where the missionaries rested in 1667, and it continued to be an important site of evangelizing activities in the years that followed. All through her teenage years, the girl inhabited a village where Jesuits were either residents or frequent visitors and where a cabin surmounted by a cross was a constant reminder of the Christian presence. And yet, for eight years she appears to have had nothing to do with the missionaries or their chapel. Why? Chauchetière attributes Tekakwitha's long resistance to the lure of Christianity partly to her uncle's anti-Christian sentiments; he muses further, "Perhaps also Catherine's timidity prevented her from approaching the fathers to seek instruction."[61] These factors may indeed have played a role, though the uncle made no move to prevent her praying and going to the chapel when she did finally start frequenting the Jesuits in 1675. Since Chauchetière is merely speculating about her motives for waiting so long to convert, we might consider another possible explanation: perhaps Tekakwitha was more fully integrated into Mohawk society than her biographers admit, less an outcast, and therefore less predisposed to seek out exotic religions and foreign connections.

Accounting for Tekakwitha's turn to Catholicism is not so difficult. By the time she began preparing for baptism, conversion was something of a mass movement among the Mohawks.[62] After five years of disappointing results, the fortunes of the Jesuit mission improved abruptly around 1672, and the missionaries themselves were hard-pressed to account for the change. One crucial development that assisted their efforts enormously was the emergence of an Iroquois settlement at Kentake (later Kahnawake) near Montreal. This relocation had begun not as a religiously motivated pilgrimage but as part of a general northward migration of population from the Five Nations lands into Canada; Catholicism took root as part of the larger pattern of migration and alliance.

Political fracturing drove many Mohawks to the Montreal region in the 1670s, and French-Jesuit influence convinced most of these migrants to adhere to the Catholic Church. Since the "new Christians" remained closely connected to the clans and longhouses of the old Mohawk lands, their frequent visits tended to generate a revival of interest in the Jesuit religion. While some Mohawks traveled north to live with their kinfolk on the St. Lawrence, others remained at home, joining the others symbolically through baptism. Excitement was greatest at the village of Gandaouagué, where Father Bruyas proudly reported thirty baptisms in 1672.[63] Acceptance of Christianity and removal to the Montreal area were two distinct gestures, both of them favored by those elements of Mohawk society inclined to strengthen ties with the French. Some individuals took baptism and then struck off for the new settlement, some migrated without converting, and others converted but stayed in their home villages. The result was that by the mid-1670s, lines of politico-religious affiliation ran between the Mohawk River and the St. Lawrence, joining Mohawks among the French and French among the Mohawks. Jesuits were a crucial link in this network, though they never really controlled it, nor did they fully understand the complex Iroquois agendas at work.

It was in these circumstances, and after large numbers of her fellow villagers had already emigrated or converted, that Tekakwitha had her momentous encounter with Christianity in the spring of 1675. She was then eighteen years old, and a foot injury had kept her confined to her cabin when everyone else was out working in the fields. The Jesuit then resident at Gandaouagué, Father Jacques de Lamberville, happened to be passing by when what was later described as a providential impulse led him to look inside the apparently deserted longhouse. There he found the young woman, a captive audience for his preaching and, as it turned out, a willing and eager listener: "The first words that Catherine spoke to the father revealed the feelings in her heart, but she explained to the father what her uncle might do to keep her from being baptized, for fear that she would do as the others did and leave the country." Lamberville invited her to come to the chapel to pray, which she did as soon as her wound had healed.[64]

"At first no one caused her any trouble. They let her come and go for prayers, like the others."[65] Here again, Chauchetière the honest chronicler undercuts the rhetorical flourishes of Chauchetière the hagiographer, for while the latter portrays his subject as a lonely Christian among persecuting pagans, the former reveals that she went to the chapel with "others," that her family made no move to prevent her (and Iroquois respect for personal autonomy was such that it would have been surprising if they had tried to restrain her), and that her "malicious" uncle was concerned only to ensure that Tekakwitha stay with him. In another context, Chauchetière notes that a "sister" from her longhouse, as well as the clan mother Anastasia Tegonhatsiongo, had already departed for the St. Lawrence; thus the uncle's worries seem perfectly well-founded.

Once she joined the Mohawks who frequented the Jesuit chapel, Tekakwitha became, from the missionary point of view, a "catechumen." Literally, the term designates one who learns the catechism in preparation for baptism, but there were no catechism manuals available in the Mohawk language at that time, and the girl could not understand French. (The biographers say nothing of her knowledge of native languages; perhaps she had some exposure to Algonquin, Huron, and other Iroquois tongues in addition to Mohawk.) Like all the Jesuits of New France, Father de Lamberville was a trained linguist, and so we are safe in assuming that he possessed a good command of Mohawk. But what would he have taught his young catechumen, and how would he have conveyed a sense of Catholic belief? Lamberville left no definite information on that score, but we know from the writings of other missionaries that words and pictures were often deployed to give Indians a sense of the pleasures of heaven and the torments of hell, and to recount the life of Jesus. Otherwise, instruction tended to concentrate on familiarizing converts with formulaic prayers, some basic behavioral prohibitions, and ritual actions such as crossing oneself.

Of this initial stage of her introduction to Catholicism, Chauchetière writes simply, "After Catherine had persevered some time in going to pray as a catechumen, the father thought he would baptize her."[66] This does not imply that admission to membership in the church was granted lightly, however. After some early mistakes when naïve missionaries baptized natives who later changed their mind about Christianity and committed the terrible sin of apostasy, the Jesuits were careful to ensure that converts were unshakably committed to a Catholic life before admitting them to that sacrament. Catechumens were put to the test, a test that was mainly behavioral rather than intellectual; besides praying regularly, applicants had to demonstrate that they had renounced "impurity" and "paganism." There were other criteria, but most were negative, which is to say they focused on determining that the subject had detached herself from native customs judged to be in contradiction to the law of God. Father de Lamberville, convinced from his first encounter that Tekakwitha possessed the qualities of an excellent Christian, nevertheless made careful inquiries about her habits and past behavior. "All the people of Catherine's cabin spoke well of her and those of the village spoke similarly; all the Christians rejoiced when the father finally decided to baptize her."[67] Because of discrepancies about dates in the Chauchetière and Cholenec texts, it is impossible to know how long Tekakwitha had to wait for her baptism—possibly half a year, possibly just a few weeks—but it does seem to have been an unusually short trial period.[68]

Along with two other Mohawks, Tekakwitha received the ceremony of baptism in the bark-covered chapel of Gandaouagué on Easter Sunday, 1676. No one objected. Indeed, as Pierre Cholenec observed, "There was less trouble than had been feared, for her aunts, far from opposing her, had already been baptized themselves."[69] She was given the baptismal name of Catherine, a popular name, "held in great veneration among the Indians."[70] (Was the name simply assigned by Father Lamberville, or did the girl choose it for herself? The biographers do not say, though the fact that it was unusually common among native women suggests that they themselves made the selection. Perhaps the French sound for "Catherine" was easier for Iroquois speakers to approximate than other saints' names.) Ceremonies in which individuals received a new name and a new identity were by no means unfamiliar to Mohawks of the seventeenth century. Rituals of adoption, requickening, and initiation were solemn occasions to mark an important transition in someone's social identity—from enemy captive to clan member, from ordinary man to league sachem, from child to adult—and always a new name was conferred on this remade person. The new name was in fact an old name, having belonged in the past to a now-deceased clan member; reviving the name meant preserving the social personality associated with it, so that the ceremony marked both discontinuity in the life of a human individual and continuity over the generations of a particular personal identity.[71] Baptism may have made sense to Mohawks in similar terms, for the rite involved an altered personal identity, a new name, and, because baptismal names always harked back to a Christian saint, connection with a personality from the past. Tekakwitha, now Catherine, was named for Catherine of Siena, and we may be sure that she would have listened attentively when the Jesuits told her of the life of that great fourteenth-century mystic-ascetic saint. By the same token, Claude Chauchetière began to adopt something of an Iroquoian attitude toward names and identities when he wrote, "The spirit of Saint Catherine of Siena and of the other saints of that name was renewed in her."[72]

Once past the hurdle of baptism, many native converts tended to return to behavior the Jesuits regarded as incompatible with Christianity. "We have even seen some who become worse than before being baptized, because they did not have the courage to disdain human respect, a common failing among these people."[73] By "human respect," Chauchetière meant the tendency to conform to the expectations of secular society, and indeed convert Iroquois did come under pressure to continue discharging their responsibilities as members of a family and a community. Mohawks would not object if some among them accepted initiation into the Jesuits' sacred society and began praying in their chapel, but they would be shocked if initiates then refused to contribute to communal feasts or to participate in collective rituals designed to help sick people; such a refusal would have seemed hostile and antisocial. The Jesuits had to tolerate many customs they disapproved of, but they drew the line where they perceived devil worship. At least, they tried to draw the line: since supernatural forces that did not stem from God were by definition "demons," and since spirituality pervaded so many aspects of Iroquois life, it was difficult for the most sophisticated priest to determine exactly which practices in a Mohawk setting defied God's law. For the converts themselves, the distinctions were even more problematic; with the best will in the world, it sometimes seemed impossible to know where civic obligations ended and sin began.

The missionaries established some basic guidelines for converts living in religiously mixed settings, and Tekakwitha/Catherine followed those rules to perfection. In detailing her exemplary conduct, Chauchetière sheds considerable light on mission practice, indicating where, in the complex world of Mohawk culture, the Jesuits chose to direct their regulatory attention: "The Christians noticed how precisely she followed the rules that the father had prescribed for them: that is, to go to prayers morning and evening every day, to attend mass every Sunday; and, concerning that which is to be avoided, not to attend dream feasts, or dances or other Indian gatherings contrary to purity."[74] It is easy to understand why Father Lamberville forbade attendance at "dream feasts." Dream guessing was a feature of many Iroquoian rituals, but the priest would have been principally concerned about the great three- to four-week midwinter festival, called Onnonhouarori by the Mohawks. Perhaps it reminded him of the disorderly carnival rites of Catholic Europe in which, to the despair of the clergy, the "lords of misrule" prevailed amid noise, drunkenness, and the playful inversion of social hierarchies. The Iroquois had no real hierarchies to invert, but their

Onnonhouarori did entail the temporary overthrow of reason and restraint (the name implied "turning of the head").[75] Groups of masked revelers would storm through longhouses, breaking up cooking fires and knocking over pots; generally these adults behaved as naughty children. A central part of the serious fun was the game of dream guessing, and that, much more than mere disorderly conduct, was what made the midwinter celebrations anathema to the Jesuits.

Iroquoian peoples put great stock in dreams, believing they could foretell the future and reveal the repressed "desires of the soul" that brought people illness and grief. In dream-guessing games, the central player would hint at the subject of his or her dreams, using riddles to elicit guesses from the other participants. Since the dream content pointed toward a sacred desire, it was up to the guessers to give the dreamer what he or she wanted once its identity was ascertained. Someone might say, "What I want is seen in my eyes," and the listeners, realizing that some glass beads resemble eyes and are designated by a word related to the word for "eyes," would give him a quantity of beads. Then the dreamer and the disguised "mad people" accompanying him would take their loot, leave the longhouse and the village, and come back later with their collective madness purged.[76]

Sometimes the Jesuits mocked dream divination and ceremonies such as Onnonhouarori as "silly," but ultimately they took them very seriously: hence their position at the top of Father Lamberville's list of prohibitions. They worried that supernatural powers, far from being illusory, really did speak to the Iroquois through dreams, and since the messages were clearly not divine, the conclusion followed that dreams were a device employed by the Devil himself to keep Indians in his thrall. What made dream guessing even more objectionable (and reinforced the conclusion that diabolical forces were at work) was its association with forbidden acts. The hidden desires that dreams revealed were sometimes aggressive and violent, sometimes erotic. A Jesuit among the Hurons told of a sick man whose dreams indicated a desire for a special feast at which dogs of a certain description had to be cooked and eaten, various dances had to be performed, "but principally he wanted the ceremony of the *andacwander*, a coupling of men and girls, which occurs at the end of the feast. He specified that there should be twelve girls, plus a thirteenth for himself."[77] Such activity, so flagrantly "contrary to purity" in missionary terms, was not a common feature of Mohawk festivities, but it was always a possibility where repressed appetites communicated through dreams were accorded sacred status.

Looking at the midwinter ceremony through Jesuit eyes and seeing people obeying instructions from the Devil, orders that occasionally culminated in public copulation, we cannot be surprised to learn that this festival was designated off-limits to Christian converts. But what about all the other customs and rituals of the Mohawks? The striking thing about the rules Father

Lamberville laid down for his flock is how few were the activities he prohibited. Almost all the rituals followed by the people of Gandaouagué—
puberty rites, condolence ceremonies, the requickening of League sachems,
to name only a few—were pervaded by a sense that human affairs were linked
to and affected by unseen forces that needed to be cajoled, appeased, or
thanked. When people planted corn, when they went hunting, when they
prepared medicines or embarked on war parties, they prayed, burned tobacco, and observed other precautions that were clearly religious, but not
Christian. Insofar as the missionaries were aware of this pervasive spirituality, they wisely chose to ignore much that might have been considered incompatible with the First Commandment. Instead they concentrated on a
few areas where Mohawk custom was flagrantly at odds with Catholic norms,
leaving converts otherwise free—or so the strategic silences of the Jesuit
writings would suggest—to continue their familiar way of life. Traditional
Iroquois may have deplored the way a growing circle of Christians under-
mined the ideal of universal participation by refusing to attend certain curing rituals and community festivities, but the impact on Mohawk unity was
hardly explosive.

Much more disturbing was the migration of large numbers of people to
Canada. Ever since the peace of 1667, some dissident Mohawks had joined
other Iroquois in settling the northern lands that were now accessible to
them and in cultivating closer relations with the French. With Kahnawake/
La Prairie now established as a predominantly Catholic Iroquois village on
the St. Lawrence, missionaries in the old Mohawk villages began encouraging
converts to relocate.[78] This new Jesuit policy, apparent from about 1672 on,
constituted an implicit admission that the Five Nations could not be converted
en masse and that a baptized minority in a "pagan" Iroquois environment
could only be expected to follow a narrow range of Christian observances.
Increasingly, the role of field missionaries such as Father Lamberville was to
dispatch dying Indians to heaven and living Indians to Canada. As the movement swelled from a trickle to a significant flow around the mid-1670s, local
leaders like Tekakwitha's uncle came to regard religious conversion as a prelude to emigration.

By the time Tekakwitha became Catherine, Mohawk communities were
tearing themselves apart. Jesuit influence played a part in provoking the split,
but the fault lines were already discernible in the social geography of clans,
ethnic origins, and political factions before missionaries appeared on the
scene. The accumulated stresses of two generations of war, epidemics, and
economic dislocation had taken their toll, and the hard choices imposed by
military setbacks in the 1660s accentuated political strife. Even in the absence of Christianity and religious divergence, the customs of solidarity and
the mechanisms for reaching consensus in Iroquoian societies were sometimes overwhelmed by deep divisions, and in such cases, it was common

for one faction to hive off and found a new village.[79] Bitterness and resentment were the normal accompaniment of such a rupture, but usually political links and clan connections remained more or less intact.

It was in this deteriorating atmosphere that Tekakwitha had to make her
choice between the faction rallying around the cross and the French alliance
and the so-called traditionalist Mohawks, never friendly to the French and now
increasingly hostile to emigration and Christianity. She had relatives in both
camps, and so the choice had to be agonizing, for either option would im-
peril important relationships (that dilemma dominated her very first conversation with Jacques de Lamberville). Eventually she decided to join the
Catholics, but her attachment to her longhouse and to Gandaouagué must have
been strong, since she remained in the village for a long time—either one
and a half or two years, depending on which Jesuit chronology we follow—
while so many other converts were flocking to Montreal/Kahnawake.

As one who stayed behind when others had left, Catherine seems to have
become a target for the accumulated resentments of those around her. Along
with other members of the small Catholic minority on the ground in Gandaouagué, she came to represent for the opposing faction the larger numbers
who had departed and the pain of conflict and separation. "The cabin began
to persecute her," writes Chauchetière, "saying that since becoming a Christian she had become lazy, for she did not go to work in the fields on Sundays. They rebuked her for this supposed negligence and then mistreated
her in various ways." The biographer mentions only two specific examples
of this "mistreatment": people in her house took away her rosary, and they
left her nothing to eat when they went out to work on Sundays. Additionally, Catherine had to endure "the jeers of the shamans and the drunkards
and of all the enemies of the prayer." Children would point at her, "calling
her, in derision, 'the Christian,' as if speaking of a dog." This mockery must
have been unpleasant, especially for a sensitive girl like Tekakwitha, but she
bore it courageously and continued to pray regularly. The only hint of danger in Chauchetière's account comes where he tells of a plan to frighten her
out of any thought of leaving for the Christian settlement of Kahnawake.
Her uncle and some others discussed the idea of sending a young man armed
with a hatchet who would threaten to smash her head. However, it is clear
that no one intended to do her any physical harm, and the wording of the
sentence suggests that even this charade was never actually carried out. Pierre
Cholenec's original Life of Catherine makes no mention of any of this "persecution," and Father Lamberville, the one eyewitness to this period of
Tekakwitha's life who left a written account, says only that she complained
to him of the "displeasure" shown by the people of her longhouse.[80]

For Chauchetière, and for subsequent hagiographers, the proper way to
narrate this phase of the life of their saintly heroine was to structure the raw
data around a plot recalling the lives of the classical martyrs. Young women

saints of early Christian times were often depicted as lonely individuals who
stood firm in the midst of an implacably hostile pagan environment, with
family opposition and the violent persecution of Roman officials putting
their faith to the severest of tests.[81] Bearing these literary models in mind
and looking past the rhetorical flourishes in order to concentrate on the
concrete details of the narratives, it becomes clear that Tekakwitha's trials
were not on the same order as those recorded in the traditional *Lives of the
Saints*. No doubt, her suffering was real, but it was inseparable from the larger
collective trauma of the Mohawk nation. During the great schism of the
1670s, all Mohawks must have felt, to some degree or another, the same
wrenching of personal loyalties as they faced the choice of staying or leaving for Canada; either way, they faced the hostility of those who took the
opposite path.

At every turn, the process of constructing a historical biography on the
basis of hagiography has required us to counteract the sources' tendency to
treat Tekakwitha as an alien presence in the land of her birth, the embodiment of Christian virtue marooned upon pagan shores. Claude Chauchetière,
who knew better in his heart, described her in the life he wrote for skeptical French readers as "a lily among thorns," implying that this anti-Indian
Indian possessed an inner self fundamentally at odds with the sinful society
in which she grew up. My point is quite the opposite: she needs to be recognized as a Mohawk girl, her existence framed by the life of the Mohawk
longhouse, her fate bound up in the vagaries of Mohawk history. Of course
this simple formulation is misleading in its own way, for there was no clear
and singular "Mohawk identity" in that age of transformation and turmoil
when Iroquois nations were reconstituting themselves with people of diverse backgrounds and divergent outlooks. Tekakwitha was not an outsider,
but neither was she an absolutely secure insider. In those terrible times of
upheaval and movement in the northeastern woodlands, there were no stable
and unambiguous identities. It was in that shifting Mohawk context that
she would go on to pursue her extraordinary career at Kahnawake as a Christian ascetic and holy woman.

Sometime after her baptism, Father Lamberville began urging Catherine to
move to the new settlement of Kahnawake. He had the same advice for the
rest of his Gandaouagué flock, for he was convinced that only there could
they experience Catholic devotion consisting of more than simply regular
prayers and the avoidance of a few specified sins. Catherine was interested
but also was reluctant to cross her uncle. Then, in the fall of 1677, propi-
tious circumstances arose, and Mohawk kin networks succeeded where
unaided missionary urgings had failed.

It began, according to Pierre Cholenec, with an "older sister by adoption" who had previously moved, along with her husband, from Gandaouagué to Kahnawake. This sister sent her husband expressly to go and tell Tekakwitha about the advantages of life in the new settlement and to escort her back if possible. The brother-in-law joined a party of three under the leadership of a prominent Oneida captain named Garonhiague (the French, familiar with this man's fiery temper, transliterated his name as "Hot Powder"), which was traveling south to visit Mohawk and Oneida villages. Gandaouagué was the travelers' first stopping place, and there they were received in the usual Iroquois style; after they had eaten, an attentive audience waited to hear their news. Hot Powder gave a speech on the beauties of Christianity and the advantages of life on the St. Lawrence. The people listened politely (even Mohawks of the anti-Christian faction would be expected to do guests that courtesy) and then left, all except Catherine, who came forward to ask for help in moving to Kahnawake. Since her uncle was then away at "Orange" (Albany) doing business with the Dutch, it was hastily decided that she would go back with her brother-in-law and his other traveling companion, a Christian Huron. While Hot Powder continued on his way westward to Oneida, the other three headed east down the Mohawk River.

Father Lamberville, the only eyewitness to these events, leaves the story at that, but Chauchetière's and Cholenec's accounts both feature a harrowing escape from the "wicked" uncle.[82] Warned that Tekakwitha had been spirited away, they write, he loaded his gun with three bullets and set off to retrieve her and to murder her escorts. In one version of the story, he passed one of the men without recognizing him; in the other version, he caught up with the whole group, but Catherine managed to hide in the woods while her companions convinced the uncle that she was back at Gandaouagué. In any event, no blood was shed—if any had, it would have been the only violent episode reported in the entire decade of internal Mohawk strife— and Tekakwitha was able to continue on her way.

So she came, at the age of twenty-one, a baptized Christian who had never seen a church, never tasted a communion wafer, never met more than two or three Europeans, to the banks of the St. Lawrence River and the newly constructed Iroquois village where she would spend the rest of her days. Her "sister" and the clan matron Anastasia Tegonhatsiongo, familiar figures from her childhood, welcomed her to their longhouse. A new missionary, Claude Chauchetière, had just arrived at Kahnawake three months earlier, but there is no indication that he was on hand to greet her. Their rendezvous would come later.

3

Poitiers: The Making of a Jesuit Mystic

ANADA. CLAUDE CHAUCHETIÈRE WAS ONLY SEVEN OR EIGHT YEARS OLD WHEN HE first heard of this mysterious land far across the sea. He and his older brother, Jean, were then pupils in the little parish school of St. Porchaire in the heart of Poitiers, and their teacher, the local curate, told them of a priest of his acquaintance who had died a holy death just before sailing for Quebec. He never forgot the powerful impression this story of devotion and self-sacrifice produced in his own young mind: "The zeal of this good priest touched me and made me feel how good it would be to give oneself to God."[1] Though the would-be missionary had never even left France, the teacher's report somehow conjured up a set of associations in young Claude's mind linking Canada, death, and a glorious and fulfilling union with God. Something of that forbidding sense of the place endured even after he had spent half a lifetime—with minimal risk of martyrdom, as it turned out—in the colony on the St. Lawrence.

It was in 1695, with old age creeping up on him, that the fifty-year-old Chauchetière sat down to write a spiritual autobiography in the form of a long letter to his brother, himself a Jesuit then serving at Limoges. (There were, in fact, three Chauchetière brothers in the Society of Jesus; younger brother Jacques had died ten years earlier after brief service as a missionary in South America.)[2] This was Claude's narrative, based on the memoirs and rough notes accumulated over the course of a long career, of his religious development, with its crises and moments of inspiration and its long and painful accretion of understanding. Claude was not entirely sure his brother wanted to know all about the periods of insight, ecstasy, and aridity that marked his interior development, but he felt compelled, like many other Christians of the time, to bear witness. His life, as he had come to understand it, had a very definite purpose, one that had been increasingly apparent to him since April 17, 1680. Accordingly, he noted at the outset that his autobiography was written in a spirit of "gratitude that I owe to God and to his Holy Mother and to Catherine."

The autobiography is one of three major texts of Chauchetière's composition that have survived: the other two were a much revised and frequently rewritten Life of Tekakwitha and a history of the mission of Sault St. Louis/Kahnawake. None was published until long after his death. The three interpenetrate to an astonishing degree, blurring genre distinctions in the process. Catherine's presence haunts all his writings, imparting significance to the history of the community where she flourished and died and giving meaning to Claude's own early life as a preparation for his providential encounter with saintliness. At the same time, the author himself is an essential and highly visible subject in the biography and the history, the essential observer from the European center bearing witness to the marvels God has wrought in a wild and distant land.

Not long before he sat down to compose his autobiography, Chauchetière had left Sault St. Louis after seventeen years in residence, an exceptionally long time for a Jesuit to remain at one posting. In 1695, he was at the Jesuit college of Montreal, living for the first time since coming to New France in a predominantly French environment, though he was still close enough to the Christian Iroquois settlement to maintain contact with the people he had come to know and admire. The Jesuits had a rather tenuous existence in Montreal, for the church in that small town at the western end of French settlement in the St. Lawrence valley was under the control of the rival Sulpician order.[3] Claude's main duty was to teach mathematics to French-Canadian boys and military officers, but he also heard confession, preached the occasional sermon, and helped administer the Jesuits' properties in and around Montreal. Perhaps because he was technically classed within the order as a "spiritual coadjutor," a rank reserved for Jesuits who had not completed their formal education, Chauchetière had never been placed in a position of command, had never served at the main Canadian college in Quebec, and had never been sent on any dangerous missions to the unconverted nations out beyond the perimeter of firm colonial occupation. His letters back to France from this period suggest that he took satisfaction from the work he was doing, and above all from his role in proclaiming the spiritual glories of Tekakwitha and other Christian Indians, but they also convey a sense of wistful disappointment with his comparatively safe and orderly existence far from the front lines of missionary adventure.[4] In spite of his image of

Canada as a place of deadly danger and dramatic self-sacrifice, Claude Chauchetière had a long and outwardly uneventful life there.

Under the surface of this rather ordinary missionary career, the spiritual autobiography reveals a truly remarkable inner life. His ceaseless pursuit of self-transcendence had entailed years of arduous preparation that allowed him, at times, to soar to peaks of dazzling insight; he also experienced recurrent periods of confusion and despair, though he always managed to make his way back up to plateaus of serenity. This interior existence, with all its dramatic reversals and desperate struggles, intersected in complicated ways with the external facts of Chauchetière's biography. On a very few occasions, there is a clear connection between an event in the world of human affairs and an important spiritual development: the crisis following his father's death was one of these; his encounter with a dying Mohawk virgin was another.

Chauchetière's hometown, Poitiers, is built on a plateau at a bend of the river Clain; from the top of rocky cliffs it looks out over the Poitou country of west central France. One of the kingdom's great cities in the Middle Ages, it had never fully recovered from the damage inflicted in the course of the sixteenth-century Wars of Religion, when Poitou had been an area of Protestant strength and correspondingly severe Catholic reaction. By the time Claude was born in 1645, the town had slipped to the rank of substantial provincial center. However, it still boasted a *parlement*, a university renowned especially for its law faculty, numerous religious orders, and important law courts.

The Chauchetières were a well-established legal family. Claude's father, Jehan, as well as his father before him, served as *procureur au siege présidial*, meaning that he was attached to the highest court in the region, which heard appeals from the lower courts of Poitou. A visiting Scottish nobleman, Sir John Lauder, went to see the opening of its sessions in November 1665 and was impressed with the speeches and pageantry as the councilors and *procureurs* took their oaths, resplendent in black robes and four-cornered hats lined with scarlet. "The Praesidial of Poitou at Poictiers is the greatest of France: yea it consistes of mo[re] conseillers or judges (to wit, about 30 wt 2 Kings Advocats, 2 Kings procureurs), is of greater extent then several parliaments."[5] To call Jehan Chauchetière a "prosecutor" would be a misleading translation, since, in addition to investigating crimes and preparing cases, a *procureur* under the ancien régime participated in judging criminal and civil cases and passing sentences.[6] Comfortable members of a prestigious profession, the Chauchetières would have looked down upon the moneygrubbing bourgeoisie of business, while they in their turn would have been looked down

Poitiers, capital of Poitou. St. Porchaire, the small parish church where Claude
Chauchetière first heard of Canada, can be seen in the background, toward the
center. Bibliothèque nationale de France, Va86, tome 3. © Photograph courtesy
Bibliothèque nationale de France, Paris.

on by the haughty nobility, with their legally recognized privileges, including exemption from taxes, the right to bear arms, and so forth.[7] Like the majority of families whose sons entered the Society of Jesus in early modern Europe, the Chauchetières belonged to the unprivileged urban elite.

Even more than judicial establishments, churches and religious houses dominated Poitiers's cityscape. A century earlier, the town had been a principal center of the French Reformation, but with the triumph of Catholicism, its Protestant faction was reduced to a barely tolerated, cowed minority. To overwhelm the Calvinist traditions of Poitiers and the surrounding district, deliberate steps had been taken to bolster the Catholic presence, with endowments and special privileges for men's and women's orders. The Jesuits were among the most prominent beneficiaries of these encouragements. Arriving at the end of the sixteenth century, they were given some disused university buildings, as well as revenue-producing rural estates from defunct monasteries. Subsidies from the king and bequests from rich citizens allowed them to establish a large college and a sumptuous church by the second decade of the seventeenth century. Carmelites, Cistercians, Augustinians, and other religious orders thrived as well, making Poitiers, in the words of one local historian, "the capital of the Catholic Counter-Reformation."[8]

"Counter-Reformation." "Catholic Reformation." "Catholic Renewal." These and similar terms have long been the focus of searching discussion as historians struggle to characterize the far-reaching transformations of Catholicism in the sixteenth and seventeenth centuries.[9] In the past, the anti-Protestant thrust, military and political as well as religious, was emphasized in keeping with the negative and reactive implications of the term "Counter-Reformation." Certainly the impulse to conquer heresy by force and persuasion was very much in evidence in seventeenth-century Poitiers, where clerics were fierce champions of Catholic positions on such controverted points as the authority of the pope, the cult of the Virgin and of the saints, and the virtues of celibacy and religious orders. But more recent scholarship has insisted that there was far more to the Catholicism of this period than opposition to Protestant "heresy." This was a time, especially following the Council of Trent (1545–63), when the church was fundamentally restructured in an effort to end corruption and create a dedicated, effective clergy. Old religious orders were reformed and new ones created, most of the latter dedicated to transforming the world through education, charity, and evangelizing work, rather than retreating from the secular world after the fashion of medieval monasticism. In this respect, the Jesuits were the quintessential Counter-Reformation order. The church's effort to refashion itself extended beyond the clergy to encompass the laity as well; "superstition," indifference, and religious ignorance were to be rooted out from every corner of the land, so that European society should become truly Christian from top to bottom. There was also an outward thrust into the "pagan" and "infidel" regions of the wider world, with the intention of bringing all humanity under the influence of the one true faith. In its radicalism and its moral earnestness, in its preoccupation with achieving Christian perfection for individual souls, and in its resolve to reshape society to that end, the Catholic Church had more in common with its Protestant rivals than anyone at the time would have admitted.

In France, the Catholic Reformation tended to be most apparent in the seventeenth century, rather later than in Italy and Spain, and so the sense of enthusiasm and renewal was still strong when Claude Chauchetière was growing up in Poitiers. Though his outlook and life course were indelibly colored by that great movement in all its aspects, he does not seem to have been personally preoccupied with "heresy"; indeed, Protestantism is never once mentioned in his surviving writings. Yet he received his Jesuit training in Poitiers, Bordeaux, Tulle, and La Rochelle, all cities close to the heart of Huguenot France in the sixteenth century. It was on this religious frontier that Catholicism, triumphant but still insecure, burned with a particularly high degree of fervor, and that atmosphere of spiritual intensity, rather than any specifically anti-Calvinist focus, seems to have influenced young Claude as he advanced through his schooling and contemplated his future.

After acquiring the rudiments of reading and writing in French at the parish school of St. Porchaire, Chauchetière entered the nearby Jesuit college at about the age of thirteen.[10] Built half a century earlier with an endowment from King Henri IV, this institution sat perched at the edge of Poitiers's plateau. It was one in an extensive network of colleges established by the Jesuits across all the regions of France in the early seventeenth century. With its large central pavilion and the adjacent Baroque chapel (really a substantial church) in the characteristic Jesuit design, it was one of the main ecclesiastical and educational centers of the city. A Jesuit college was never a purely educational facility; lacking monastic houses, the Jesuits used their colleges as residences and administrative headquarters for all their various charitable and proselytizing activities. The college at Poitiers was affiliated with the university, and it offered Jesuits-in-training from southwestern France, the region designated by the Jesuits as their province of Aquitaine, the higher education that occupied them between the completion of their novitiate and their ordination as priests. However, its main business, like that of any other Jesuit college, was in providing a high-quality secondary education to boys from the town and the surrounding region.[11]

Like the majority of pupils, Claude Chauchetière attended as a day scholar—there were also boarding facilities for boys from outside Poitiers—and, as such, he paid no tuition fees. Other religious orders operated local

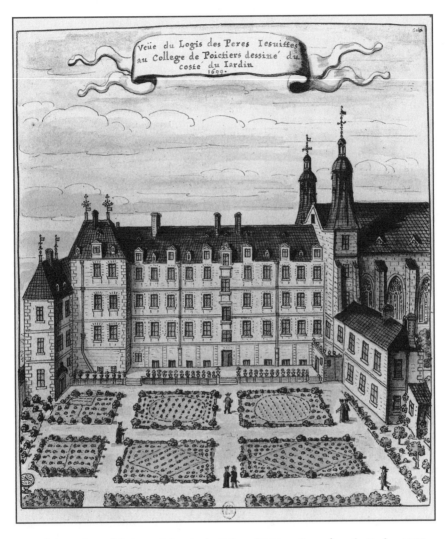

View of the Residence of the Jesuit Fathers in the College of Poitiers, Drawn from the Garden, 1699. Bibliothèque nationale de France, Va86, tome 3. © Photograph Bibliothèque nationale de France, Paris.

schools, and his father might have sent him to any of them, but the Jesuits were famous across Europe as educators, and so he chose the Jesuit college for Claude and his brothers. The curriculum for all Jesuit schools had been set out in the famous *Ratio Studiorum* of 1599, a program of humanistic learning that proceeded through the various subjects one at a time. The *Ratio Studiorum* was hardly a program of religious indoctrination, for it focused mainly on

the works of non-Christian classical authors. It incorporated the latest thinking, shaped by Renaissance humanism, on what young men destined for
the clergy or for the other professions needed to know before they began
their specialized training. There was nothing uniquely Jesuit about this conception of education, and so the *Ratio Studiorum* has to be seen not as an inno-
vative departure but as a systematic consolidation of prevalent approaches.[12]

The first three years of the program, "grammar," were devoted to learning the Latin language, its rules of grammar and syntax. After an introduc-
tory period in which some French was allowed, Latin became the sole
language of instruction, and even in recreation periods students were supposed to speak Latin among themselves. They used texts by Cicero, Caesar,
Virgil and Ovid. The fourth year, when Claude would have been fifteen,
was called "humanities," and it involved deeper literary study of classical
Latin works, as well as an introduction to Greek. The basic program ended
with a year of "rhetoric," a subject in which the French Jesuits emerged as
acknowledged masters in the seventeenth century.[13] At this stage, too, the
focus was on classical writings, with an emphasis on the techniques of ele-
gant and persuasive expression; a variety of subjects such as history and
geography entered the curriculum under this rubric. After rhetoric came
"philosophy," a challenging course encompassing mathematics, logic, ethics,
and physics; only boys intending to join the clergy were likely to take philosophy. Chauchetière took his philosophy after he had joined the Jesuits
and completed his initiation as a novice.[14]

The Jesuits' pedagogical methods were fairly conventional for the times.
Claude would have spent much of his time in school listening to a teacher
lecturing, or rather dictating notes, usually as a commentary (in Latin, needless to say) on a classical text. He also had to perform oral and written
exercises, especially in the humanities and rhetoric years, when students
composed Latin odes, elegies, and other writings. Jesuit pupils learned the
techniques of verbal debate and put their skills on display at public dispu-
tations. Claude likely participated also in the theatrical productions the Jesuit
colleges were famous for; both classic and Christian plays were performed.
All this learning took place in an atmosphere of rivalry—the Jesuits awarded
distinctions and prizes on the belief that emulation stimulated learning—
and stern discipline. This being the seventeenth century, generally regarded
as the peak period for corporal punishment in European history, there was
frequent recourse to the rod. Jesuits themselves were not supposed to hit
students (though some did), but every college had a prefect to beat negli-
gent or disobedient boys.[15]

More important to the Society of Jesus than the intellectual content of its
curriculum was the educational process more broadly conceived. The order's
Constitutions ordained that all students take confession and mass regularly and
"imbibe, together with learning, morals becoming Christians."[16] Regard-

ing children as unformed matter tainted by original sin, they sought to shape their charges in the habits of virtue and civility. A Spanish Jesuit frequently quoted by his French colleagues referred to youth as "soft like wax, easily taking the form that one imprints upon it."[17] Their education therefore aimed to isolate boys from external influences (even looking out the window was forbidden) and to keep them under close surveillance in school, controlling behavior and perception in the hope that a particular type of man, virtuous, learned, and articulate, would be the end product. In this field as in their overseas missions, the Jesuits revealed their aspirations as engineers of humanity. However, judging by the reports of pranks, disobedience, and even occasional open revolts that crop up in the college annals, the schoolboys of Poitiers were, on the whole, less malleable than warm wax.

In addition to turning out future lawyers, officers, and officials solidly grounded in virtue and piety, the Jesuit colleges served as a recruiting ground for members of the society itself. Claude Chauchetière, an apt pupil from a good family, was one of those encouraged by the teachers to consider whether he might have a calling. Marriage, a family, and an honorable legal career beckoned as an alternative, but in the personal turmoil following his father's death, the sixteen-year-old boy concluded that something more was demanded of him, a life dedicated to the pursuit of Christian perfection. The prospect of joining a tightly knit substitute family of admired priests must have had strong appeal for a bereaved orphan, but his main concern, as he deliberated his future, was not supposed to be whether or not he wanted to become a Jesuit. The question was, did God want him to be a Jesuit? After a period of supervised soul-searching at the end of his rhetoric year, he made up his mind to join the Society of Jesus as a novice. Along with other new recruits from different corners of the province of Aquitaine, he therefore made his way in the fall of 1663 to the college of Bordeaux, site of the two-year novitiate. On September 7, Claude's eighteenth birthday, he took his initial vows and began the long and arduous process of becoming a Jesuit.

If we were to judge by the anti-Jesuit "black legend" propounded by a battalion of influential enemies, Protestant, Catholic, and atheist, from John Donne to Blaise Pascal and Voltaire, Chauchetière was about to descend into a religious boot camp designed to turn him into a mindless fanatic, blindly obedient to the pope and to megalomaniac superiors. Anti-Jesuitry, like the cold war anti-Communism of a later century, was about a subtle and devious organization, ruthlessly bent on unlimited domination and adept at infiltrating governments and subverting all agencies of power to its selfish ends. And there was just enough evidence in the spectacular success of the

Society of Jesus from its founding in 1540 to its dissolution by the pope in 1773 to make the slander plausible. The growth in Jesuit numbers, the rami- fying network of colleges across Europe, the widely publicized overseas missions, and the close connections the Jesuits cultivated with kings and popes (in Chauchetière's day, Louis XIV turned to a succession of Jesuit confessors for spiritual advice) all seemed to suggest that the society was not a religious order but a diabolical conspiracy. But in many important respects—the propensity for political intrigue to advance corporate inter- ests, for example—the Jesuits were like other religious orders of their day, only more successful. Many of their rules and procedures—for instance, the vows of chastity, poverty, and obedience—simply continued centuries-old traditions of Western monasticism. But ever since the little knot of follow- ers gathered around the Spanish mystic and ex-soldier Inigo de Loyola (Ignatius Loyola) coalesced into the Society of Jesus in 1540, the Jesuits displayed a number of characteristics that set them apart from other Catho- lic religious.[18]

Whereas medieval monks withdrew from "the world" (secular society) into an enclosed space where existence was structured around a regular routine of prayer, Jesuits sanctified themselves by going out into the world wherever and in whatever way the cause of Christianity could be advanced. There was no room in Loyola's scheme for cloister walls or for the immo- bility of a rooted life; as his successor, Jéronimo Nadal, put it, "The world is our house."[19] In theory, a Jesuit had to be available to go wherever he was needed at a moment's notice, and for that reason he could not accept the constraining responsibilities of a parish appointment. To be a Jesuit, according to the organization's initial ethos, was to be a traveler, indeed a pilgrim, one who followed the example of Loyola himself and renounced security in favor of sanctification, though a growing emphasis on educa- tion introduced tensions between the ideals of poverty and mobility and the need for stability.[20] Even in Claude Chauchetière's time, however, the comparatively settled and sedate Jesuits still prized the detachment from familiar surroundings, from friends, family, and established routines, that comes with the knowledge that every place of residence is only a tempo- rary stop. In practical terms, the society still maintained great flexibility, which allowed it to respond to changing circumstances and new opportu- nities. The vow of obedience by which a Jesuit submitted his will to that of his superiors similarly contributed to the society's effectiveness by facilitat- ing the coordination of members distributed across Europe and around the globe. Like the vows of obedience required in virtually every Catholic order, their purpose was primarily to help members overcome self-will rather than to empower those in command. Any acquaintance with Jesuit practice in this period reveals that orders from superiors were often formulated in consultation with the Jesuit "under obedience" and that, in many situations, notably in overseas missions, Jesuits required far more in the way of initiative and resourcefulness than of submission of the will.

Many commentators have remarked on the precocious modernity of Jesuit "practices of the self." Though actuated by long-standing Christian aspirations to imitate Christ and unite with God, they were innovators when it came to the technical procedures for shaping individual personality and subjectivity. Just as a Jesuit cultivated expertise in reengineering the school-boy and fashioning him into a particular sort of man, he also concentrated on remaking himself, constantly monitoring his progress and modifying his habits in a lifelong campaign of self-creation. Loyola's *Spiritual Exercises* was the classic expression of this aspect of Jesuit practice. It was a program for periodic retreats in which the subject goes through a series of visualization exercises, imagining scenes from the lives of Jesus and of the Virgin, conducting internal conversations with these figures, and examining his own conscience. Solitary meditation alternated with consultation with a spiritual adviser in an intensive effort to find out what was coming between the individual and a perfect union with Christ and to devise the appropriate routine of prayers, fasts, and other devices for removing those obstacles. The *Spiritual Exercises* also contains marvelous techniques for considering important life decisions on questions such as whether one has a clerical vocation.[21]

During his two years at Bordeaux as a novice on probation, Claude Chauchetière underwent the spiritual exercises regularly as one component of a larger program of self-fashioning, the most thoroughgoing one that the Society of Jesus could offer. Learning the techniques of confession and mass, practicing preaching, and mastering other priestly skills was only one part of the process. The main business of novices was to advance in "grace and spiritual gifts" under the supervision of a seasoned spiritual director.[22] Because this was a period of probation, novices were monitored to see whether they should be encouraged to continue their training or gently eased out. Claude spent his two years perpetually amazed that he had not been ejected, for he had a low opinion of his spiritual and intellectual attainments. His superiors thought otherwise, as revealed by their evaluation, forwarded to Rome toward the end of his novitiate. The Jesuits compiled, every three years or so, detailed reports on each member in a given province, and in the "triennial catalog" of the province of Aquitaine for 1665, Claude is assessed this way:

Ingenium: bonum (character: good)
Iudicium: bonum (judgment: good)
Prudentia: in spe magna (discretion: great hope, good potential)

Profectus in litteris: supra mediocr. (advancement in learning:
    above average)
Naturalis complexio: suaviter malincholica (natural complexion:
    pleasant and melancholy)

"Melancholy" did not necessarily imply a mood of gloom and depression;
rather, it was a medical term derived from the Galenic theory of natural
"humors." To have a "melancholy complexion" was to be constituted with
an excess of black bile, a condition that usually went along with a reserved
and studious personality, as opposed, for example, to a hot-tempered "colic"
humor. Note that Chauchetière's talents received a positive rating—and there
was no modern "grade inflation" here; plenty of his colleagues were assessed as below average—at the conclusion of his novice years.[23]

Chauchetière's own view was that he was not making progress toward
"the perfection that I aimed at." He dealt easily with the inevitable "temptations against purity," feeling no need to "mortify the flesh" with severe
self-flagellation; instead, Claude followed the approved Jesuit technique of
moderate mortification. To master the natural impulse to seek bodily comfort, he deliberately adopted uncomfortable postures whenever he sat down.
His major problem, as he recalled thirty years later, was one of "scruples,"
a false and excessive sense of humility. It could be sent by the Devil to prevent a Christian from doing good through a crippling sense of inadequacy;
and of course an insecure boy like Claude, passing through a rigorous screen-
ing process designed to test his vocation, was particularly susceptible. His
challenge, as he went through his daily examination of conscience and his
periodic spiritual exercises, was to sort out the illusory from the real in
his internal sense of his limitations and of his unworthiness in the sight of
God. The spiritual director no doubt helped him with this, encouraging him
to regard his insecurities as a sign that God wished him to cultivate the virtue of humility. Taking the advice to heart, Claude prayed for the success of
his classmates in their academic competitions and volunteered for all the
"lowest jobs" the college could provide. But he stayed in the order and,
despite his misgivings, took his second vows in 1665, and then returned to
Poitiers as an "approved scholar."

At the age of twenty, Claude was now a Jesuit, but his advanced education was only just beginning. More years of arduous study, interspersed with
a series of increasingly responsible teaching assignments, still lay ahead
before he could be welcomed into the order as a full and permanent member. His hometown of Poitiers was where the student Jesuits of Aquitaine
came for their academic training, consisting in theory of a three-year course
in philosophy, followed by four years of theology. Under the rubric of
"philosophy" came a number of fields of study, including what we would
call science, as well as mathematics, a subject Claude excelled in and enjoyed,

though he considered his enthusiasm for math a "fault" insofar as it nur-
tured his pride and distracted him from spiritual concerns. Another source
of pleasure at about this time was welcoming his brothers Jean and Jacques
into the society as novices. With their parents dead and their stepmother
now remarried and building a new family, there was a sense in which the
three brothers were reconstituting a family of sorts within the Society of
Jesus. They seem to have maintained a close relationship, though they were
hardly ever together in the same physical location.

Before moving on from philosophy to theology, Chauchetière had to
complete his régence, an interlude between stints of higher education when
the Jesuit-in-training worked as a teacher at a junior level. He drew the short
straw and was assigned to the college of Tulle, a backwater deep in the Corèze
and "the most despised place in my province." Here he had to teach beginning Latin, starting with the intake class and continuing with the same group
of boys as they advanced through the grammar program. He did not like
Tulle, nor did he enjoy teaching at such an elementary level, finding it "a
great trial because of the limited ability of the scholars."[24] After three years
of drilling conjugations and declensions into resistant skulls, Claude was
finally allowed to move up the educational hierarchy to the humanities and
rhetoric courses. With older students, more stimulating subjects, and, no
doubt, a higher level of confidence and pedagogical skill on his part, he seems
to have derived satisfaction from this phase of his teaching career. Contrib-
uting also to the boost in morale was his transfer from the "despised" Tulle
to more congenial colleges: first Saintes and then La Rochelle. At the conclusion of this extended period as college instructor and trainee Jesuit, the
twenty-eight-year-old Chauchetière returned to Poitiers, ready to tackle his
theology course, the one remaining hurdle before he took the final vows
that would make him a Jesuit father.

Teaching, studying, mastering classical languages, acquiring academic credentials and professional qualifications: from his late teens to his early thir-
ties, Claude Chauchetière was caught up in the strenuous process that turned
a talented boy into a Jesuit priest. But these activities were only one dimension, and not necessarily the most important one, of his education. The
founder of the Society of Jesus, for all his insistence on rigorous intellectual
training to enhance the order's reputation and to make it effective, still considered learning, refinement, and prestige to be only a means to an end for
the individual Jesuit. What counted ultimately was the achievement of a state
of religious perfection, the union with Christ, that had been the goal of
Christian monasticism since the hermits of the ancient church first went out
into their desert retreats. Ignatius Loyola's originality lay in developing a

mysticism of *engagement* with the world rather than *withdrawal* from it, but in fundamental respects the aim was a traditional one.[25] For himself and for the society he established, Loyola tried to combine an intense inward-looking spirituality with an outward and worldly orientation, bequeathing to future generations a legacy of creative tension in the continual struggle to maintain a balance between the two dimensions of religious life. Inevitably, there was a tendency for the Jesuits in particular historical circumstances to lean collectively toward one pole or the other, and everywhere there were differences in personal temperament that led some Jesuits to concentrate more on cultivating the spirit, others to strive more for practical success in learning, preaching, or administration. Chauchetière's autobiographical writings leave no doubt that he was located at the mystical end of the spectrum.

When he sat down in 1695 to sum up his life, the story Claude found in the yellowing notes and fragments of text he had been carrying with him since the time he was a novice was one of hard-won spiritual development. His progress toward union with God was slow but by no means gradual; rather, it proceeded by leaps, interrupted by periods of stagnancy and regression. Nor was it a complacent narrative, for Chauchetière always seemed aware that his achievements were incomplete and provisional.

Looking back on his student days, just after the completion of his novitiate, Claude saw himself as a spiritual child, striving to "detach myself from the world" and from everything, including his studies in mathematics, that might draw his attention away from heaven. He wanted to go further and "detach myself from myself" but felt he was making no progress toward that goal. Practiced in humility and fighting down all the temptations of selfishness and complacency, he still felt distant from God and suffered long periods of "aridity" when his prayers seemed empty. When he took the spiritual exercises during his philosophy studies at the Poitiers college, he found he had nothing to say: "For a long time, I was like an animal that thinks of nothing."[26] Moving to Tulle for his *régence* only cast his spirits lower. Cut off from his brothers and from his mathematical studies in an out-of-the-way town, performing thankless work with hopeless students, Chauchetière hit a low point; indeed, he went through just the sort of personal crisis that typically precedes a breakthrough for spiritual seekers in the Christian tradition.[27]

For five years, he had been preparing for this moment without ever knowing when it would come; or, for that matter, if it would come; or what form it would take if and when it came. Struggling to overcome the promptings of ego, the desires of the flesh, the comforts of family and friends, the distractions of everyday life, he had studied sacred texts, had taken the sacraments, and had prayed regularly with all the fervor he could muster. Throughout, his aim had been to submerge himself, evacuating from his person all that came between him and perfect union with God.

He could prepare the conditions and did so to the best of his ability, but of course he could not gain his end simply through his own efforts.

Then, one Christmas night it happened. He was lying in bed listening to the sound of the church bells, and suddenly he was swept away. Claude's autobiography is vivid and precise on this, more than on any other point:

> In the year 1668, about 9 or 10 at night on Christmas Eve, I heard the bells tolling the hour. At first I found this sound pleasing, and then, I know not how, I was hurriedly transported to this mystery. All of a sudden, my soul was completely changed and reordered. My body was embalmed in the fragrance I smelled. I spent the entire night in a state of ravishment. I wept for joy and I thanked our lord for having guided me as he had done. My transports kept increasing, though I did nothing but follow the spirit conducting me. I had nothing to do myself, but simply to watch myself in amazement as I was charmed by God.

All night and all the next day, the transport continued. So pleasing was this rapture that he had the greatest difficulty tearing himself away when morning came and it was time for him to assist with mass. He went through the ceremony in a daze until the point when he swallowed the host, whereupon his chest began to hurt, and he felt he would suffocate. In retrospect, he realized this may have been the effect of holding his breath, but at the time, the painful sensation felt like an intensified "grace" as the body of Christ entered his own body. Tears flowed freely as he followed the priest around the church, holding the lamp for the distribution of communion bread and desperately praying to God not to let him break down completely in public. He managed to make it back to his room, but the minute he had loosened the band of his surplice, he was overcome: "I could never explain the reciprocal caresses that occurred then within me."[28]

The mystic ecstasy seems to have lasted a night and a day. It would be followed by others, though never as overwhelming as the first one. As never before, Chauchetière now felt the presence of God when he prayed, and ever since that Christmas, as he put it, "I was touched more by love than by fear."[29] Love is the constant theme of Christian mysticism: not dutiful, cerebral love but intimate, personal and, very frequently, erotically charged love; love in the form of a complete body-and-soul experience; love that gives one's self without reserve, seeking only to merge with the beloved. In the late Middle Ages and early modern period, it was mostly women— Catherine of Siena and Theresa of Avila are two well-known examples— who manifested this loving mysticism in its most spectacular forms, but men too partook. The mystical experience required long, intense preparation but also a certain passivity at the crucial juncture. Commonly, it went together with asceticism, another practice with a bodily focus and another devotion that appealed particularly, though not exclusively, to Catholic women.

Needless to say, mysticism was not simply a kind of spiritual thrill seeking. It was a serious, and very demanding, form of religion, understood by its adepts to provide profound and lasting (though ineffable) knowledge, even as it confirmed and strengthened the practice of Christian virtue. But because of its emphasis on unmediated contact with God, mysticism tended to raise the suspicions of vigilant churchmen who feared its subversive potential, especially in the hands of women and other "ignorant" lay-people.[30] No matter how vehemently mystics protested their orthodoxy, their subjectivism seemed to imply contempt for theological learning and for the authority of the ecclesiastical hierarchy. Moreover, there was always the possibility that the sense of inspiration and oneness with God could be a delusion or a trick of the Devil. Accordingly, a well-regulated Jesuit mystic like Chauchetière was careful to report his experiences to his spiritual adviser and watch for danger signs in the form of wild or sinful inclinations. The rule was, hide nothing from your confessor, but reveal nothing to anyone else, for boasting about divine "favors" of this sort, succumbing, in other words, to the sin of pride, was an indication that something was amiss.

Claude says little about his confessor in the autobiography, but it is likely he would have had a sympathetic hearing, for mysticism was rife within the Society of Jesus in France at that time. In the seventeenth century, it has been said, mysticism found a home in France, just as it had thrived in Spain in the sixteenth century and in Germany in the fifteenth.[31] While mysticism flourished across Catholic France, a specifically Jesuit version developed, arising in association with an internal reform movement that, in the first half of the century, set out to challenge complacency and worldliness within the order. In the decades just before Chauchetière was born, the college of Poitiers and the Jesuit establishments of the surrounding region had been a hotbed of the "extraordinary devotions," ascetic and mystical practices pursued by a circle of young men dedicated to religious interiority. The movement was partly inspired by the Life of Saint Theresa, recently translated into French, with all its lush descriptions of mystical transports, but it was also a reaction against what its adepts considered an excessive emphasis within the society on the raising of funds, the construction of buildings, and the relentless effort to secure prestige in the eyes of secular society. They wanted to get back to a "purer" Ignatian focus on the spiritual development of members, rather than the institutional success of the order.[32] As a semiorganized program for institutional reform, the "extraordinary devotions" were suppressed, but the mood and style of mysticism continued to influence French Jesuits through the second half of the century, when Claude Chauchetière's religious outlook was taking shape.

For mystics more than for most Catholics of the period, the self was a fundamental problem to be solved.[33] All Christians tried to obey the law of God and overcome the sinful impulses that were natural to fallen humanity, but mystics felt the need to go beyond mere obedience—a resolution through fear of the contradiction between God's will and the subject's will—to a merging of wills, through love, that would eliminate the need for obedience. Rather than strive for *resignation* in the face of the pain, death, frustration, and humiliation that God had ordained, they sought to achieve *indifference*. "Indifference" was a fundamental concept in the mystical Catholicism the young Chauchetière imbibed. It implied, as the pinnacle of Christian perfection, not the mere curbing of the self's sinful tendencies but an *annihilation* of the self as an entity separate from God. Much behavior that seems bizarre when viewed from a vantage point outside this mentality—fasting and self-flagellation, but also more subtle behaviors such as Claude's prayers in favor of his opponents in school competitions or the vow of a Jesuit missionary to spend the rest of his life among the Indians of Canada *because* he had discovered within himself a deep aversion to the country and its people[34]—all need to be understood in light of this aspiration to eradicate the self.

"The world," with its allurements of comfort and conviviality and, most dangerously of all, its ability to confer approval and prestige, was filled with traps for those who sought "indifference" of this sort. Jesuit mystics did not want to fit comfortably into the society that had given them birth, nor were they without ambivalence toward the institutional church that was their home. They accepted orthodox doctrine and the authority of the pope and of their superiors, and they accepted the religious hierarchy dividing themselves as priests (or priests-in-training) from the lay masses, and yet they worried about the threat to "indifference" posed by their own elevated situation as respected clerics. They prized their ordination, their membership in a prestigious order, and their higher education, but at the same time they felt the need to denigrate these in the interests of humility. Their feelings about book learning and theological expertise, a pillar of the ideology of clerical superiority and a field in which the Jesuits particularly excelled, were particularly complicated. Even as they pursued their extremely demanding studies, Jesuit mystics like Chauchetière had to remind themselves that these were ultimately insignificant. At every level, paradox abounded as mystics struggled to achieve spiritual glory that could only come with humility, pursued "consolation" available only to those who had renounced desire, worked to acquire the very theological expertise they regarded as an instrument of human pride, circulated letters, and published books proclaiming that the most important insights could never be put into words.

In the mystical writings that passed through Poitiers, Tulle, and the other Jesuit colleges of France, the spiritual superiority of the "ignorant" and the "humble" was a recurrent theme. According to historian Michel de Certeau, this mystical discourse was a symptom of the general spiritual crisis of the period: a nostalgic hankering on the part of the religiously sophisticated after an unqualified faith that now seemed available only to "simple" folk. It was the expression of a movement "that led 'spiritual' learned men and theologians towards witnesses who humbled their competency: maids, cowherds, villagers, and so on. These characters, real or fictitious, were like pilgrimages to an alternative 'illumination.' . . . A humbled theology, after having long exercised its magistracy, expected and obtained from its other the certainties that eluded it."[35] One of the most famous mystical texts of the time was a letter by the Jesuit professor Jean-Joseph Surin describing his encounter on a long coach journey with a poor, completely illiterate lad. This former servant, "simple and extremely crude of speech," nevertheless instructed the Jesuit theologian on sacred mysteries.[36] Certeau notes that the "young man on the coach" may well have been a fictional creation; and even if he did exist in reality, his role in Surin's letter is as an alter ego, a projection of the antirational, anti-intellectual side of the author's thought.

In a society structured by hierarchies of honor and wealth, one where men ruled over women and where educated clerics claimed exclusive religious authority, male mystics were fascinated by the notion that the poor, the despised, and the uninstructed might be closer to God. By the same token, they were inclined to idealize women. But these men were far from suggesting that women should perform sacraments or that beggars should rule the kingdom; the powerless and the unlettered were, for them, more abstractions than living, breathing human beings. Moreover, these deprived characters entered mystical writings primarily for purposes of negation, personifying all the qualities of simplicity and humility that these religious sophisticates feared they lacked. In Surin's letter on the coach journey, his enlightened/illiterate interlocutor is identified only in the vaguest terms; the central character in the narrative remains the author himself: Surin looking and listening, Surin being amazed, Surin accepting his lesson in humility.

In religious, and even in social, terms, mystics like Surin and Chauchetière were insiders looking out, scholarly initiates with a sense that something was missing in the ordered, rational, and bookish world they inhabited. In his analysis of French mystical writings from the period, Mino Bergamo discerns a basic interplay between persons and qualities familiar to both reader and writer and associated with their bounded sphere of order, law, and authority, on the one hand, and, on the other hand, a wider, limitless world beyond, imagined as the antithesis of the familiar sphere. This second sphere suggests savagery and chaos; it is associated with the female and the nonrational; and in this discourse, it is infinitely preferable to the world of boundaries and constraints.[37] "I want to appear in this world as a savage," wrote Surin in one of his poems.[38] Of course Surin knew even less about real "savages" than he did about the mysterious youth who shared his coach. Like other representations from the external dimension, his savagery was an imaginative inversion, an upside-down projection of the familiar. Mystical writers conducted an imagined journey out into the realms of anti-order and found an Other that represented the antithesis of their own excessively controlled world. In important respects, their works resemble the literature of travel and exploration that was so popular in Europe at the time, and Bergamo underlines the parallels, labeling this tendency in religious literature "mystic exoticism."[39]

It was in this environment of Jesuit mysticism that Claude Chauchetière matured, struggling to annihilate the self and achieve perfect indifference. Before him were inspiring images of an "out-there," a place far away that was the negation of here; images of savage people, the uninstructed, strangely attired, dangerous "not-me." When academic study and social conformity seemed stultifying, when the promptings of ego raised insurmountable barriers to the achievement of indifference, these exotic locales and alien cultures beckoned to Claude with their promise of help in conquering the self.

Claude's first mystical experience at the age of twenty-three was only an initial step in a long and arduous spiritual ascent. For the next few years, as he moved from Tulle back to Poitiers and then on to the colleges of Saintes and La Rochelle, his spiritual life was disturbed by recurrent inner struggles. After that first ecstatic and erotically charged experience in his chamber at Tulle, he began to be troubled by powerful sexual urges: "I found myself so full of disorder as to become insupportable to myself." This led to "insensitivity" toward God, a sense that his prayers and devotions were empty gestures: "I had entered a labyrinth and could not find a way out." Then he would feel close to God once again, experiencing an illuminating sense that his hardships were in fact correctives to willfulness; God was teaching him to surrender himself more completely. Up and down he went, ever "sighing for the hidden life," but experiencing "an alternation of consolation and desolation" until 1671–72, when he reached what he called "my second stage" of mystical enlightenment.[40]

The turning point came during the festival of Saint Francis Xavier, December 3, 1671, when "God gradually dispersed all my clouds." Praying at the altar of that Jesuit missionary-saint as he had done so often since childhood, Claude felt anew the ecstatic sensation of oneness with God, in all its spiritual and bodily manifestations. This time the transports succeeded one another in a regular sequence and were accompanied by a more steady and enduring sense of insight and assurance. During prayer, he sometimes felt a feverish heat, his breathing almost stopped, and he seemed at times to float. Often he woke in the middle of the night, feeling the presence of God at the end of the bed; this occurred most commonly when he was to take communion the next day, and he would lie awake for hours hungering for the host. Other food, indeed, everything that was not God, seemed "insipid," and so asceticism began to come naturally: Claude stopped eating and drinking for intervals, "as if I did not have a body." At the cognitive level, he gained illuminating insights that, as a typical mystic, he could never adequately convey in words: "God gave me such clear knowledge of himself and of his mysteries, that he seemed to me completely new." This general knowledge of divine mysteries, as well as the physical transports that accompanied it, were intimately bound up with Chauchetière's understanding of God's special plan for him: "The door which admitted me to a state of habitual fervor was a total abandonment of myself to God, giving myself to Him, to come to the missions."[41]

Francis Xavier, the immediate inspiration for Chauchetière's mystical renewal, was one of the great Jesuit saints, and he symbolized the society's missionary tradition. One of Ignatius Loyola's original disciples, Francis had been dispatched, about the time the Society of Jesus was officially established, to go with the Portuguese fleet to India and there work to spread Christianity. Claude would have been thoroughly familiar with his life and writings for Xavier's letters from Asia were regularly read aloud in the refectory when student Jesuits took their meals. Xavier's ten-year career overseas was indeed awe-inspiring. Following in the wake of the armed Portuguese commercial penetration of India, Ceylon, Malaya, and the "Spice Islands," he baptized crowds so large his strong arm and equally strong voice sometimes failed him before he could get to the end of the long line of would-be converts. Seething with restless energy, he pushed beyond the last European outposts to enter distant Japan; then, as he came to realize how much prestige Chinese culture enjoyed in East Asia, he turned to the mainland in one final, ill-fated expedition. Sick and weakened on arrival, he died on the beach near Canton in 1552.

Francis Xavier's letters display none of the ethnographic curiosity and sensitive descriptions of foreign cultures that characterize French Jesuit reports from North America in Claude's day (though there was enough information on exotic lands in Xavier's letters for the Jesuits to print them for the benefit of lay readers; so began the tradition of missionary publication that continued through the *Jesuit Relations* from seventeenth-century New France). Instead, the missionary comes across as a powerful personality, plunging through ancient civilizations with bullheaded determination, tearing the idols from Hindu temples and ordering children to urinate on them, baptizing the cowed or curious masses without inquiring much into their state of mind, then moving on to the next remote destination. As a fervent believer with an urgent sense of purpose, Francis Xavier could create a powerful impression, not least upon the minds of Jesuits in Europe whom he addressed directly and bluntly:

> Many fail to become Christians in these regions because they have no one who is concerned with such pious and holy matters. Many times I am seized with the thought of going to the schools in your lands and of crying out there, like a man who has lost his mind. . . . "How many souls fail to go to glory and go instead to hell through their neglect!" And thus, as they make progress in their studies, if they would study the accounting which God our Lord will demand of them and of the talent which has been given to them, many of them would be greatly moved and, taking means and making spiritual exercises to know the will of God within their soul, they would say, conforming themselves to it rather than to their own inclinations: *"Lord, here I am! What would you have me do? Send me wherever you will, and if need be, even to the Indies!"*[42]

It was by no means every Jesuit who dropped his studies and other duties to venture out into infidel lands following Francis Xavier's example; in fact, the majority of seventeenth-century Jesuits stayed in Europe in their respective countries of origin.[43] Yet the sense of mission and the ideal of self-sacrifice through travel to accomplish God's purposes remained central to the society's corporate identity. Even within Catholic Europe, Jesuits acted as missionaries, sponsoring confraternities in the cities to promote piety among the laity and operating itinerant missions in rural districts to convert the peasantry from religious "ignorance" and "superstition."[44] For English Jesuits and others operating in Protestant-controlled areas, "domestic" mission work was fraught with deadly danger. But even when there seemed to be so much to do close to home, many Jesuits felt drawn to overseas postings where they could imitate Francis Xavier and the early apostles of Christianity.

By the time Claude Chauchetière joined the order, Jesuit missions extended across the five continents known to Europeans. Substantial portions of Japan had been won for Catholicism and then lost again in the anti-Christian reaction of the early seventeenth century. In China, a succession of sophisticated missionaries such as Matteo Ricci had infiltrated the mandarin class, and though they won few converts, their achievements as cultural go-betweens connecting China and Europe were impressive. Meanwhile, another Italian Jesuit and accomplished cross-cultural chameleon, Roberto di Nobili, mastered the ways of a Hindu holy man in southern India. Though Asia taxed Jesuit talents for linguistic and cultural adaptation, it was in the Americas that the largest numbers of converts were gained. Portuguese Jesuits labored in Brazil from the 1550s, herding Indians into sheltered Christian villages where they enjoyed some protection from enslavement in the colony's plantations. In the vast Spanish domains of New Spain and

South America, Spanish Jesuits shared the mission field with other orders, concentrating their efforts mainly on frontier areas such as northern Mexico, Florida, and the vast interior regions known as "Paraguay." It was in this last location that they achieved their greatest successes in the seventeenth century: some hundred thousand Guaraní accepted baptism and came to live in highly regulated *reducciones* where the Christian god was worshiped and his commands strictly obeyed. Though they denounced the violence and cruelty that were so central to Spanish and Portuguese colonialism, the Jesuits benefited greatly from the proximity of brutal conquerors whose depredations had the effect of making mission life seem comparatively attractive to natives.[45]

As an organization, the Society of Jesus conducted missions with clear-headed rational planning: they chose their targets carefully, taking account of political and diplomatic constraints, assessing the adequacy of supply routes and transportation facilities, and endeavoring to avoid duplicating the efforts of other missionary orders. Though frequently regarded as cosmopolitans loyal only to the pope, the Jesuits actually organized their missions mainly within a national framework, attempting as much as possible to cooperate with the imperial projects of Europe's Catholic monarchies. Thus French Jesuits, their efforts coordinated from Paris with only the most distant supervision from Rome, generally went to Canada and the French West Indies, as well as to areas outside European control, such as the Ottoman Empire and Indochina. But whereas the Jesuits as a corporate body planned their overseas evangelizing "objectively," individual Jesuits came to the missions through highly personal and subjective mental processes. Theoretically, any member of the Society of Jesus was sworn to go wherever in the world he was required, but in practice missionaries were volunteers responding to a divinely inspired calling.

As a twenty-seven-year-old teacher of rhetoric at the college of La Rochelle, Claude Chauchetière pondered his missionary vocation. This was generally a good time for him: instructing older boys in an interesting subject, he was also called upon, as the resident rhetoric specialist, to give public lectures and sermons at the magnificent Jesuit chapel. It was here at La Rochelle, moreover, that he enjoyed his second plateau of mystical experience, more stable and serene than the wild flights that had marked his earlier encounters with the divine. When not busy with his students and his books, Claude liked to wander in the gardens that adjoined the college. Since La Rochelle was one of France's premier Atlantic ports and the main depot for colonial shipping, it served as an important way station in the Jesuit global network, with missionaries preparing for embarkation or arriving from abroad and letters arriving from across the Atlantic. It was just the place to think about a career overseas.

In December 1672 the college of La Rochelle played host to two returned missionaries, Father Joseph-François Le Mercier, former superior of the Canadian mission, and another Jesuit, who had been working in the French West Indies. Both were looking for recruits for their respective missions. The visit occurred between the feast of Francis Xavier and Christmas, two salient dates on Claude Chauchetière's personal calendar (like so many of the events recounted in his self-narrative, this one seems providential). Claude made his choice without hesitation. "I chose Canada, the rougher, more obscure option; at that time, it was not highly regarded, except where the sanctification of missionaries was concerned; it was believed that not much could be done there."[46] For his missionary self-surrender, he sought a dark and forbidding place unlikely to bring fame and success. Among French Jesuits who submitted official applications for mission work, more asked to be sent to Constantinople or to the East Indies than to the French North American colony,[47] and so Claude's attachment to what he was already referring to as "mon cher Canada" was certainly the minority choice.

What, beyond the indistinct impressions formed by a teacher's anecdote when he was a small child, would "Canada" have meant to a young man whose life had, up to now, been rather circumscribed? Generally, French people of the seventeenth century regarded New France as an unattractive place of exile, partly because of what they heard about its forbidding climate, but also because of the terrible reports of wars with the Iroquois.[48] The *Jesuit Relations*, a series of annual volumes published between 1632 and 1673 and widely read by clergy and laity alike, were a major source of this frightening image. The *Relations* and the missionary letters that circulated through the Jesuit colleges of France contained fine-grained ethnographic description of the customs of the "savage" peoples of North America, as well as chronicles of the Christian missions, and biographical sketches of heroic missionaries such as Isaac Jogues and Jean de Brébeuf stood out. The inspiring deaths of the New France martyrs were commemorated, too, in the "martyrology" that was read out in Jesuit refectories and in widely reproduced lithographs showing Brébeuf and his colleagues gazing calmly heavenward as naked Indians chopped pieces of flesh from their bodies and burned them with flaming brands.[49] More Jesuits had in fact been killed in Japan, South America, or England than in New France, but the French Jesuits did a brilliant job of dramatizing the deaths of the North American missionaries, skillfully highlighting resemblances linking these with the Passion of Christ. As a consequence, the idea of "Canada" had become intimately linked to martyrdom in French minds of the seventeenth century.

There was more to the colony's forbidding reputation than the association with violence and death, however. Young Chauchetière thought that "not much could be done there," and indeed the *Jesuit Relations* do leave an impression of disappointing results that contrasts with the triumphant sense of spiritual conquest conveyed by the letters of Francis Xavier, as well as the chronicles of the Latin American Jesuits. Instead, one reads of the ill-fated attempt to establish *reducciones* on the South American model for the Montagnais and Algonquin near Quebec; by the late 1640s, most of the Indians had either died or fled, leaving these highly regulated convert communities virtually empty.[50] Meanwhile, the Jesuits were directing the bulk of their efforts to Christianizing the Hurons, a populous Iroquoian nation located inland, far from the French settlements. Most Hurons held the missionaries responsible for the epidemics that afflicted them, and for many years they regarded the Jesuits and their religion with unmixed horror. Only after fifteen years of thankless exertions among people who held them in contempt did Brébeuf and his colleagues finally convince a significant number of Hurons to accept baptism. Not long after that, however, in 1649, the weakened and divided Hurons were attacked and destroyed by their Iroquois enemies. Then, about the time of Claude's novitiate, there was a modest breakthrough as peace with the Iroquois allowed the Jesuits to convert some members of the Five Nations and to establish Christian Iroquois settlements on the St. Lawrence.

Whether dealing with Christian natives or confronting unconverted Indians, the French Jesuits always felt hampered by their comparative powerlessness.[51] In a Mohawk village, they could not count on the deference and respect their education and clerical status would command in Catholic Europe, nor could they lord it over cowed natives as the Spanish Jesuits of Paraguay did. They had to endure being addressed as equals by unlettered hunters; they were made to feel incompetent as they struggled to master the art of the canoe and the snowshoe; frequently their exhortations produced contemptuous laughter. For some proud priests, such humiliating experiences seemed a subtle form of torture, no less painful than the torments inflicted by fire and knife. But for those who sought humility and self-annihilation, this aspect of the Canadian missions, combined with the deadly dangers and the frustrating pace of conversion, formed a package that was both appalling and—for that reason—irresistibly appealing.

Thus, the reader Claude Chauchetière had before him images of a "Canada" that seemed designed for someone with his spiritual needs and predilections. Its associations were with savagery—savage land and savage people—in all the contradictory and powerfully evocative senses that term suggested to Europeans of early modern times. In Chauchetière's imagination, the repellent/ attractive outer world of anticivilization, a place where rationality and dry formality found their opposite, acquired a specific location: it was to be found across the ocean and up the River St. Lawrence. Furthermore, Canada was a place associated with death: not banal, meaningless death but sacrificial death, the death of martyrs and saints. It was where one went to annihilate the self, possibly in a glorious and bloody martyrdom, more likely in a more modest acceptance of the risk of violence and of the certainty of hardship and frustration. Other mystics of the period, Jesuits and non-Jesuits alike, were drawn for similar reasons to the same destination. For the Ursuline nun Marie de l'Incarnation, it was "an earthly paradise where crosses and thorns grow so lovingly,"[52] attractive to the spirit precisely because it was so repellent to the body and to the ego. Chauchetière put it this way: "Thinking of Canada, my nature [i.e., his nonspiritual side] was horrified by the things Our Lord had in store for me."[53]

In the wake of Father Le Mercier's visit to La Rochelle, Chauchetière was in a fervor of excitement, now certain of where his future lay. Sometimes he had to flee the college for the breezy alleys of the adjoining gardens "to evaporate the fire that was consuming me."[54] The returned missionary had promised to inform New France's Jesuit agent in Paris of Claude's interest in Canada, and before departing he gave Claude some basic instruction in the Huron language. He also left him with handwritten Huron prayers and other manuscript writings of the sort that Canadian Jesuits used to initiate new missionaries into the complexities of Amerindian languages. Claude devoured these materials and soon developed the habit of saying his rosary in Huron: "I preferred reciting it in that language rather than in Latin because of the spiritual consolation that this method of praying God caused in me."[55]

Linguistically, he was clothing himself in the persona of the Indian Other, an experiment in identification that gave him great satisfaction. At one level, he was simply preparing himself for a future in Canada, but his remark about "spiritual consolation" suggests a process with deeper personal meaning. By no means the first Christian mystic to engage in a version of "cross-dressing," Claude was playing with his self-identity, venturing symbolically into a sphere where the learned language of theology was never heard. For others, transgression had more commonly involved gender lines, with male clerics putting themselves temporarily into a woman's position in order to approach God in a mood of enhanced humility, but for a Jesuit in seventeenth-century France, putting oneself on the other side of a great cultural divide could be equally stimulating. Hence Surin's wish to "appear in this world as a savage" and Chauchetière's impulse to address God in the language of the Hurons. For the gender cross-dressers as for the cultural cross-dressers, the imaginative projection was typically "downward" from a situation of higher to one of lower status and power; and though there were good religious reasons to "humble" oneself in this way, there may also have been an unavowed thrill in temporarily shedding the burdens and responsibilities of power without really relinquishing its privileges.[56]

Chauchetière soon discovered there were other, less pleasant, ways of cultivating humility when he returned to Poitiers for the dreaded theology program, an intellectually daunting ordeal he needed to endure before embarking as a missionary. Of his three-year battle with the abstruse doctrines of Catholicism he wrote, "God worked to annihilate me and to make me become nothing." He did his best to accept the "pain" involved as another disguised "blessing." Claude could be excessively severe in his self-assessments, but the periodic reports contained in the "triennial catalog" suggest that he really did have difficulty with the challenges of theology. When Claude was a novice, his college rector had rated him "above average" in the "advancement in learning" column, and the same notation applied in 1669 when he was teaching at Tulle; but in 1672 he received the notation "not great," and by 1675, in the midst of the theology course, it had sunk to "medium."[57] Yet Claude had made an effort to renounce intellectual ambition, and he seems in fact to have attained a level of tranquillity by this time, feeling "grace flowing through my soul as if from a great river that has carved out its course."[58] He completed three years and then dropped out of theology one year short of attaining his degree. It was, in fact, quite common for Jesuits to curtail their studies in this way, especially those who were not destined for academic duties in Europe; indeed, the order positively encouraged trainees to renounce unnecessary degrees. When he emerged from the Poitiers college in 1677, Chauchetière could nevertheless be considered a highly educated man, with three years of philosophy plus three years of theology beyond the secondary level; additionally, he had five years of teaching experience.

Fired with a youthful missionary enthusiasm, Claude was nevertheless a mature man of thirty-two when the call came to join the New France mission. His autobiography is silent on the circumstances surrounding his departure from Poitiers and his voyage to the land that had so long served as the focus of his spiritual fantasies. It appears that he landed at Quebec in the summer of 1676 and that he served for a time at the nearby Jesuit mission of Lorette; there he studied the Huron language, a good linguistic base, as it would turn out, on which to build a knowledge of the related Iroquois languages that were spoken at Kahnawake. Having given himself a head start before leaving France, Claude was able to lead Huron children in prayer by the end of his first week. After a year at Lorette and Quebec, Claude was sent up the St. Lawrence to Sault St. Louis (Kahnawake), the mission for Iroquois converts that had recently been established across the river from Montreal. Curiously, he remained a student Jesuit for a year and a half after arriving in Canada, only taking his vows to become a full-fledged Jesuit priest in February 1678.[59] There is no obvious explanation for the delay. Was he hesitating to take the final step in dedicating himself to the Society of Jesus and its evangelizing mission?

When Claude arrived at the Sault in the summer of 1677, the mission superior was Jacques Frémin, a veteran missionary already suffering from failing health. Within months, Frémin had returned to France for medical treatment, leaving Chauchetière alone with only one colleague, Pierre Cholenec. The two remaining Jesuits, roughly the same age and both comparatively new to Canada, were destined to lead closely intertwined careers in the Montreal/Sault St. Louis area for the rest of their lives. Cholenec, a Breton Jesuit educated at the Collège Clermont (later Louis-le-Grand) at Paris, was in every respect the senior partner. Four years older than Claude, he had a longer experience as a missionary, and his university degree and status as a "professed father" gave him a higher position in the Jesuit hierarchy. In spite of this disparity, the two were nevertheless colleagues;[60] Claude was never really under Cholenec's command. They seem to have had quite different temperaments: Pierre comes across in the surviving documentation as relatively stable, hardheaded, and businesslike, more or less immune to the alternating moods of enthusiasm and depression that are so prominent a feature of Chauchetière's personality (though it must be said that Cholenec left no truly personal writings; this characterization is based mainly on his treatment of Tekakwitha and her memory).

Living in the Jesuit residence at the Sault with Cholenec—they were joined in 1679 by a new superior, Jacques Bruyas—Chauchetière launched into the busy round of duties that fell to a missionary in this burgeoning native settlement: celebrating mass on a daily basis, taking confession, visiting the sick, instructing newcomers, tending to the dying and dead, supervising work on the farm, writing reports. No doubt he could appreciate the importance of all these repetitive tasks in the larger scheme of things, but he may have had difficulty squaring his unheroic situation at the Sault with the Xavieran conception of the missionary vocation and the overblown image of Canada that had inspired him. Surely at some level, he must have realized before coming here that his colleagues would not all be saints; that the natives would be neither pure embodiments of natural virtue nor religiously empty vessels grateful to be filled with the truths of Christianity. Surely someone must have warned him that the colony was more than just a battleground for the contending forces of God and the Devil. But would he have been fully prepared for the mundane realities of colonial life, especially now that peace had been established with the Five Nations, life was comparatively secure, and the last Jesuit martyrs had been in their graves for more than twenty-five years? And how would he have fared as he deepened his acquaintance with real Indian people, glimpsing outlooks, traditions, and experiences that could not easily be reduced to a negation of civilization? Here he was at last at his longed-for destination, among real Indians in the land that for years he had thought of as "my dear Canada." Disappointment was almost inevitable.

For whatever reasons—and his writings reveal little of the specific circumstances—Chauchetière experienced a severe crisis of adaptation in the late 1670s, a year or two after landing at Quebec. He poured out his soul in letters to his brothers, then still in the midst of their Jesuit training in France, and though the letters have been lost, they must have conveyed a sense of deep despair.[61] Jean Chauchetière felt it necessary to write back with elaborate arguments proving the existence of God and reminding his brother how to examine his conscience for indications of what the Lord required of him. His younger brother, Jacques, less sympathetic, simply told him to cease this unedifying correspondence, which was causing consternation as it circulated through Jesuit circles in France. All indications are that this was the worst period of despondency and the most serious crisis of faith in Claude's long and disturbed career. Like earlier periods of darkness, however, this one ended with a sudden, providential reversal, which he could date precisely: April 17, 1680.

As usual, Claude Chauchetière came away convinced that God had planned his rescue long before he got himself into difficulties. Had he not felt called to the missions in 1668, just when the New France Jesuits were beginning to convert the Iroquois? Had he not come to Sault St. Louis in 1677, within months of Tekakwitha's arrival? Even though he had not recognized her as the instrument of his salvation while she still lived, he came to believe that God had sent Catherine "to deliver me from a great interior affliction that lasted an entire year, to the point where I doubted my vocation; but I was delivered from all my scruples and from all my affliction and I was pulled from my hell, when I went, in spite of myself, to recommend myself to the prayers of that servant of God who died on the seventeenth of April 1680 and whom I cared for during her illness." Mediated by death, Chauchetière had experienced his intimate encounter with the Other. "After that, I was in an endless paradise, [entry to] which cost me only one year of pain."[62]

Looking back much later from the vantage point of his fifty-first year, Claude Chauchetière could discern meaning and purpose in his life as the chosen herald of Catherine Tekakwitha. Fifteen years of his life had been devoted to repaying his debt to the Mohawk virgin, testing, proving and proclaiming her holiness, but also writing about other, living, Christian Iroquois with the warmest admiration. It was a remarkable breakthrough, unique in the annals of early modern missionary history, to exalt a native in this way and in explaining it we have to consider both the extraordinary religious career of Tekakwitha, the subject of the next chapter, and the unusual receptivity of Chauchetière to the idea of Indian holiness.

The Jesuit's attitude toward Catherine was surely inseparably connected to his ideas and feelings about her people more generally. After 1680,

Chauchetière wrote about the Iroquois of Kahnawake in the most glowing terms, more unreservedly positive than any of the other French missionaries of the seventeenth century. Here is a characteristic passage from one of his letters:

> We see in these Indians beautiful vestiges of a human nature that has been entirely corrupted in civilized peoples. Of all the 11 passions they have only two; anger is the greater of these and even so they only display it to excess in wartime. Living together without lawsuits, lacking avarice and being content with their small portion, and applying themselves diligently to their work; no one could be more patient, hospitable, affable, liberal, moderate in speech. Indeed all our fathers, as well as the French who have gone among the Indians, agree that their life is sweeter than ours.[63]

Though framed, of course, according to the standards of Catholic religion and European civility, these effusions are not simply a recitation of noble savage clichés: Claude knew the Iroquois of Kahnawake very well, as his descriptive/ethnographic writings make abundantly clear. The conventions of hagiography prevented Claude from doing justice to the Iroquois context of Catherine's life in the biography he composed; thus he praises the "saint" in isolation, while saving his appreciative portrait of her people for other texts. Non-Christian Iroquois still seemed evil to him and, for that reason and to win over European readers, he presented her in the land of her birth as "a lily among thorns." And yet it seems clear that his revelations about Catherine were the product of, were indeed the personalized expression of, a new appreciation of native culture that was forming in this Jesuit's mind. "What I have said about Catherine," he wrote in his 1695 autobiography, "could be said of several Indian men and women now still living."[64]

According to my speculative reconstruction of Chauchetière's spiritual and personal crisis of the late 1670s, it was the collision of mystical pro-savage expectations with the concrete realities of Canadian Indian life that had brought the missionary to the brink of despair. What rescued him, I suggest, was a deeper acquaintance with the Iroquois Christians of Kahnawake. Mastering their language and learning about their outlook and way of life allowed him to appreciate them in a less naïve way. As he recovered, then, from his initial shock and disappointment, Claude seems to have found ways to reconcile his initial stance of mystical exoticism, the projection outward of inverted forms of European norms, with his personal experience of a real human community struggling to find its way in a shifting world of war, epidemics, and colonialism. The result was a modified, an enriched and grounded, form of exoticism, one in which the central viewpoint was somewhat uncertain, where cultural difference was not pure otherness, and where there was room for a "savage" saint.

After seventeen years of service at the mission of Kahnawake, followed by a further fourteen years at the Montreal college, Claude Chauchetière was moved to the college at Quebec, the main Jesuit establishment in New France, where sick and infirm missionaries were cared for. There he died in 1709, aged sixty-three.

We know little about the exact circumstances of his death, but we do know the date. We know, further, that dates and anniversaries mattered to this missionary. Ever since Catherine's death on April 17, 1680, his writings had displayed a preoccupation with that date and with what he came to see as correspondences between significant dates in his life and hers. This is what he wrote in his spiritual autobiography: "But the greatest grace the God granted me was the relation he willed me to have with Catherine Tegakouita, for I became aware that, at the same time that God called me from France to come to this country, the Jesuit fathers took possession of the Iroquois missions. And at the same time that God granted me further blessings, he called Catherine to the faith. And at the very season of the very year that I arrived at the mission of the Sault, it was at that same time and year that Catherine arrived at the mission." The chain of correspondences in fact continued long after Claude Chauchetière ceased recording them. I do hope that, on that day in 1709 when he drew his last breath, he was conscious and fully aware that the calendar read "April 17."[65]

4

Kahnawake: A Christian Iroquois Community

Wʜᴇɴ ᴄʟᴀᴜᴅᴇ ᴄʜᴀᴜᴄʜᴇᴛɪÈʀᴇ ᴀɴᴅ ᴄᴀᴛʜᴇʀɪɴᴇ ᴛᴇᴋᴀᴋᴡɪᴛʜᴀ ꜰɪʀꜱᴛ ᴄᴀᴍᴇ ᴛᴏ Kahnawake in 1677, both could feel they were at the outer edge of their respective worlds. From Claude's point of view, Kahnawake was "the mission of Saint Francis Xavier at Sault St. Louis," a Jesuit establishment housing an Indian community just at the point where French civilization met the wild North American forest. When he looked out over the broad St. Lawrence, he could make out the clearings where Canadian *habitants* (settlers) were establishing their farms in the parish of Lachine. Coming from his left, he could hear the roar of the rapids—the "sault" that gave the mission its French name—where the river plunged over and around the scattered boulders, then calmed down, just as it reached the place where he stood, before proceeding on its placid way, past the little town of Montreal, past the capital and port city of Quebec, and on to the Gulf of St. Lawrence, where the sea lanes led back to La Rochelle. To the east of Lachine, the young Jesuit could see the mountain that loomed over Montreal, one of the few bumps on Kahnawake's generally flat horizon. Atop the mountain was a wooden cross, a reminder of the Catholic idealists who had come to this war-torn land in 1642 to found the "City of Mary" as a perfect Catholic society of French settlers and converted savages. That utopian vision was never realized, but Montreal remained; with the surrounding agrarian settlements, it marked French Canada's farthest extension to the southwest. French imperial claims, and the native alliance system that underpinned them,

extended inland over half the continent, but this is where solid French occupation ended.[1]

Since long before the French appeared on the scene, Mohawks had ranged
this stretch of the St. Lawrence, a crossroads where the waterway linking
the Great Lakes to the Atlantic met streams from the far northwest (the
Ottawa) and from New York (the Richelieu and Lake Champlain). There is
no clear evidence to suggest that they occupied the region—since the mid–
sixteenth century, it was something of a no-man's-land, traversed by many
nations, controlled by none—but it certainly formed part of their strategic
perimeter.[2] Mohawks came here to hunt game or to encounter other peoples,
either to trade, to fight, or to negotiate. They were highly affronted when
the French laid claim to Montreal and erected a fort there, and at every opportunity through the long years of Franco-Iroquois war the Mohawks attacked the settlers and damaged their installations. With the establishment of
peace in 1667, the region resumed its old function as a space of encounter
and exchange, and Mohawks and other migrants from the Five Nations flocked
north to see how they might benefit from the new situation. Kahnawake was
the result, a peaceful Iroquois response to the colonization of Montreal that
implied both friendship with the French and the staking of a rival claim to
control this strategic section of the St. Lawrence.

The village was only a year old when the two newcomers made their way
here from their respective starting points. It comprised twenty-two longhouses arranged in two rows, plus a French-Canadian-style wooden house
for the missionaries and a small chapel, soon to be replaced by a more substantial log structure. There were three Jesuits here, Father Jacques Frémin,
the superior, Pierre Cholenec, and now Chauchetière; the Indian population fluctuated widely as people came and went, moving freely between
Kahnawake, the northern hunting grounds, and the older villages of the Five
Nations.[3]

Though newly established at this location, the community already had a
nine-year history at nearby Kentake, a location claimed by the Jesuits as part
of the seigneury of La Prairie, where natives and French-Canadian *habitants*
settled side by side in the 1660s. The move to Kahnawake was dictated partly
by the normal Iroquois practice of managing resources through relocating
villages, partly by the Jesuit desire to isolate the natives from the contaminating effects of French-Canadian brandy traders.

Kahnawake, like Kentake/La Prairie before it, was both a Jesuit mission, that
is to say an instrument of directed religious change, and a self-governing
Catholic Iroquois community. If that double designation seems slightly
contradictory, think how many ambiguities lurk within the terms "Catholic"

and "Iroquois" in this historical setting. If we ask exactly how a community might manifest both a "Catholic" and an "Iroquois" nature at the same time, the difficulties are compounded. In an effort to gain a better understanding of the environment in which Catherine Tekakwitha came into her own and achieved fame as a holy woman, we need to go back to the initial movement of people from the Five Nations to the St. Lawrence. Because the sources for this history come almost entirely from Jesuit pens, it is important to make a special effort to counteract the Jesuits' tendency to exaggerate the degree to which they controlled events. Insofar as it is possible to reconstruct the migration and religious conversion in the light of Iroquois history, rather than as an episode in the history of the missions, it becomes clear that the Jesuits, at least as much as the natives, were improvising, compromising, and making the best of situations they neither created nor fully understood.

In searching for the roots of Christian Kentake and Kahnawake, we shift the scene back to January 1668, shortly after twelve-year-old Tekakwitha first set eyes on French missionaries. One of the Jesuits who had passed through her village of Gandaouagué the previous summer, a young father named Jacques Bruyas, was now installed among the Oneidas, at their populous town near Lake Oneida.[4] While his two colleagues stayed to evangelize the Mohawks, Bruyas had traveled on farther west to the neighboring Iroquois nation, "younger brothers" to the Mohawks. Bruyas was now writing to his superior in Quebec, and his news of the Oneida mission was mostly bad. Communication was his greatest problem: a French-Canadian fur trader named Bocquet had accompanied him from Montreal, but this "interpreter's" knowledge of Iroquoian languages turned out to be next to nil. Bocquet spent most of his time hunting and fishing, leaving the inexperienced Bruyas struggling to make himself understood with a little handwritten book of prayers and sermons in phonetic Huron. Huron may be related to Oneida as English is related to Dutch, but the languages were hardly identical, and Jacques Bruyas does not seem at this point to have had a firm grasp even of Huron. When Oneida people came in small groups to see this French emissary in the longhouse where he lodged, they could make no sense of the sounds he uttered, and so, once their visit was concluded, few bothered to return. In these circumstances, the Oneidas and their guest seem to have formed unfavorable impressions of one another. Bruyas described them in his report as "barbarous" and "cruel," immersed in "Drunkenness, dreams, and Impurity," and they seem, for the most part, to have shunned him.[5]

Eventually, he was befriended by a woman named Gandeacteua. She gave him meat when her husband's hunt was successful and—most important from the missionary's viewpoint—helped him learn Oneida. Gandeacteua had been born an Erie before that nation was destroyed by the Iroquois in 1654–57, but she had been adopted by the Oneidas and had married

Tonsanhoten, another captive adoptee, though he was originally Huron.
Perhaps because of her husband's influence, or possibly because the large
number of Hurons incorporated into the Five Nations had made their
language widely known, she understood Huron and was therefore able to
translate the words the Jesuit read out from his book. We can only guess at
Gandeacteua's motives in attaching herself to the Frenchman. It may be simply that he rewarded her with presents; more likely, she and her husband
may have been interested in cultivating a special relationship with the French
in order to reap any political and commercial advantages that connection
might bring.[6] Tonsanhoten of course came from a nation that had been
closely allied to the French, and it appears further that he had already lived
for a time in or near Quebec, perhaps at the Jesuit mission of Sillery, where
many Hurons had taken refuge.

With Tonsanhoten usually away from the village, Father Bruyas came to
depend on Gandeacteua for practical assistance and as a teacher of Oneida
language and customs. In return, he wanted to give her the gift of eternal
life. Gandeacteua gladly recited Christian prayers with him and even helped
him minister to and baptize her dying aunt, but she showed no interest in
securing baptism for herself. Yet they must have spoken extensively about
myth and metaphysics, for the Jesuit's sole reference work (the Huron
manuscript) dealt with no other subjects. And so the two of them carried
on their colloquy about the cosmic order: he a Frenchman armed with a
text he could scarcely comprehend, she a trilingual Iroquoian trying to bridge
the gap between her second language (Oneida) and her third (Huron), each
of them far from the land of their birth, living among people who had once
been their deadly enemies. The cultural complexities of this scene are characteristic of this "contact zone" in the seventeenth-century Northeast.

Claude Chauchetière recounts the story of Gandeacteua as a subplot in
his biography of Catherine Tekakwitha, for the purpose of recognizing the
instrumental role she played in establishing the sanctified environment in
which the Mohawk saint would flourish. The two women never met, however; Gandeacteua died before Catherine made her journey north. In the
biography and in his history of the Sault St. Louis mission, Chauchetière
praises Gandeacteua as an exemplary Christian, kind, virtuous, and courageous, but he acknowledges that her conversion to Catholicism was by no
means instant.[7]

As the months passed, Bruyas continued to make progress in his language
studies under Gandeacteua's tutelage. But then, one day in the autumn, he
received the devastating news that his teacher was leaving Oneida to visit
Canada. The "interpreter" Bocquet was heading home, and the village council
had decided to organize an escort party to accompany him as far as Montreal.
Tonsanhoten, with his Canadian Huron connections, was quick to volunteer, all the more so because he had a sore leg that he hoped might be treated

in Montreal. Gandeacteua went with him, as did five other Oneidas. Clearly this expedition was much more than a simple courtesy to a departing visitor. The escort offered itself ostensibly to guarantee Bocquet's security, but the more likely Oneida motive was to ensure their own safety as they ventured into the settlements of a former enemy. The French traveler's departure presented the Oneidas with a golden opportunity to test and cement a still-fragile peace and to assess the prospective benefits of closer connections to the lands and the peoples of the north. But where did all this leave poor Jacques Bruyas? Far from encouraging this liaison with Catholic French Canada, the frustrated Jesuit could think only of the trouble the loss of his tutor and friend would cause to the stalled Oneida mission.

All across the Five Nations, probes were going out in the direction of Canada about this time. Almost the minute it was safe to do so, small parties ventured up into what are now the provinces of Ontario and Quebec. After decades of warfare, they certainly knew the way, but now they came north equipped for hunting and trading rather than fighting and raiding. Senecas rounded the western end of Lake Ontario, then plunged inland to the depopulated territories of the Neutral and Huron nations, while groups of Cayugas and Oneidas went by the eastern end of the lake to reach landing places such as Toronto and Cataraqui (Kingston, Ontario, today). Meanwhile, Mohawk and Oneida canoes were making their way into the French and Algonquin areas on the St. Lawrence and Ottawa Rivers, stopping at Quebec, Three Rivers, and Montreal. Though hunting was primarily a male activity, women went along on these expeditions, and the temporary camps they established became, in many cases, the bases for more permanent year-round settlements. By the end of the 1660s, tentative reconnaissance had given way to solid occupation, with six new Iroquois villages dotted along the northern shore of Lake Ontario, while others were taking root farther east near Montreal. All of the original Five Nations contributed to the colonization, and there was considerable intermixing in the new settlements.[8]

This uncoordinated northward drift of population would eventually give rise to the village of Kahnawake. It was neither directed nor even foreseen by the Jesuits. Some astute missionaries were nevertheless able to turn to advantage a situation they had not created. Trolling the stream of migrating humanity, they managed to hook a number of Iroquois, and then set to work trying to convert them to Catholic Christianity.

Winter had already arrived by the time Gandeacteua, Tonsanhoten, and the other Oneidas arrived at Montreal, and so they were able to cross the frozen St. Lawrence on foot. They spent the winter of 1668–69 in Montreal; during a visit to the church, according to Chauchetière, they were impressed by the pageantry of the Christmas services. In the spring, the party moved on to Quebec, where the resident Jesuits instructed the visitors in the ways of their religion. Gandeacteua agreed to be baptized, and she received the

The First Six Indians of La Prairie Coming from Oneida over the Snow and Ice. Chauchetière's drawing shows Gandeacteua, Tonsanhoten, and one of their companions arriving at Montreal in the winter of 1668–69. Behind the three figures a settler's ox is hauling a load of firewood to the French settlement. © Archives départementales de la Gironde, H Jésuites.

Christian name favored by Iroquois converts, Catherine. The missionaries did their best to persuade the newcomers to settle at their "Huron" mission just outside Quebec, but for whatever reasons—a location too remote from their homeland? limited hunting resources? a lack of kin connections with native converts on the spot?—they declined. However, when they were making their way back through Montreal, the Oneidas did succumb to the blandishments of another Jesuit, Father Pierre Rafeix.

The Jesuits possessed a seigneury, La Prairie, on the south shore of the St. Lawrence, almost opposite the town, which had been unoccupied and neglected during the wars as it stood exposed to Iroquois raids. With the return of peace, Father Rafeix wanted to develop the potential of La Prairie, and so he had a house constructed there, hoping to attract French-Canadian *habitants* who would clear the lands and begin establishing rent-paying farms on the estate. At just that point, Gandeacteua's party happened along, and the Jesuit invited them to join the nascent community. For some months, they lodged at his house while Gandeacteua sowed corn and Tonsanhoten built a small longhouse, which the couple moved into in the summer of 1669. (It is not clear what became of the other Oneidas.) With prospective settlers coming from the east to look over La Prairie and with Iroquois coming by from the south, the cabin served as an inn for guests, both native and French. A new community was beginning to take root, with Gandeacteua as its central figure.[9]

Habitant families began clearing the forest, building their square-timber cabins, and preparing the land for plowing so that they could raise wheat and other European crops and livestock,[10] while in another sector of La Prairie, Indian people were erecting a growing village of bark houses and planting fields of corn, beans, and squash. By 1671, several native families had been baptized, and work began on a simple wooden chapel. With Jesuits acting simultaneously as missionaries and parish priests, the mixed flock gathered for services, the French on one side of the church, Indians on the other. The Jesuits were also the local seigneur, collecting rents and other exactions once the settlers brought their land into production. Natives remained exempt from feudal dues.

There was much interaction between the two groups but few signs of any tendency to merge. Intermarriage was notably rare, even though the Iroquois had a surplus of women while the majority of French Canadians were male. This might seem surprising in view of the well-known tendency for French-Canadian fur traders living in the western interior to take partners from among the Algonquian women they encountered there, not to mention government policies that favored interracial marriage.[11] Anthropologist Dean Snow suggests that Iroquoian women were much less inclined than Algonquians to become fur trade wives because their culture placed women at the center of kinship networks; they could hardly be considered, as Algonquian women sometimes were, appendages of male-centered family units.[12] Iroquois women did not "marry out." Rather, they brought husbands into their households, and few Canadian settlers, interested though they might have been in a native wife, would have been prepared to enter a longhouse family in an accessory capacity.

Even by the standards of seventeenth-century Iroquoia, the native population of early Kentake was exceptionally heterogeneous and rather unstable. People came here from the Seneca, Cayuga, Onondaga, Oneida, and Mohawk nations and were joined by some passing Algonquins. Moreover, many—perhaps most—of the Iroquois were of captive origin, and a large number tended to consider themselves Huron.[13] One could not begin to express this diversity in statistical terms, since individual identities were so resistant to simple classifications. Consider the example of Gandeacteua, an Oneida of Erie origin married to an Oneida of Huron origin; her sense of herself as Oneida may not have been absolute, but she could hardly feel Erie when the Erie people had been obliterated; and if she felt inclined, contrary to the usual tendency among Iroquoian women, to identify with her husband's people, she would have to face the fact that the Hurons, too, had been vanquished and dispersed by the Iroquois. Nevertheless, people of variously ambiguous backgrounds did tend to identify with particular ethnic categories; consequently, politics in Kentake revolved around negotiations among these somewhat contrived groupings. Whether ethnic divisions created political divisions or politics to some degree fomented ethnic divisions is not at all clear.

The delicate balance of this multiethnic community was upset in 1673–74 when the great Mohawk leader Kryn, hero of the war with the New England Indians, moved here from Gandaouagué, drawing two hundred Mohawks in his wake. Others clearly resented the sudden Mohawk predominance, even though assimilated captives made up a substantial portion of the new contingent. There appears to have been a great flare-up that resulted in a senior Huron chief leaving the settlement and moving to the Sulpician mission of La Montagne, on the island of Montreal.[14] Many families went with him, especially those who considered themselves "Huron." Over the years, there were attempts at reconciliation, and Christian Iroquoians continued to move between La Montagne, Kentake and Kahnawake, and Lorette, the Jesuit mission near Quebec City. All this migration tended to reinforce the Mohawk character of Kahnawake, but there was still a sizable Oneida and "Huron" presence when Tekakwitha lived there, with the result that maintaining internal cohesion remained a challenge.

Under these circumstances, the Jesuits seem to have had an important role to play as mediators, thanks to their situation somewhat outside the interethnic tensions and squabbles and to their position as privileged intermediaries with the French colonial regime. Beginning in 1671, they

helped to organize elections of "captains" to represent and lead the Oneidas, Mohawks, Hurons, and others at Kentake. In a variation on the Iroquois
tradition of selecting separate leaders for war and for peaceful civic functions, the regime that emerged at Kahnawake featured separate chiefs for
religious and secular functions.[15] Undoubtedly the missionaries had a hand
in instituting that allocation of responsibilities. At the same time, as Father
Chauchetière freely acknowledged, unity depended on the peculiar "genius"
of the Iroquois: among these people, he observed, charity prevailed over
private property and "sociability, visits, hospitality, festivals and reciprocal gift-giving are highly developed."[16]

In 1676, the native component of Kentake/La Prairie's population
moved a few miles to the west, making its new home at Sault St. Louis,
another Jesuit seigneury, though one granted to them in trust by the French
crown for the use of the resident Indians. The relocation had the effect of
emphasizing the sense of separateness from lay French society, for the new
settlement—henceforth known to Iroquois as "Kahnawake"—would be
exclusively native (mostly Mohawk) and Jesuit. And though individuals,
especially men, still tended to come and go, Kahnawake acquired a degree of stability, a distinctive identity, and a more complete set of Iroquois
community institutions.

Along with the ethic of hospitality and reciprocity that Claude Chauchetière
admired so much, the unity of Iroquois communities depended on institutions and rituals of solidarity and conflict resolution, most of which could be
found at Kahnawake when Tekakwitha lived there. There was a council of
elders, just as there was at any other Iroquoian village, and discussions were
conducted there according to the same etiquette—dignified rhetoric, a clear
order of speakers, avoidance of interruption and direct contradiction—and
with the same aspiration to achieve consensus. Clans played a fundamental
role in the life of the community, a fact that was reflected in the layout of
the village, with longhouses arranged in rows by clan and by moiety.[17] The
overwhelming predominance of the Turtle clan caused problems in early
Kahnawake, since the choice of marriage partners, as well as all sorts of ceremonial matters, hinged on the interaction of two or more roughly balanced
clans. A solution was soon found in a restructuring operation that subdivided
the Turtles into a greater and a lesser branch.[18] Obviously, there was much
improvisation, and doubtless many native festivals were modified to avoid
offending Jesuit sensitivities, but it is clear that Iroquoian traditions provided
a basic framework for collective life at Kahnawake.

As an Iroquois salient thrusting into a French colony, the new community was bound to have complicated relations with both the French and the
old Five Nations. Like the other mission communities of New France, Kentake
and its successor, Kahnawake, were intimately involved in the French fur
trade. Trapping expeditions, which took small parties of men and women

far into the interior during the winter and spring seasons, became central to the local economy, much more so than had been the case in Five Nations villages before 1667. Unlike the colonized natives of the Spanish empire, however, these Indians were not integrated into the colonial labor system. They did not work for wages, and the government did not try to force them to serve colonists. There was no labor service requirement here, nor were Indians subjected to any form of tribute. Instead, they supported themselves independently through selling furs and handicrafts to pay for their purchases of imported goods.

Farming, with the traditional "Three Sisters" predominating, remained basic to subsistence, and though some Iroquois acquired horses and other farm animals of European origin, cultivation generally followed time-honored Iroquoian traditions. Signs of trade with the French could be seen everywhere at Kahnawake, in the broadcloth shirts people wore and in the metal tools they wielded, but similar signs could be discerned in the old country of the Five Nations. Most striking is the degree to which this community, on the very doorstep of French Canada's second city, remained staunchly Iroquoian in its manners and customs. Government officials who wanted mission Indians Frenchified complained that they remained completely "savage" in their way of life and unable to speak a word of French.[19]

Politically, too, Kahnawake retained a high degree of autonomy. Accepting that the king was its "father," the convert community resolutely refused to subject itself to his laws and his courts. A Kahnawake man was charged in 1689 with the rape and murder of a young French girl, but the governor of New France ordered the trial suspended and the prisoner released after he received protests from the village elders.[20] Instead of punishing the perpetrator, native justice focused on compensating the victim's family. The governor's concern was to maintain the goodwill of the Christian Mohawks as he prepared for war against the English and their Five Nations allies, and so he allowed the continued judicial autonomy of the natives. They in return manifested their loyalty to the French monarch by taking part in his wars from the late seventeenth century on, doing so as allies, not as subjects; they counted on rewards for their support and always reserved the right to withhold it.

The Kahnawake Iroquois hardly fit the conventional description of a "colonized people." Yet to speak of their relationship with the French empire only in terms of independence and defiance would be to gloss over a fundamental fact: they had come to live on the St. Lawrence in the full knowledge that this entailed close alignment with the French. There were some parallels between their situation and that of the young French-Canadian men who were at the same time making their way through the Great Lakes and the Upper Mississippi. Without really ceasing to be French, these *coureurs de bois* had to adapt to the customs and cultural expectations of the Algonquian societies in which they took up residence.[21] The correspondence with Kahnawake and the other mission settlements of the St. Lawrence is not perfect, but we might still label this "the Indians' Middle Ground," for here in the French-Canadian heartland, the "natives" were also "newcomers," and they had to find ways of adjusting to the expectations of the ambient society without melting into it.

Alignment with the French did not mean that the people of Kahnawake and of the other Canadian missions had to cut themselves off from their relatives back in the old homeland. The "pagan" Iroquois, for their part, and notwithstanding some lingering bitterness over the way the emigrants had abandoned their nation, came to appreciate the value of the new settlement as a listening post and as a diplomatic intermediary in relations with the French. Goods, news, and people moved easily between the northern and the southern settlements, and, in typical Iroquois fashion, loyalties could be complex and ambiguous. In but not of French Canada, tied still to the League Iroquois by fraying bonds of clan loyalty, the Kahnawake Iroquois had to be agile diplomats.

When the French and the Five Nations were on friendly terms, as they were in the decade that followed 1667, the Kahnawake Iroquois could work their ambiguous external connections to good advantage, but when relations soured, as they did in the late 1670s, these in-between Indians felt torn in their loyalties and vulnerable in their intermediate position. In 1675, the Mohawks, together with the other nations of the Iroquois League, forged an alliance with the new English governor of New York, thus strengthening their hand vis-à-vis the French and emboldening them to challenge the latter's incursions into the regions to the south of the Great Lakes. Tensions built in the late 1670s and the early 1680s, leading to all-out war after 1684, with the result that the converts of Kahnawake were dragged into a deadly struggle against their own kinfolk. Members of the community did manage to minimize their own direct participation in the conflict and successfully weathered the storm, perhaps more terrible in anticipation than in the event. But Kahnawake, perched at the edge of New France and lying open to attack from the south, went through a terrible and extended waiting period. Catherine Tekakwitha's two and a half years at the Sault were passed in the shadow of this looming threat, and the great bursts of collective penance that she participated in at Kahnawake coincided almost exactly with the war scare.[22]

For this breakaway group of Iroquois, issues of identity and affiliation were perennially challenging in the seventeenth century. Who are we? What holds us together and distinguishes us from others? Where, if anywhere, do we fit in the clan connections and the alliance system of the Five Nations? How are we linked to, how separate from, our French-Canadian neighbors and their Algonquian allies? These were questions that the people of

Kahnawake faced on a perennial basis, and religion was one of the ways they addressed them. In this context (and of course there was far more to religion than its sociopolitical function), Catholicism should be understood as one of the fundamental constituents of a collective identity. More than simply reflecting the complexities and perplexities of Kahnawake's in-between colonial situation, religion served as a medium through which internal belonging and external affiliation were negotiated.

When newcomers first came to Kahnawake, they were shown two trees growing near the entrance to the village. At one tree, they had to leave their "drunkenness," for the Jesuits were convinced that alcohol had brought violence and disorder to the Iroquois and that it counteracted their own evangelizing efforts. It was said that many Iroquois came to the St. Lawrence precisely to escape the ravages of liquor in their homeland; indeed, prohi-bition may have been imposed in Kahnawake as much by the natives as by the missionaries. The second tree was where the newly arrived were sup-posed to deposit their "impurity," a set of sexual practices the Jesuits were reluctant to enumerate, though they seem to have had in mind mainly po-lygamy, not common among the Iroquois in any case.[23] Non-Christians were not barred—restricting admission in that way would have been at odds with the Jesuit conception of Sault St. Louis as a site of conversion—but they were expected to observe these specific prohibitions. There were lapses, though no one seems to have objected in principle to the idea that visitors should respect Jesuit susceptibilities in this way. Once lodged in Kahnawake long-houses, however, unbaptized visitors could expect to face persuasive efforts aimed at converting them to Christianity.

Whenever they could spare the time from other pressing duties, the Jesuits would visit the Iroquois cabins to talk with any residents prepared to learn about Christianity. However, any attempt at conventional preach-ing was doomed to failure by the baffling linguistic barriers that separated priest and listeners. Kentake and Kahnawake were polyglot communities, and so missionaries tended to rely on a version of Huron to communicate, imperfectly no doubt, with people of various Iroquoian tongues. But even a perfect knowledge of the listeners' language could not solve the deeper problem of the untranslatability of many basic Christian concepts such as "God the father," "commandment," and "sin."[24] Instead, the Jesuits tended to rely on pictures, especially vivid depictions of the torments of hell, as well as stories about the life of Jesus and of the saints, to attract people's attention and convey a message.[25] Their instruction concentrated on prac-tical lessons: how to recite prayers, when to abstain from meat, what native customs to avoid as sinful. Until formal catechism classes were instituted in

Liquor Is Banned. Chauchetière's drawing of a council meeting at Kahnawake where the decision is taken to prohibit alcohol combines realistic detail—men seated in their robes in front of the log chapel—with a fanciful touch in the form of a devil impaled through the groin by a cross. Though prohibition was never entirely successful, the picture suggests that it was a measure adopted by the natives, and not simply imposed by the Jesuits. © Archives départementales de la Gironde, II Jésuites.

1682—that is, until the mission was thirteen years old and Catherine Tekakwitha was already two years in the grave[26]—conversion tended to be more about gestures and behavior than about theology.

Moreover, once the initial stages of missionary work at Kentake had passed, the Jesuits were usually too burdened with parish work among the *habitants*, and with ministering to the burgeoning Iroquois Catholic population—celebrating mass, conducting funerals, weddings, and baptisms, visiting the sick, administering the mission's temporal affairs—to spare much time for the instruction of neophytes. They left it mainly to resident natives themselves to persuade non-Christians to join in prayers and prepare for baptism. As Pierre Cholenec reported,

> Any passing Iroquois who happen to stop by their cabins are forced to submit to instruction. Both men and women take part, cleverly instructing, exhorting and convincing them. Their own good examples constitute their most effective weapon of assault, one which we find none can resist. Thus, all the Iroquois who come here and then become Christians owe their conversion mainly to the zeal of their relatives; the father assures me that they do a hundred times more than he.[27]

Those who withstood this pious assault and declined to join the Church tended to drift away from Kahnawake, while Iroquois who stayed generally accepted baptism sooner or later. Apparently adherence to Christianity was more than simply a gesture of accommodation toward the Jesuits; it seems to have become a requirement for full citizenship in this native community.

For those who were not already Christian before coming to Kahnawake, baptism served as a crucial ceremony of initiation into the community. It also implied affiliation with the French, as symbolized by the priest's role in administering that sacrament and by the frequent presence of French colonists as godparents. Yet baptism did not erase clan affiliation and the name and personal identity that integrated an individual into the lineages of Kahnawake. Thus, everyone received two names, an Iroquois name bestowed by the women of their clan, as well as a Christian name conferred by the church, with the result that residents of the village carried double names: "Catherine Tekakwitha," "Anastasia Tegonhatsiongo," "Martin Skandegorhaksen." These names had the appearance of a European-style pairing of a personal name and a family name, but they were something quite different, a badge of layered identity. A name in this style proclaimed that an individual was simultaneously Tekakwitha, the current embodiment of a resuscitated personage who had belonged for generations to the Turtle clan, and a Christian baptized in memory of Catherine of Siena.

Many other Catholic rituals served the function of binding the community together in shared observances. The Jesuits reported in enthusiastic tones on the virtually universal attendance at Sunday mass; many Iroquois went

Confirmation Administered for the First Time. François de Laval-Montigny, bishop of Quebec, came to Kahnawake in 1676 and confirmed more than eighty Christian Indians. The pastoral visit was a great ceremonial occasion, one with both diplomatic and religious significance, for in welcoming this important French dignitary, the Iroquois community reaffirmed its alliance to New France. © Archives départementales de la Gironde, H Jésuites.

to mass during the week as well, and most participated in public prayers each evening. "They live like angels," gushed Claude Chauchetière, well aware that such unanimous and regular churchgoing was unheard of in Catholic Europe. In Kahnawake's chapel, the men stood on one side, the women on the other, forming two choirs that sang alternately through the entire service.[28] An Iroquois *dogique*, or "prayer captain," took the leading part in the ceremonies, frequently delivering a sermon in place of the priest. At Christmas and Easter and on the occasion of a visit from the bishop or the intendant, there were special festivities recalling in their social functions the calendrical feasts of the Iroquois tradition.[29]

Similarly, the material trappings of Catholicism could work as emblems of group identity in ways that were not unfamiliar to Iroquoians. Though they dressed very much like their pagan relatives in the old Five Nations lands, residents of Kahnawake were instantly recognizable by their Christian accessories such as crucifix pendants and rosary beads; the latter were either attached at the waist or, in a stylish aboriginal flourish, worn as hair ornaments. Items of apparel with sacred or magical associations were as familiar to Iroquois people as were seasonal festivals featuring prayers of thanksgiving for life and sustenance. These gestures and affectations, actively promoted by the Jesuits because they lent themselves, in a way that language-dependent matters of belief did not, to adaptation and cultural compromise, served as visible badges of identity uniting the disparate elements that made up the Christian village of Kahnawake.

Catholic identity looked outward as well as inward, defining relations with others even as it worked to give villagers a collective sense of themselves. Christian rituals and emblems served first of all to accentuate the division of the Iroquois and to assert the separateness of the breakaway settlement vis-à-vis the Five Nations rump. Looking in another direction, it embodied connection, most obviously with the French but also with other converted native nations in the French orbit. Christianity, in some of its most basic gestural and symbolic aspects, functioned as the religious component of the alliance relationship by which Iroquois bound themselves to the French. More than simply an *expression* of affiliation, it was a vital constituent of the association connecting the groups. In the Iroquoian tradition, a treaty of peace and alliance is not an arrangement agreed upon at a given time and fixed for the future; it is a living relationship requiring the parties actively to implicate themselves in the affairs of the other, constantly reaffirming and, when necessary, renegotiating the alliance.[30] For the Sault Iroquois, it would have seemed natural to adopt Catholicism in order to partake of what their allies presented as a central element of their identity.

In this case, the acceptance of Christian religion did not imply submission to European rule, as it did to some extent in colonial New England.[31] In the Spanish empire, spiritual conquest generally followed military con-

quest and was intimately connected with imperial rule.[32] The Mohawks
and the other Five Nations, by way of contrast, had never been conquered,
even though they had suffered defeat at the hands of the French. Adherence to the Catholic Church therefore had different political overtones for
the Iroquois than it did for Mayan, Quechua, or Nahuatl people, overtones suggesting alliance rather than sovereignty.

Connected to the French partly through a shared Catholicism, the people
of Kahnawake remained separate from them, and quite deliberately so.
Accordingly, their array of socially integrating customs drew on Iroquois
as well as Christian traditions. Kinship structures, marital customs, and even
burial practices were only lightly affected by conversion. People continued
to define their families through female parentage (a situation that shaped
even the Jesuits' evangelizing strategies, as they sought out families with
many daughters, refusing to waste their time on sons)[33] and chose their
mates outside their own clan. Native marriage ceremonies prevailed for many
years, with church weddings only gradually gaining popularity. Likewise,
burial and condolence rites, of crucial importance in maintaining social
cohesion within an Iroquoian village, continued largely unchanged for many
years.[34] At the Huron mission of Lorette, a year's crop of corpses was disinterred every November on All Souls' Day and reburied in a common grave;
the Jesuits did their best to wrap the ceremony in Christian apparel, but it
was, to all intents and purposes, a native Feast of the Dead.[35]

In Kahnawake, it seems apparent, Christianity served political and social
purposes as it reinforced the lines of connection that crossed clan and tribal
boundaries and aided in the age-old effort to counteract divisive tendencies
within the village. It also provided a vocabulary of symbol and ritual for
negotiating connections with the French and others. But can we leave it at
that, as though such a momentous religious change were about everything
except religion? Certainly the actors involved would have had difficulty
accepting such an exclusion. For all the great differences in their respective
outlooks, French Jesuits, Iroquois converts, and non-Christian natives would
all have seen human affairs as framed within a broader reality that included
a sacred side, a sphere populated with other-than-human personalities,
supernatural forces, and mysteries.

In the Iroquoian cultures of the seventeenth century, very few important
aspects of life lacked a spiritual dimension. Rarely was human endeavor
treated as exclusively human. A hunter, for all his experience and skill, depended also on the cooperation of the animals' spirits, secured through
prayer and the observation of certain taboos. A successful warrior needed
the assistance of other-than-human beings, connected to him perhaps

Superstitious Burials are Banned. The 1673 funeral of Catherine Gandeacteua was the occasion on which the Iroquois of Kentake decided to Christianize their burial practices. Claude Chauchetière's history of Kahnawake, from which this illustration is taken, makes it clear that the change was superficial. Totemic emblems were removed from grave markers, and possessions that would have been buried with the deceased were instead distributed to "the poor." © Archives départementales de la Gironde, H Jésuites.

through an amulet, to reinforce his own strength and bring him luck. Similarly, medicinal remedies, though formulated on the basis of generations of experiment and observation, had to be made of herbs collected in certain phases of the moon and by individuals in the proper ritual state. Technology, skill, and strength were understood to be the product of human effort working in conjunction with unseen forces, the latter subject to human influence through ritual. Misfortune, loss, and death could also come about through the intervention of other-than-human persons.

Mohawks and other Iroquois who gravitated toward the French therefore had an additional motive, beyond diplomatic courtesy, for accepting initiation into the Catholic Church; such a step could be a means of gaining access to the sources of French power.[36] Whether they converted, as Catherine did, in the Iroquois homeland or migrated to the St. Lawrence before accepting baptism, these people had every reason to think that the French enjoyed mysterious advantages over Indians. The Europeans were accompanied by deadly diseases yet always escaped the worst ravages of the resulting epidemics. They possessed wonder-working substances such as iron and alcohol, and they had access to endless supplies of useful objects. Moreover, in the mid-1660s, they had bested the Five Nations militarily. Since it was logical to assume that secret forces were at work in all these phenomena, it made good sense to affiliate with the French religion to enhance one's likelihood of avoiding harm and gaining benefits. Then, of course, there were the Jesuits' predictions about an afterlife of torture for those who refused baptism, which provided one more reason to embrace Christianity.

There is no shortage of testimony to suggest that Iroquois converts took the spiritual content of Catholicism very seriously indeed. Jesuits compared them to "Christians of the primitive church," suggesting by that phrase something of the pure faith of an ancient golden age with none of the negative connotations later acquired by the adjective "primitive": "Not only are there more true Christians among these savage peoples, but they are proportionately more numerous than in our civilized Europe." Writing shortly after Tekakwitha arrived at the Sault, Father Frémin thought he detected a strong "inward" spirituality on the part of recent converts still learning the ways of the church. "Is there anything more pleasing than to see these good catechumens the foremost and most ardent at prayer, and, when everyone has left the church, to see them stay behind? Even though they do not yet know their prayers, they praise the Lord from the bottom of their hearts."[37]

On the other hand, there is no indication that Iroquois people were in any general sense in awe of the French. They knew that the latter had been vulnerable to Five Nations attacks in the past and that they might be again in the future. Moreover, while they readily adopted steel needles, iron axes, and copper kettles, these products were integrated into an evolving Iroquois way of life; women used metal pots as a convenient way to cook traditional corn *sagamité*. Though profoundly changed through their encounter with European technology, Iroquois people were not about to turn into Europeans. They had no such desire, and, in any case, intention has little to do with it; culture cannot be discarded like a worn set of clothes. Religious change was, in this respect, similar to other aspects of cultural change: Christian beliefs and practices were incorporated into an indigenous religious framework. Short of a genuine miracle that wiped out existing cultural identities at the moment of baptism, there could be no other form of "conversion."

Native converts may have been assiduous in their devotion to Catholic prayer and regular in their attendance at mass, but they did not necessarily abandon all their indigenous techniques for approaching the sacred. Claude Chauchetière was largely silent on that subject, either because he was unaware of such "pagan survivals" or because, in preparing his various texts for French readers, his enthusiasm about their Catholic devotions led him to overlook lapses into non-Catholic devotions. However, another Jesuit, Joseph-François Lafitau, who served at Sault St. Louis from 1712 to 1717, just after Chauchetière's death, recorded some of those strictly Iroquoian practices that were never mentioned in the writings of Claude and his contemporaries. A major figure in the history of comparative ethnology, and the author of *Moeurs des sauvages américains comparées aux moeurs des premiers temps* (1724), Lafitau gathered most of his material about the "American savages" through observing the convert Iroquois of Kahnawake.[38] Unlike the previous generation of New France Jesuits, he wrote with an anthropologist's intellectual agenda and thus tended to concentrate on notionally primordial Indian customs.

What did this precociously modern field researcher reveal about the natives he knew at Sault St. Louis?[39] "Among christianized Iroquois," Lafitau noted in the course of a discussion of Indian curing rites, "it should be regarded as a heroic act when, in illnesses, one does not have recourse to shamans [*jongleurs*], especially if there is some indication or dream which causes a suspicion of sorcery." Sorcery, shamanism, and dream divination are all signaled in this one brief sentence; all were considered flagrant contradictions to Christianity, and none were ever mentioned in the earlier Jesuit reports from Kahnawake. Lafitau wrote of Iroquois shamanism with the familiarity of the eyewitness: "The shamans have some innate quality which partakes still more of the divine. We see them go visibly into that state of ecstasy which binds all the senses and keeps them suspended." For a Jesuit who spent his entire missionary career in this Catholic village, Lafitau knew a great deal about non-Christian Iroquois religion. On sacrifices to the sun, he observed, "Sometimes our Iroquois [our Iroquois, please note, not the Iroquois] expose to the air on the top of their lodges strings and belts of wampum, braided strings of Indian maize and likewise animals which they consecrate to the Sun."[40]

"They are like angels," said one Jesuit in 1682; they worship the sun, follow the advice of dreams, and call on shamans to cure their ills, said another Jesuit in 1724—two reporters, each with a particular agenda, focusing selectively on one portion of the broad range of techniques available to Iroquois converts attempting to gain the assistance of unseen forces. Possibly, the eighteenth-century shamans wore crucifixes and invoked saints—the sources are mute on such points, though Latin American examples suggest the possibility—but even tinges of Catholic coloration would not alter the fundamentally Iroquoian nature of the practices described. Depending on the circumstances, these native converts might appear to a European observer as devout Catholics, saintly ascetics, or superstitious pagans. Rival missionaries of the Recollet order concluded that Indians were simply "fickle and inconstant," and that the Jesuits' stories of convert piety were a hoax,[41] but in fact, the Iroquois were simply displaying their traditional openness and spiritual eclecticism. Catholic styles had become integral to the identity of the Kahnawake people, and church ceremonies were valued for their sacred qualities, but in some dimensions of the religious field Iroquois traditions simply seemed to work better than anything the Jesuits had to offer.

If this eclecticism made the Kahnawake people imperfectly Christian, then the same could be said—and was said at the time—of the majority of Catholics in seventeenth-century Europe.[42] The peasantry in particular, but not only the peasantry, was notorious for its ignorance of basic Catholic dogma and its devotion to lucky charms, healing springs, and secret incantations. Across early modern Europe, an official Catholicism aspiring to uniformity and universality coexisted with various local systems of belief and practice.[43] Many elements of local religion in the Old World setting may have derived from ancient pre-Christian traditions of paganism; reforming clerics called this "superstition" and did their best to eradicate it. It tended to be pragmatically oriented, providing the sort of magical assistance to the ill, the distressed, and the lovelorn that the more austere "translocal" religion of the Counter-Reformation church withheld.

Iroquois converts would have had minimal exposure to this important dimension of European religion for two reasons. First, the settlers of Canada came from different regions of France and had not lived together in the colony long enough to have developed a rich local religion; second, the natives' main point of contact with French culture was the Jesuits, representatives par excellence of translocal Catholicism. The proper response to danger and suffering, they taught, was not manipulation but resignation before the will of God. One could ask, through the Virgin Mary or one of the saints, for luck in hunting or protection from smallpox, but there were no grounds for counting on the request being granted. The main thing was to embrace the divinely ordained outcome, even—especially—when it brought pain and suffering, and remember that life after death was what really mattered. Faced with this sort of advice, ordinary Catholics in France were inclined to turn to the seemingly more helpful remedies of magic and "superstition." Iroquois Christians tended to have recourse in similar circumstances to their own version of local religion.

What made the Catholicism of Kahnawake distinctively Iroquoian was not just the admixture of indigenous rituals and beliefs; it was the way in which the Indians made Christianity their own. Virtually all Kahnawake converts dutifully recited their prayers and went to mass; many turned to shamanism and divination in times of need; some (or was it the same individuals in different circumstances?) set out to plumb the deepest mysteries of Christianity.

5

Body

and

Soul

Modern scholars sometimes treat Christianization as something imposed upon hapless native victims, but the history of Kahnawake suggests a very different process. Converts might better be viewed as active investigators probing the exotic myths and arcane rituals of a complex foreign religion. Jesuits seem to get all the credit for their ethnographic achievements in coming to terms with the strange ways of the Other, but parallel native efforts to bridge the gap of cultural difference and comprehend the European Other are just as noteworthy. Both before and after baptism, Indian converts faced formidable challenges to their intelligence and to their religious imagination as they struggled to apprehend the intricacies of Catholicism. And like the missionaries, they examined the Other, necessarily, from the vantage point of their own culture, and with their own purposes and concerns.

One lesson the Iroquois seem to have learned at an early stage of their research is that there were basically two distinct versions of Catholic Christianity: the rites and knowledge that the Jesuits wished to share with Indians and another, secret, religion that the Jesuits kept to themselves. During the course of visits to Montreal and Quebec, it must have been evident to them that a similar split prevailed within the French population. The majority, including even eminent war leaders, had mainly indirect access to the powers associated with Jesus and Mary; heavenly protection came to them mostly through the intermediary of a class of spiritual specialists. In addition to the Jesuits, this latter category included other groups of male priests, as well as religious women, hospital nuns, and others. All these people resembled the Jesuits in their distinctive costumes, their renunciation of sex and of recognizable kin connections, their special quarters, their control over buildings dedicated solely to religious purposes, and (in the case of the male priests) their exclusive right to perform elaborate rituals featuring strange gestures and incantations in a language that could not be understood by the uninitiated. Quite evidently, they were uniquely equipped to act as intermediaries between the community and the heavens.

The Iroquois had no priestly class that corresponded exactly to the Catholic clergy, but they were certainly familiar with spiritual specialists possessed of extraordinary ability to manipulate supernatural forces. By means of powers acquired by accident of birth or conferred by an animal spirit communicating through a vision, some men and women were able to foretell the future, cure illness, or find lost objects. Such shamans, as individuals or associated together in a society, might have fetish objects of peculiar potency, as well as songs or dances that functioned as a means of activating their powers. These objects and rituals were generally proprietary; in other words, the person or group owned certain songs, dances, and other sacred procedures. The spiritual/magical powers they invoked were not inherently "good" or "evil"; in theory, they could be used to help or to harm others, though malicious magic was considered a heinous crime, whereas beneficial magic brought public esteem and gifts. Iroquois people counted on their shamans to use their powers for the good of the community, though they may have felt some apprehensions about the potential for harm that always accompanied spiritual powers.[1]

Without suggesting that natives would have equated Catholic priests and Iroquois shamans, we must assume that their perceptions were colored by their experience with their own spiritual/magical specialists. That being the case, a degree of ambivalence about the Jesuits and their priestly authority was inevitable.[2] In view of the ritual potency and supernatural connections of the missionaries, it would have made sense to follow their expert instructions in matters of prayer, mass, confession, fasting, and the like to derive full benefit from Christianity's heavenly forces. Moreover, it might have seemed prudent to stay on the good side of such ritually powerful men as the Jesuits. The difficulty, from an Iroquois point of view, is that the latter were not truly part of the community. In spite of honorary ceremonies of adoption,[3] they did not really belong to any of Kahnawake's clans. No one's husband, no one's son: could they be trusted with complete control over Iroquois access to the European deity?

Not all converts were content to accept their assigned position as objects of pastoral care. While some continued to engage in shamanistic healing practices and sacrifices to the sun, others made efforts to bypass the priestly monopoly and gain direct access to the wellsprings of European spiritual power. In neither case did this imply contempt for the Jesuits or a rejection of their role as religious leaders. On the contrary, the Kahnawake Iroquois generally acted as though they felt themselves to be apprentices with a great deal to learn from their missionaries about the complexities of the Christian religion. They willingly accepted guidance and instruction from the Jesuits and, on the whole, did their best to earn the benefits available to dutiful Catholic laypeople. Yet at the same time, they—at least some among them—cultivated other channels. It was a delicate matter of learning what the Jesuits wished to teach but also—and without causing offense—what they intended to conceal.

Why not simply join the Catholic clergy or, in the case of women, apply for admission to a religious order? There were no racially based rules in New France, as there were in the Spanish empire,[4] barring the ordination of Indians. On the other hand, the French missionaries made no serious effort to recruit a native priesthood. Early experiments in bringing up native boys and girls in church-run boarding schools only convinced them that the children and their families would not accept European styles of educational discipline.[5] The Jesuits and their colleagues in other orders appear to have concluded that the cultural gap was too wide for Indians to be integrated into the Christian clergy, and though their attitude was shaped by colonialist arrogance, it was not entirely unfounded. There is no indication that Iroquois Catholics were eager to become priests and nuns,[6] and their lack of interest is quite understandable. Preparing for ordination would have posed monumental challenges to people unfamiliar with even the French language, let alone Latin, reading, and writing. More to the point, it would have demanded a willingness to place oneself deep within European culture. Even forming the desire to take such a step presupposes a degree of cultural assimilation that was completely absent from the missions of seventeenth-century New France.[7] Iroquois Christians were not about to become French; instead, they would explore the potentialities of the new religion in their own way, as Iroquois.

The Jesuits were by no means blind to these realities. Sometimes they tried to harness native traditions, as well as the converts' drive to penetrate the mysteries of Christian ritual, for their own evangelizing purposes. Chauchetière records that, in the early 1670s, a Jesuit colleague temporarily resident at La Prairie passed out special rosaries, without any explanation of their purpose.[8] If there was a deliberate strategy to invest the beads with an intriguing air of mystery, it succeeded brilliantly, for Iroquois people were accustomed to looking for important words and sacred significance in the arrangement of beads on strings. The rosaries were taken up and prized as potent objects by those who received them. Eventually, it became clear that they were designed for the confraternity of the Holy Family, a devotional group for laypeople featuring regular meetings with particular prayers, lay preaching, and mutual confession of faults. The Jesuits sponsored hundreds of chapters in the cities of Europe and New France, and now they were experimenting with the confraternity as an instrument of native evangelization.[9]

If Chauchetière is to be believed, a number of Iroquois got together and, armed with their rosary/wampums, organized themselves into a devotional society before the missionaries had explained what a confraternity was and how a rosary was used to recite prayers. Their circle, led initially by Catherine Gandeacteua, the Oneida founder of La Prairie, would provide an associational framework for the settlement's Christian elite in the years that followed. Catherine's leadership suggests that the group was predominantly female, just as it tended to be in Europe and French Canada. But can we really believe the claim that recently converted natives spontaneously formed themselves into something like a Catholic confraternity? The women involved might well have made some accurate deductions about rosaries and confraternities by observing their settler neighbors and by picking up on clues dropped by the Jesuits. Their own cultural background not only would have prepared them to see beads as potentially meaningful and sacred but also would have provided them with rich associational traditions connected with Iroquois shamanism and medicine societies.[10]

"The Iroquois are particularly well known for their elaborate medicine societies," writes Dean Snow, referring to the exclusive clubs that are organized around special rituals, usually healing rituals for curing the sick.[11] In modern times, a number of such societies have been active—the False Faces, the Company of Mystic Animals, and the Little Water Society, to name only three—each with its own rules, procedures, and formal membership. Some ethnohistorians suggest that their seventeenth-century ancestors may have had more loosely organized and short-lived bands of devotees grouped around a particular shaman. Nevertheless, concludes an archaeologist, "shamanistic curing societies . . . were probably the dominant religious form during the precontact Iroquoian period."[12]

Medicine societies were exclusive but not closed; new members were recruited, often from among those who had benefited from one of the society's cures, and inducted through an initiation ceremony. Membership crossed clan lines. Each medicine society possessed its own songs or chants, as well as its specialized paraphernalia such as masks or medicinal potions; these were forbidden to nonmembers. Though they guarded their secrets jealously, there was nothing antisocial about a medicine society; its powers were available to outsiders in need of help, though usually at a price. Thus there were many formal similarities between an Iroquoian medicine society and a Catholic devotional confraternity: defined membership that brought together people from different sectors of society, sacred objects, special prayers or chants, a benevolent role within the community, prestige and influence for members. There were also some basic differences, notably in the way Iroquois culture tended to treat songs, prayers, sacred objects, and the spiritual powers that went along with them, as property. Little wonder, then, that Kahnawake converts would seize upon the Holy Family rosaries and place them at the center of an exclusive devotional group.

Over the years, the Christian elite of Kahnawake went well beyond the Holy Family rosary in its quest for spiritual empowerment. Who exactly was involved, beyond a few named individuals such as Gandeacteua, the Jesuit sources do not reveal, nor do they indicate how many people participated. Three years after it was initiated, the missionaries began to exercise some control over entry into the confraternity, but around that time it appears to have ceased functioning as the primary framework of Iroquois Christian devotion. There continued to be a circle of spiritual seekers at Kahnawake; quite possibly, following the medicine society pattern, there was more than one circle. Numbers fluctuated, and there seem to have been varying degrees of involvement. The sources are rather vague about all this, perhaps because the Jesuits were not fully aware of what was going on at any given moment. What they do indicate quite definitely is that the converts most deeply implicated were predominantly female and that, by the late 1670s, they were engaging in quite astonishing spiritual experiments.

Chauchetière's mission chronicle for 1678 speaks of a circle of women who resisted sin and embraced a demanding life of Christian virtue:

> Several of them, having passed the nubile age and having repeatedly refused good offers of marriage, gave themselves to God, body and soul, in a spirit of great poverty; they depend upon charity for their food and clothing. This year, as many as thirteen persons were united in this spirit. Aiming at the highest level of perfection, they meet together and one of them delivers a little exhortation, or else they point out one another's faults. They proceed in the same way as the Ladies of Charity do in France, taking it upon themselves to discharge acts of charity toward their neighbors. Above all, they care for the poor and the sick to whom they carry firewood, doing so secretly and quickly running away to escape notice. They sit up with the sick and give them as alms anything that they need. Their method relies on the avoidance of the pleasures of the body and the mortification of the flesh, something which they hate as a snare of the Devil. And when they go to excesses, they say that the reverend fathers, who want to make them give up the belt and the discipline [i.e., flagellation], are filled with compassion and do not understand how heavily they were burdened with sin before they were taught how to live properly. Thus, we see

them, always busy carrying firewood, stringing wampum beads, planting, grinding [corn], sewing, or making bags and other handiwork.[13]

This passage, with its emphasis on collective labor, suggests that the thirteen
women may have drawn upon another Iroquois institution, the women's work
group, as well as the medicine society, in organizing their pious activities.
At the same time, their association was also modeled on European Catholic
organizations, the confraternity of the Holy Family and the Ladies of Charity. The sources that gave shape to this pious sect may have been diverse,
but its members joined collectively for a very serious program of chastity
and penitential asceticism.

Whereas the foregoing passage emphasizes similarities to European
women's benevolent societies, most other descriptions of these women's
activities make it clear that "charity" in the modern sense was not a primary
focus. The devotions of these "new Christians" revolved around "severe
penances," as an excerpt from one of Chauchetière's letters reveals:

> You will be pleased to hear about the austerities practiced by certain
> Indian women. Although there may be some indiscretion in their
> behavior, it will show you their fervor. More than five years ago some
> of them learned, I know not how, of the pious practices followed by
> the nuns of the Montreal hospital. They heard of disciplines, of iron
> girdles, and of hair shirts. . . . The one who first initiated [these as-
> cetic practices] began around Christmas of the year 1676, when she
> went to the foot of a large cross that stands beside our cemetery, took
> off her clothes and exposed herself to the air. This was during a snow-
> storm and she was pregnant at the time; and the snow falling on her
> back caused her so much suffering that she nearly died from it, along
> with her child, who was thoroughly chilled inside the mother's womb.
> It was her own idea to do this, and she said it was to do penance for
> her sins. She has since then acquired four companions who imitate
> her in her fervor. In the depth of winter, two of them made a hole in
> the ice and threw themselves into the water, where they remained dur-
> ing the time that it would take to say the rosary slowly and deliber-
> ately. One of the two, returning to her cabin and fearing that she would
> be found out, did not venture to warm herself at the fire, and so she
> lay down for the night with the ice still adhering to her shoulders.
> The men and women have invented several other such means of mor-
> tification by which to torment themselves as part of their habitual
> penance, but we have made them give up any excessive mortification.[14]

This particular report dwells on voluntary exposure to cold, but other sources
speak of whipping ("Some of them made their bodies bloody several times
a week by long and severe discipline"),[15] burning, fasting, and the use of

European penitential devices such as the hair shirt and the "iron girdle" (a belt fitted with points on the inside to scratch the wearer's skin).

The Jesuits reported similar practices in the other missions of New France— Huron, Algonquin, and Iroquois converts lacerating themselves, exposing their bodies to ferocious cold, or simply refusing to have a decayed tooth removed in order to savor the pain—but nowhere was the ascetic movement as strong as it was at Kahnawake.[16] This behavior, extreme by any standard, appears to have been confined to a comparatively short period in the late 1670s and early 1680s, beginning sometime before Catherine Tekakwitha came to live there and falling off a few years after her death.

Chauchetière attributed these "austerities" to the example of French nuns, and though he insisted, when writing of the first Kahnawake ascetic, that "it was her own idea to do this," the suspicion is bound to arise that French Jesuits played an instigating part. Officially, the Society of Jesus since the time of Loyola frowned on extreme mortification of the flesh,[17] and it is unlikely that the behavior of its missionaries, men like Claude Chauchetière, whose asceticism consisted mainly in sitting in uncomfortable chairs, would have directly inspired the Iroquois converts to feats of spiritual athleticism. On the other hand, flagellant devotion was a feature of many Jesuit-sponsored confraternities in Europe, and it shows up in the records of some of their overseas missions.[18] No doubt the Jesuits helped prepare the ground for the outbreaks of ascetic extremism in a variety of ways, for example, with stories of saints and Good Friday orations about the bodily agony of Christ that may well have conveyed the impression that the most estimable Christians imitated these models of voluntary suffering. But would the Indian converts have taken away such lessons?

The idea of "paying" for sin through personal suffering would have been quite foreign to people raised as Iroquois. Unlike the Nahua cultures of central Mexico,[19] the Iroquoians did not have a concept of personal transgression of divine ordinances that required confession and atonement. Violations of ritual and taboo required remedial action to restore threatening imbalances, but the onus was on the group rather than the individual offender. In human affairs, injuries called for compensation for the victim rather than punishment of the perpetrator; thus the Iroquois concept of doing justice, centering as it did on the presentation of gifts to, for example, the relatives of a murdered person, was incompatible with the European idea of making the wicked suffer for their crimes. Accordingly, the convert women of Kahnawake tended to "mortify the flesh" in couples or in groups, and when they explained their actions to the Jesuits, it was usually in terms of the "sins of their people" rather than strictly personal offenses. Father Cholenec was horrified to discover that one woman jumped into the frozen St. Lawrence clasping her three-year-old daughter so that the child could participate in penance for sins she had not yet committed. The missionary's utter bewilderment at the extended sense of self that led the Iroquois mother to include an infant in her frigid baths suggests that these ascetic exercises had meanings for the Indians that French Christians could not fully comprehend.

Seventeenth-century Iroquois were, in fact, expert torturers, well versed in the methods of making captive enemies suffer, but they also had experience in withstanding pain and discomfort deliberately inflicted on their own bodies. Some early Jesuit visitors to the Five Nations recorded the following scene, which seems to foreshadow later "Christian" practices:

> Not long ago, a man of the [Cayuga] town of Oiogouen had a vision one night of ten men plunging into the frozen river; they entered the water through one hole and came out by another. The first thing that he did on waking was to prepare a great feast to which he invited ten of his friends. . . . Thereupon he recounted his dream to them; they were not at all taken aback, but instantly volunteered to fulfill it. Accordingly, they went to the river and pierced the ice, making two holes fifteen paces apart. The divers stripped. The first man led the way, jumping into one of the holes and emerging, most fortunately, from the other one. The second man followed suit and then the others, until the tenth, who paid the price for all the rest: he could not find his way out and perished miserably under the ice.[20]

This same 1656 text goes on to describe another incident, in this case part of the mid winter festival at Onondaga:

> Immediately upon the announcement of this festival by these public cries, nothing was seen but men, women, and children, running like maniacs through the streets and cabins, though in a far different way than masqueraders in Europe, for most of them were almost naked; they seemed insensible to the cold which is nearly unbearable even to those who are warmly clothed.[21]

Well before Catholicism had made any impact on the Iroquois, freezing baths and voluntary exposure to cold air appear to have formed part of their repertoire of gestures connected with the sacred.

Some reports on the "penances" of the Iroquois of Kahnawake also mention burning. This particular form of "mortification of the flesh" was virtually unknown in the European Christian tradition, but it too had ample precedents among the preconversion Iroquois. In curing rituals, Huron and Iroquois shamans frequently plunged their hands into fire and brought them out grasping coals and hot ashes.[22] There was also much burning as part of the ceremonial preparation for war.[23] Anticipating their own possible capture by the enemy, warriors accepted "practice" burns and blows with a show of bravado clearly designed to address their own deep apprehensions. Women and children trained similarly, knowing that they, too, might be

taken prisoner: "Their constancy in torments is beyond all expression," wrote
a Jesuit. "This the Indians exercise themselves in during their whole lives,
and accustom their children to it from their tenderest infancy. Little boys
and girls have been seen to tie themselves together by an arm, and to put
between a red coal to see who should shrink first."[24]

The collective penitential practices of the Catholic Indians of New France
reached a peak in the midst of an extended war scare, and this behavior was
most intense at Kahnawake, the mission settlement most exposed to attack
from the direction of the Five Nations, making it appear that there was a
close connection with indigenous customs. Not only the form but also the
occasion of self-torture can be understood to some degree in Iroquoian
terms.[25] Knowing that an enemy was readying the fire and the torture stake,
the converts of Kahnawake may have been engaged in preparatory burning
and laceration designed, at least partly, to toughen themselves.

And yet it would be too simple to reduce the ascetic episode to traditional Iroquoian war preparations and nothing more. For one thing, the
gender balance is wrong: men led the way in war, whereas women played
the central role in this religious movement. We should therefore consider
the possibility that the "penitents" were preparing themselves for the fires
of hell as well as those of the enemy. There is no direct evidence in support
of this hypothesis,[26] but it is certainly plausible, since missionaries in a hurry
often made use of pictures showing sinners suffering the miseries of damnation. Even the most pious converts, such as Catherine Tekakwitha, felt
they had reason to fear damnation, and given the resources her culture had
developed to cope with the dread of torture, a hell-inspired training program seems a natural response. It may seem that the idea that they were
preparing for hell conflicts with the notion that war fears fueled the women's
asceticism, but there is no real contradiction. Just as European Catholics might
engage in group flagellation at times of emergency when fears focused simultaneously on the plague or the invader and the ultimate judgment of God,
so the Iroquois of Kahnawake may have been addressing, in their own way,
terrors of more than one order.

Finally, a third dimension to Iroquois flagellant Christianity, perhaps the
most important, should be considered. In addition to its role as a mechanism for coping with the fear of pain, self-torture seems to have been part
of a quest for the sacred. The convert women of Kahnawake combined their
Iroquois-style self-torture with fasting, sexual abstinence, and collective
prayer, gestures that were by no means foreign to their native traditions,
but which, taken together, suggest something more spiritually ambitious
than a program of hardening oneself against the prospect of bodily suffering. Scholars working within the European tradition distinguish between
two sorts of asceticism, the classical stoical version, which trains the subject
to regard bodily comfort as unnecessary and evil, and the Christian version,

in which comfort, regarded as good, is renounced in favor of a greater, eternal benefit.[27] In the Iroquoian tradition, by contrast, there is no such radical distinction: self-denying behavior can be pursued both to strengthen the self and to gain spiritual benefits; there is no rigid separation, as in Europe, between a human/material sphere and an extrahuman/spiritual sphere. Warriors preparing for campaigns avoided sex to enhance their physical strength, but also their luck, while hunters reduced their food intake in the belief that hunger would improve their eyesight, as well as their fortunes. According to the Iroquois ethnologist A. C. Parker, overeating was considered "a religious offence" that would also "destroy the capacity to withstand hunger."[28] Thus, it is quite reasonable to suppose that the ascetic women of Kahnawake were engaged in a hardening exercise designed both to enhance their physical courage and to help them achieve mystical ecstasy and spiritual power.

Clearly, something more was going on at Kahnawake than "penance" in the sense of discharging the debts of sin and accumulating credit against a future term in purgatory. These women appear to have been in pursuit of direct and profound religious experience. Claude Chauchetière must have understood this. He knew the reality and the unforgettable power of mystical transports, and even though he had personally experienced these effects without recourse to severe asceticism, he was well aware that others in the European Catholic tradition combined mysticism and painful self-denial. In the late medieval and early modern centuries this was a religious style that appealed particularly to saintly women. Fasting, beating herself with chains, sleeping on a narrow board, and drinking the fetid water that had washed the oozing wounds of lepers were among the practices favored by Catherine of Siena.[29] She and other mystic-ascetics suffered self-inflicted torments that tested the limits of bodily endurance as they strove to break through the confines of mundane existence and partake of the divine.

It can be difficult for modern people to come to terms with such behavior as anything but a symptom of psychological disorder. The glib post-Freudian response is to sexualize ascetic practice, to see it as an attempt literally to "beat down" sexual urges or, alternatively, as an actual sexual performance in a bent masochistic form.[30] Enough eroticism does indeed suffuse most versions of ascetic mysticism to give these unhistorical interpretations a degree of plausibility, but they remain reductionist and utterly inadequate to the task of understanding asceticism on its own terms.

Friedrich Nietzsche is one thoroughly modern writer who, despite his contempt for Christianity and his tendency to treat asceticism as disease, offered a penetrating analysis of the psychological appeal of self-mortification. Ascetic Christianity is surrounded by paradoxes, according to Nietzsche: favored by people in a position of weakness, justified by its adepts in terms of submission and self-denial, it actually involved a supreme assertion of will. Billed as an expression of love, it drew its energy from undercurrents of hatred, the weak and the sickly redirecting toward their own bodies the "insatiable resentment" they felt toward the strong and the healthy. Nietzsche's greatest insight is in recognizing the search for meaning that lies at the heart of ascetic practice. Frequently those who punish their bodies are individuals whose lives are already filled with suffering. Voluntarily inflicting pain on oneself is then part of a process of transvaluation by which suffering ceases to be pointless and random and becomes deeply meaningful to the sufferer. "Not suffering, but the senselessness of suffering was the curse which till then lay spread over humanity—*and the ascetic ideal gave it a meaning!*"[31]

Nietzsche manages to avoid the pitfall of associating mortification of the flesh with the supposedly Christian principle of "dualism." Reality, it is sometimes claimed, was divided into two distinct and mutually antagonistic dimensions: the soul and matters spiritual, which were considered "good," and the flesh and all things material, seen as "bad." Writings by and about saintly women of the past do sometimes speak of "despising the body and exalting the spirit," language that might give the impression that the subject was a purely mental/spiritual being, her own flesh and blood an alien object. However, that is certainly not the way Iroquois Catholics of Kahnawake understood themselves and their bodies. Then again, according to recent scholarship, that sort of dualism was also foreign to the ascetic Christianity of ancient and medieval Europe. Peter Brown, writing of the desert fathers of Egypt and other ancient Christians, and Caroline Bynum, with reference to religious women of the Middle Ages, insist that there was no fundamental conflict pitting the soul against "the flesh." In both these periods, they declare, the body was understood to be an integral part of the self; through the body, rather than against it, the soul sought sanctification.[32]

Recent research in neuropsychology suggests that pain can have a profound effect on the embodied self and its consciousness. An overload of "sensory signals," reports Ariel Glucklich, can "progressively weaken the body-self template." She continues: "If you scourge your body repeatedly, the sensory over-stimulation would not eradicate your thoughts, sense perceptions, and so forth. But your experience of being a self, an agent who undergoes these perceptions and thought, would gradually disappear, until it seemed that these belonged to someone or something else. You would enter a dissociative state, which could be modulated through pain." Such effacement of the self was what mystics such as Claude Chauchetière had always sought to achieve by one means or another; Glucklich's work suggests that neural science has much to offer anyone seeking to understand the role of voluntary pain in that enterprise.[33] However, these intriguing scientific insights still leave us having to come to terms with the specific varieties of ascetic practice in their different cultural and historical contexts.

Saintly women like Catherine of Siena seem to have been attracted to these extreme practices by their very extremism. The religious value of acting counter to the normal tendency to seek comfort and sensory gratification lay in its extraordinary quality, and the more painful and uncomfortable the experience, the more it had the effect of removing the practitioner from ordinary, mundane existence. This made it what some anthropologists label "liminal" experience: it took place on a threshold dividing all that is familiar and bounded from that which is unknown and limitless. Moderate self-denial was of no interest to women such as Catherine of Siena and Theresa of Avila, for they felt a heroic version of "the ascetic impulse," defined by Bynum as "the desire to defy corporeal limits by denying bodily needs."[34] Such an interpretation of ascetic extremism lends itself to a cross-cultural analysis that might extend beyond European Christendom and encompass similar patterns of mysticism in the religions of Africa, Asia, and America. Without overlooking the diverse variety of religious asceticism over time and around the globe, a common tendency toward self-imposed agony can be discerned as part of a deep religious experience that engages the bodily senses as well as the conscious mind.

In many settings, self-mortification was understood to confer a kind of freedom.[35] It suggested liberation from physical limitations but also defiance of social conventions and even of the laws of reason (the assertion of will, Nietzsche would say; divine folly, from another point of view). In spite of their thirst for the sacred, ascetics were still part of a particular human society and so the willful and anticonventional aspects of their behavior were bound to create difficulties in their relations with others (and, reciprocally, family and social tensions probably fueled their asceticism in many cases). Indeed, there was frequently an element of hostility and aggression as "the weak" (often women in the Middle Ages) confronted "the strong"—typically churchmen at the time. Caroline Bynum argues that women's self-mortification carried an implied critique of the soft worldliness of the church and the clergy. Alarmed by the subversive overtones, and no doubt worried about the health risks to the women themselves, confessors tried to moderate the penances of saintly ascetics, but sometimes this only intensified behavior that was "in part a response to the injunctions to moderation."[36] Likewise, a certain degree of competition between holy women tended to spur the saintly on to ever more extreme behavior. Of course, good Christians, ever mindful of the sin of pride, were supposed to keep their mortification secret—indeed, showiness about self-mortification was taken as prima facie evidence that the inspiration was diabolical, not divine—but women nevertheless found indirect ways of making their penitential achievements known.

Ascetic Christianity was never about only one thing. It was suffering individuals imaginatively transcending their suffering; it was people making use of their bodies as a means of experiencing mystical ecstasy; it was a weapon of the weak struggling with the male church establishment; it was a vehicle of self-glorification by which one triumphed over others. These observations have been made about women's self-mortification in Europe, but do they apply to the native women of Kahnawake? Strange as it might seem, given the enormous cultural differences, some basic similarities emerge on almost every count. People who had lived through—and were continuing to live through—the epidemics, wars, and dislocations occasioned by colonization were purposely adding to their pain. To all appearances, they sought not only to invest their suffering with meaning but also to cross the threshold of the divine. Finally, they too waged covert struggles, with one another perhaps, but certainly, as the missionaries' correspondence makes abundantly clear, with the clergy.

Whenever Jesuits wrote about Indian penitential practices, their words conveyed a sense of anxiety and ambivalence. They were clearly impressed by the women's ascetic achievements but also worried about the implications. When mortification reached a peak in the early 1680s, Claude Chauchetière thought he detected diabolical tendencies. "The Devil, seeing the glorious success of this mission, made use of a new weapon; transforming himself into an angel of light, he pushed the devotions of some persons . . . to the point of excess in order to give this nascent Christianity a repugnant appearance."[37]

Father Cholenec introduced European instruments of self-torture to Kahnawake—whips, irritating hair shirts, and "iron girdles"—to moderate and regulate practices the natives had already taken up, not to stimulate more bodily penance. Through the confession, he would prescribe to those who wanted to expiate their sins in this way a specified number of strokes of the whip or the wearing of an iron belt for one day a week. The most fervent converts still continued with their indigenous styles of self-torture but now added these European techniques to their repertoire, thus effectively defeating their confessor's attempt to restrain them. Cholenec wrote of one woman who, in addition to practicing flagellation, would freeze herself by rolling in the snow and then cut herself with a knife. His penitents continually eluded control.[38]

> In truth, the majority of these individuals were under my direction, but all this usually took place in the woods where these Christian women believed that anything was permitted. The woman who went diving under the ice on three consecutive nights was someone who did not normally go on hunting expeditions, but she departed with the hunt this year because I would not allow her to do what she wanted to do in the village. She said to herself, "At least in the woods I shall be mistress of my own body."[39]

"I shall be mistress of my own body." It is important to note that this evocative phrase is not a direct quotation but rather an internal monologue the

Jesuit imagines for a penitent who seemed to be eluding his regulatory efforts. Unquestionably, Pierre Cholenec saw himself as engaged in a power struggle.

Much as it might seem satisfying to contemplate native women in defiant rebellion against missionary tyranny, the relationship was rather more equivocal than that.[40] The ascetics of Kahnawake esteemed their priests, accepted their direction on some points, misunderstood them on others, evaded their control in certain areas, and, on the whole, went about their pursuit of sacred experience with and without the Jesuits' support. In other words, there was far more to their encounter with Christianity than anything that can be measured on a scale of acquiescence and resistance. In the French-Iroquois religious encounter of the seventeenth century, there were obviously great chasms of mutual incomprehension. It was more than just a matter of differing beliefs about creation, the order of the cosmos, the nature of the soul; there was a more basic incommensurability in areas such as the division between the natural and the supernatural, the nature of the human self, the concept of truth. So much of religion grew out of and expressed metaphorically certain social arrangements—family, state, law, and so on—that were not analogous. Small wonder, then, that many French dismissed Indian religion as paganism and that most natives turned their backs on Christianity. And it is all the more remarkable that a circle of Iroquois women recently arrived in Canada were able to tunnel their way into some of Christianity's mystical strongholds. The spiritual/somatic experience of using pain and discomfort to cross the line into sacred ecstasy was an area of commonality linking Indian converts at Kahnawake, nuns in Montreal, and saints in medieval Italy.

6

Catherine
and
Her Sisters

ARRIVING WITH HER BROTHER-IN-LAW IN THE AUTUMN OF 1677, TEKAKWITHA PRE-sumably went straight to her sister's longhouse for a dish of *sagamité* and a warm welcome. This dwelling at Kahnawake was to be her home for the two and a half years that remained to her on earth. The sister (never named in the sources) had a cooking fire and a portion of the longhouse for her nuclear family, and that became the focus of Tekakwitha's life as a producer and consumer of material goods. Her work in the fields and her handiwork belonged, in the first instance, to that family and she shared the food cooked on its hearth. All around were other domestic units, which together made up the extended family of the longhouse society. The new physical surroundings in which Tekakwitha found herself—the bark walls, the pots and baskets, the corn hanging from the rafters—would have had a basically familiar look, and many of the longhouse residents would have been people she had known back in Gandaouagué before they had left for the St. Lawrence. Among the familiar faces was that of her mother's old friend, Anastasia Tegonhatsiongo, the ranking matron in the longhouse.

Tegonhatsiongo immediately took the newcomer in hand, bringing her along on the daily round of women's work, which at that time of year centered mainly on the gathering of fuel for the coming winter. Chauchetière's biography concentrates on the religious side of their developing relationship:

Their long acquaintance, Catherine's desire to learn what was most pleasing to God, together with Anastasia's talent for teaching, attracted Catherine to this Indian woman. First she learned the regular obser- vances of the mission, for the feast days as well as for the workdays. She learned more in a week than others learned in several years. She took advantage of every moment: whether she was in the cabin, out in the fields or in the woods, she could always be seen in the com- pany of her dear instructor, a rosary in one hand, going and coming with her load of wood. The most menial chores were exalted by the fervent spirit in which Catherine did them. . . . The subject of their conversations was the way of life of the good Christians, and the moment Catherine heard that Christians performed some particular actions she tried to put them into practice herself, just like a holy bee who goes gathering the honey from every species of flower.[1]

In sketching this account of the early stages of Tekakwitha's introduction to Kahnawake and to the ways of the Iroquois Christians, Claude Chauchetière drew on the memories of Anastasia herself. Of course, we need to bear in mind that the old woman was telling her story to a priest and that their interview took place after the death of someone both informant and recorder had come to believe was a saint. That is no reason to dismiss the testimony out of hand, but it does suggest that there may have been other topics of discussion—news from Gandaouagué? gossip about the Jesuits? informa- tion on where to find local supplies of herbs, berries, and roots? advice on healthy living?—and other dimensions to the relationship than those that Claude and Anastasia chose to report.

The older woman told Catherine about the ways of the Christian com- munity and about how one behaved in church. Since they had left La Prairie so recently, the Jesuits were using a longhouse-style bark hut built for them by the Iroquois as their temporary chapel at Sault St. Louis, but prepara- tions were under way for a more solid log church. It seems clear that Chris- tian observances were much more elaborate here in a predominantly Catholic environment than anything Tekakwitha had known as part of the convert minority at Gandaouagué.

Their talks about the "way of life of the good Christians" also ranged far beyond local subjects. As they trudged along, the loads on their backs strain- ing at the burden straps on their foreheads, Anastasia would relate stories she had heard about the lives of the Catholic saints. Indeed, the ambiguous phrase "the way of life of the good Christians" seems to refer more to the culture of Catholic Europe than to the newly emerging customs of the na- tive converts. Anastasia's lessons then must have been about more than simply how to comport oneself in the mission chapel. She was giving Catherine the benefit of her long years of experience observing the Jesuits, examining their pictures, and listening to their myths; presumably she drew also on information she had gleaned from visits to Montreal and from the reports of Indians who had gained access to other aspects of Euro-Canadian ways.

From Father de Lamberville, Tekakwitha had already gathered that many of the Mohawk customs she had grown up with were considered bad from a Christian point of view, but Anastasia seems to have had a longer, more exacting, list of prohibitions. Like a practiced confessor, she put probing questions to the girl, trying to discover how deeply she had been implicated in the sinful customs of pagan Gandaouagué. Did she, for example, need to atone for participating in some dream-guessing ceremony? Was she addicted to slander, supposedly a common weakness among unconverted native women? The answers Tekakwitha returned convinced Anastasia that the girl was quite exceptional: she did not even seem to know what slander was. Failing to find any "faults" requiring correction, Anastasia at last turned her appraising eye to the girl's appearance. What about the colored beadwork that decorated her hair? Was this pretty adornment more important to Catherine than God's approval? Tekakwitha quickly removed the beads the minute she realized they might be considered inimical to Christianity.

What seems remarkable about this phase of her initiation into Catholicism is the way it took place entirely among Iroquois women. Jesuits (or any other Europeans, for that matter) are nowhere to be seen in this crucial chapter of Tekakwitha's life story, though they clearly lurk in the background as the main source of Anastasia's stock of legends and anecdotes, perhaps also in her confessional style of interrogation. Even though she had been baptized at Gandaouagué, Tekakwitha does not appear to have picked up any deep sense of Christianity there; her religious reeducation began in earnest at the new settlement and through contact with other Iroquois converts. She learned about what to do and what to avoid, how to act in accordance with Christian standards, and she learned all this in the same way that she had learned sewing and beadwork and non-Christian Mohawk lore, at the side of an older woman from the longhouse. At Kahnawake, Catholicism came to her mainly as an Iroquois religion, a set of procedures for living that were apprehended within the familiar setting of female work routines.

Soon enough, Catherine would have direct dealings with Fathers Frémin, Cholenec, and Chauchetière, but these could not be frequent or sustained. For the community as a whole, the missionaries were crucially important figures, privileged mediators with the French governor, king, and God, as well as indispensable ritual performers needed for the celebration of church ceremonies. Whenever possible, a Jesuit would visit the cabins to dispense "instruction," but these indoctrination sessions tended to be hit-and-miss affairs, subject to the often conflicting work schedules of the Iroquois and the missionaries themselves. Theoretically, three Jesuits lived and worked at Sault St. Louis in the late 1670s, but they all had other duties, and at least

Working in the Fields. Chauchetière's drawing of a springtime scene in the vicinity of Kahnawake. While the woman in the foreground uses a native hoe to heap up earth into hillocks where corn will be planted, a woman or girl nearby is climbing a tree to gather birds' eggs. The structures in the background may be field cabins, used as temporary sleeping quarters during busy agricultural seasons. © Archives départementales de la Gironde, H Jésuites.

one of them was liable to be absent or incapacitated at any given moment. Pierre Cholenec, the one fully effective missionary at Kahnawake throughout the period, was so busy he could only provide the mission with a kind of general management; the rest, according to Chauchetière, was left to the Indians and to the workings of the Holy Spirit.[2]

This overworked priest was supposed to be Catherine's confessor—hers and that of a thousand other Iroquois converts. Relying on the recommendation of the Jesuit who had baptized her at Gandaouagué, as well as on Anastasia's favorable reports, Cholenec rushed her through the usual trial period for neophytes. New converts arriving from the Iroquois country normally had to prove themselves over a long period before they were allowed to take communion, but since Catherine appeared to be an exceptional case, she was admitted to communion on Christmas Day, 1677. After that, the Breton priest continued to hear her confessions; retrospectively, he considered himself her "spiritual director," though at most times he was unable to give her close attention.

Once admitted to communion, Catherine became devoted to the Eucharist and took communion often. The Jesuits undoubtedly encouraged this habit, for they were known in Europe as the staunchest advocates of "frequent communion," as against those within the church who feared that excessive familiarity tended to lessen the solemnity of the occasion. According to Pierre Cholenec, familiarity bred not contempt but deeper love for the sacrament. He described the Mohawk girl in terms that recalled the behavior of women saints of late medieval Europe, spending long hours at the altar rail, praying, and contemplating the host: "She would go there every morning at four o'clock, even during the severest winter weather. She heard the first Mass at the break of day and the Mass for the Indians at sunrise. She returned often during the day, interrupting her work to satisfy her devotion." In prayer, the Jesuits relate, she radiated fervor: "She prayed very little with her tongue, but a great deal with her eyes and her heart; her eyes were always filled with tears."[3]

Setting aside the mildly misleading suggestion that there was something special in Catherine's regular attendance at mass—Chauchetière's manuscript history of the mission makes it clear that *everyone* came at least once a day— as one of the distortions inherent in hagiography, it is worth pausing to consider how the mass might have looked to this Mohawk convert. Though it is unlikely that she (any more than the millions of European Catholics who had never been schooled in such matters) would have understood the theory of transubstantiation or the elements of the ceremony, she could not fail to grasp its importance as a ritual opening between the mundane and the sacred. There were ample signs to support a cross-cultural "reading" of the rite: smoke (incense rather than tobacco) rising to heaven; special chants, the exclusive property of initiates; strange utterances in an esoteric language; offerings of food; a feast in which every last morsel had to be consumed. All these components of the mass recalled forms of worship she must have seen as a child at Gandaouagué. Beginning with these vaguely familiar characteristics as a point of entry into the mysterious ritual, Tekakwitha could begin to feel its emotional power and, in the long run, its comforting sameness. It is not implausible to think that at times she would have been brought to tears.

Not long after that first Christmas communion, the winter hunting parties set off from Kahnawake, bound for destinations up the Ottawa River and various other parts of Canada where game remained plentiful. Iroquois men had long been accustomed to procuring meat supplies and animal skins on hunting expeditions that often took them far from home; an additional advantage was the easing of pressure on village food supplies when so many men were off foraging in the woods for their subsistence. With the advent of the fur trade in the seventeenth century, hunting assumed a growing importance; it loomed particularly large in the economy of Kahnawake at this time. Along with the commercial interest in furs, hunting also made an important contribution to the community's subsistence, since Iroquois agriculture seems to have been less productive on the St. Lawrence, where the climate and soil were only marginally suited to corn and to their style of cultivation.

Though hunting was traditionally a male pursuit, many women went along on the seasonal hunts out of Kahnawake. The female presence was partly a reflection of the rapid commercialization of hunting and the consequent need to clean and process large numbers of pelts. This had always been women's work, and it required every bit as much time and effort as tracking and killing animals. Women trekked off to the forest that much more readily knowing that their departure made it easier for the remaining villagers to eke out their stock of corn. There was the added attraction of a break from routine and the opportunity to partake of a more varied and more appetizing diet than the usual day-in, day-out regimen of corn soup.

Accordingly, Tekakwitha went along with her sister, her brother-in-law, and some others on one of these hunting expeditions, leaving sometime in late December 1677 or early January 1678 and not returning until the spring. At the camp, everyone lived in a temporary bark shelter. The men would go off in search of moose or beaver during the day, while the women remained at the camp, preparing the food, gathering firewood, and cleaning and processing pelts. When they had time, Tekakwitha and her companions also busied themselves with quillwork and moose-hair embroidery. Two decorated bark boxes, which she made at the camp and brought back to Kahnawake, hung in the mission chapel as a memorial to her after her death.[4]

Far from the chapel and the mass and far from the supervising presence of the Jesuit missionaries, the converts nevertheless endeavored to nurture and maintain their Catholicism with regular prayers. A piece of wood served as their calendar. "When they are in the woods," Chauchetière observed, "they keep track of the Sundays and holidays by marking small lines to the number of seven, one for each day of the week. We put crosses on the lines that indicate the feast-days and the Sundays, and they observe these exactly."[5] These basic observances were not enough for Catherine, however, and so she made herself a little "oratory" for private prayers. It consisted of a cross carved in the bark of a tree next to a stream near the camp; there she would go early in the morning and attempt to participate at a distance in the mass she knew was being celebrated back at Kahnawake.[6]

This vignette featuring Catherine praying at her rustic chapel in the forest came to be the favorite image in modern versions of her life story; it seemed to epitomize all the most appealing qualities associated with the "Indian maiden" as an innocent woodland creature at one with nature. All the more reason to note that the seventeenth-century Jesuits attached a very different meaning to this scene. Chauchetière and Cholenec worried about the moral and religious dangers of long hunting trips, even though they recognized their economic necessity for the convert Iroquois. Not only did the hunt pose practical problems for their ministry in that it kept people physically removed from the mass and from the supervision of the missionaries, but it took Indian neophytes into a wild environment with perilous associations. For the original biographers of Catherine Tekakwitha, space had moral meaning: the Christian village at Sault St. Louis, together with the fields that surrounded it, was good, whereas the forest was almost entirely evil, the dark haunt of demons and pagan savages. Thus, far from "communing with nature" in her woodland oratory, they saw Catherine doing her best to commune with civilization. She was literally out of her element at the hunting camp, according to Pierre Cholenec: "Though her body was in the forest, her soul was wholly at the Sault."[7]

Solitude and secretive habits were generally frowned upon in Iroquoian societies of this period, and so Tekakwitha's peculiar behavior roused suspicions. One morning she woke to find a hunter asleep beside her. In the tightly packed hunting shelter, this was not an especially unusual situation; the man had returned late the night before, exhausted from a long day spent tracking an elusive moose, and he simply collapsed in the first available spot he could find on the floor. However, the man's wife began to feel that something was amiss, and when her husband later asked Tekakwitha to come and help him fetch his canoe, she jumped to the conclusion that they were carrying on a sexual liaison. There was no confrontation at the time, but since the incident occurred just as the party was preparing to return to the Sault, tongues were soon wagging in the village and, behind her back, Catherine was being spoken of as a seducer of married men. The wife took her complaint to Father Cholenec, who later summoned Catherine to answer the charge of adultery. Her denial, he says, was so simple and direct that he instantly concluded that the allegation was groundless. In Chauchetière's account, however, his colleague was not quite so sure; outwardly, Cholenec dismissed the accusation of sin, but inwardly he still harbored doubts until long after Catherine died. By the time they came to write their biographies, both Jesuits were convinced that the young woman was completely innocent and that God had allowed this "calumny" to arise as an occasion for his chosen one to sacrifice her reputation in the eyes of the world, the better to bring out her real virtue as she suffered injustice without bitterness or complaint.[8]

In the wake of this scandal, Catherine began to develop a heightened self-consciousness about her own virginal purity. After that one winter hunt, she never again strayed from the village and the church. Faltering health and a morbid fear of sin, together with her devotion to the Eucharist, conspired to keep her at home in the sanctified environment of Sault St. Louis.

Returning to Kahnawake in the spring, Tekakwitha resumed her new role as a confirmed Catholic taking regular communion. Gradually, she became aware of a whole dimension of Iroquois Christianity that had, until now, been hidden to her. According to Chauchetière, "The horror that the new Christians of the Sault felt for the life they had led among the Iroquois before they were baptized so aroused them against sin that they did not spare themselves. Some of them were then practicing severe penances but Catherine knew nothing of this except by surmise." No one told her of the ascetic activities that a small circle of native women had been pursuing from about the time she arrived at Kahnawake, "because her innocence was great and the weakness of her body provoked compassion."[9] Benevolent concern for Catherine's health was Chauchetière's explanation for this secrecy, but it was more likely Iroquoian tendencies toward exclusiveness where spiritual knowledge is concerned that kept her in the dark.

The spiritual athletes of Kahnawake appear to have been mostly young women. Certainly the dour old Anastasia was not of their number; though considered an excellent Christian and a pillar of local society, she was not temperamentally suited to immoderate behavior, especially at her stage of life. Tekakwitha always remained close to her longhouse clan mother, but she needed younger companions if she was to penetrate the mysteries of

Iroquois Catholic mysticism. She found such a friend when she encountered Marie-Thérèse Tegaiaguenta one day in the spring of 1678.

Strolling along the river by the site where the new chapel was under construction, Tekakwitha stopped to look inside. There she came upon another woman, a little older than herself, who had also been curious to see how the work was progressing. Looking over the unfinished building, they fell into conversation, speculating on how the interior would be arranged, which section was to be for the women and which for the men. Catherine's earnest sentiments suffused even this casual chat with a stranger; she expressed herself with such deep feeling that Marie-Thérèse, a baptized Catholic with a guilty secret, could not help opening up. According to the hagiographic accounts, the two of them talked of how they had kept God out of their hearts for so long, to the point where both were soon in tears. Together they went off to a private spot on the riverbank and poured out their souls to one another, telling of their respective pasts before baptism and of their aspirations to reach a purified state.

Marie-Thérèse, Tekakwitha learned, was a young widow from the Oneida nation. She had been baptized by a Jesuit missionary in her native village and had subsequently moved with her non-Christian husband to La Prairie. Her career as a Christian had been rather more eventful, however, with ups and downs that included periods of drinking and other, unspecified, "sins." Marie-Thérèse was an energetic and exuberant person, more given to enthusiasm and sharp reversals than the quiet and steady Catherine. Furthermore, she had undergone one horrific experience: an ill-fated hunting trip up the Ottawa when all the game vanished, food supplies dwindled, and, one by one, the hunters—Marie-Thérèse's husband among them—succumbed to starvation. She herself had special reasons for "survivor guilt," for the living had been forced to eat the flesh of the dead. It is not clear exactly when these ghastly events had unfolded, but obviously Marie-Thérèse was still a desperate individual when Tekakwitha encountered her, and one highly susceptible to the appeal of penitential practices and the promise of personal renewal.

The two young women, both of them apparently peripheral to Kahnawake's Catholic-ascetic medicine society and both of them hungry for powerful spiritual experiences, quickly became intimate friends. They spent every day together, keeping one another company in their various chores and recreations and discussing whatever was on their minds. Father Cholenec, officially Catherine's spiritual director, had to admit that Marie-Thérèse was "the only one in whom she truly confided; ever since they were united, it was to her that she communicated all the secrets of her heart."[10] It was to her, therefore, that the biographer Claude Chauchetière turned in later years for information on phases of his subject's life that had eluded Anastasia Tegonhatsiongo and Pierre Cholenec.

One Saturday afternoon the two women were sitting together in Marie-Thérèse's longhouse, waiting for the bell that would summon everyone to evening prayers. Marie-Thérèse had already begun to develop the habit of self-flagellation in preparation for confession and mass, and she suggested that Catherine join her so that they could chastise themselves together. Though she had never tried such a thing herself, Tekakwitha apparently had some idea what this was about and readily agreed, rushing out to break off some branches for the purpose. Hiding their instruments under their mat, the friends waited until the bell rang and everyone filed out to prayers, leaving them alone. Since time was short, they got straight down to business. Catherine dropped to her knees and begged her companion not to spare her; and then, when Catherine's shoulders were covered in blood, it was Marie-Thérèse's turn. When they were done, the two got dressed and hurried off to the chapel in a shared state of elation.

After that, mutual flagellation became a central feature of their relationship. In the middle of the village cemetery, they discovered an abandoned cabin, once used by a French-Canadian trader, and there they found they could pray and perform their penances in private. "Several times a week, over the course of nearly a year and a half, she went with her companion in devotion and they used large switches to make one another's shoulders bleed." Of Catherine specifically, Pierre Cholenec goes on to note that her "bloody disciplines" consisted of between one thousand and twelve hundred blows at each session.[11]

It is difficult to describe this ritual for modern readers without sounding lurid, without seeming to suggest kinky sexuality. The fact is that Catherine and Marie-Thérèse loved one another—the hagiographic texts make this abundantly clear—and though there is no reason to think they were "lovers" in the sexual sense, their relationship did have strong emotional, physical, and spiritual dimensions. The intimacy that they shared appears to have energized their joint pursuit of the sacred.

The close bond between Tekakwitha and Marie-Thérèse Tegaiaguenta would have seemed normal to fellow villagers, for in the Iroquoian societies of the time, close friendships between individuals of the same sex and of approximately the same age were valued highly.[12] The Jesuit hagiographers understood their relationship as a "spiritual friendship," a form of chaste intimacy through which partners helped one another to achieve higher states of devotion. The European Catholic ideal for saintly figures called for a more diffuse love with a heavenly focus, one that was at odds with "particular attachments." Catherine, however, tended to specialize in intimate, same-sex friendships—in addition to Tegaiaguenta and the maternal Anastasia, there was another, younger, woman who took on the role of bosom companion in the last months of Tekakwitha's life—and to develop her unique spiritual personality in and through them.

←

Unsure how to proceed in their devotions, the two spiritual partners decided to seek guidance from someone more familiar with the ways of Christianity. Significantly, it was not the Jesuits to whom they turned. A conception of spiritual knowledge as proprietary and exclusive suggested the necessity of cultivating other channels as well. But there was another reason, apart from the generally secretive tendencies of priests and shamans, to look for alternative sources of enlightenment: the Jesuits were all men, specialists in what appeared to be specifically male rituals; Tekakwitha and Tegaiaguenta needed to find out how women could draw insight and power from the Christian deity.

Accordingly, they sought out as their chosen agent of intercultural espionage a native woman by the name of Marie Skarichions who happened to be resident at Kahnawake in the spring and early summer of 1678. Marie seems to have been a little older than the other two; more important, she had been a Christian for many years and possessed a comparatively wide experience of life in the missions and among the French. For a time, she had lived at the Jesuit mission of Lorette near Quebec City, where a bout of illness had led to her confinement at the Hôtel-Dieu de Québec, a hospital-convent run by nuns who cared for Indians and French settlers, where she had observed Christian spiritual specialists who were women.

Marie-Thérèse and Catherine eagerly pressed her to join them in their enterprise. Marie assented, and the three of them made their way to the banks of the St. Lawrence and sat down at the same spot where Tekakwitha and Tegaiaguenta had met sometime earlier for their first conversation.

> There the elder companion spoke first, expressing her desire to join them and proposing that they follow some procedures modeled on the way of life of the nuns as she had observed them when she was in Quebec, sick. She said that they must never separate, that they should all dress in the same style, and that, if possible, they should live in the same cabin. They were then facing an island called Heron Island and they chose that place to be their home. All these things entered into their deliberations for they had no real understanding of what the religious life was about.[13]

From the native point of view, much about the hospital-convent must have appeared enigmatically significant to Marie Skarichions: the enclosed, carefully guarded house; the all-female nuns' quarters; the uniform costume; the daily round of ceremonial singing; the withdrawal from marriage, sex, and family. There were probably ample clues, in the nuns' own demeanor and in the deference paid to them by other French people, to suggest that these were women of exceptional spiritual power. Having noted the outward

The First Chapel Is Built. The chapel was under construction about the time Claude Chauchetière first arrived at Kahnawake in the summer of 1677. The Jesuit conferring with the French carpenters in the lower right corner is probably the artist himself. And could those three figures looking out across the river be a projection forward to 1678 when Catherine Tekakwitha, Marie-Thérèse Tegaiaguenta, and Marie Skarichions met to hatch plans for a native convent? © Archives départementales de la Gironde, H Jésuites.

characteristics of female monasticism, Marie later passed on suggestions to her new friends about how to organize themselves after the fashion of the French virgins. Did she, one wonders, add any further information about the content of nuns' ritual practices?

As a patient in the hospital wards, she would not have been able to see what the sisters did in their private cells, but she might have caught an inkling of what went on behind closed doors. The nursing sisters saw themselves as missionaries; as such, they took advantage of every opportunity to save the souls and stimulate the fervor of all who came under their care. They liked to tell patients about lives of exemplary piety, including that of Sister Catherine de St.-Augustin, one of their own who had died only a decade earlier, a mystic-ascetic figure of whom they were excessively proud. This Catherine was famous for her extreme penances, her inner struggles with demons, her achievements as an exorcist, and her prophetic visions. A dream she reported in 1663 featuring monstrous figures shaking the four corners of the world was taken as a portent of the violent earthquake that struck Canada shortly afterward. For sixteen years, until her death in 1668, this sickly nun had followed an austere program of fasting and bloody self-flagellation. A decade later, when Marie came to them for assistance, the nursing sisters were guarding the remains and revering the memory of Catherine de St.-Augustin; it is unlikely Marie would have escaped from the hospital without hearing something on the subject.[14]

The hospital nuns of Quebec were not the only religious women from whom natives might have learned about mystic-ascetic practices. There were also Ursuline sisters at Quebec and Three Rivers and another, quite separate, hôtel-dieu establishment at Montreal. A letter by Claude Chauchetière on the marvels of Iroquois Catholicism spoke of a group of pious women who had "learned, I know not how, of the pious practices followed by the nuns of the Montreal hospital."[15] Did they take their cue from the Quebec hospital or the Montreal hospital? It hardly seems to matter, since the two institutions were essentially similar. Yet the discrepancy reveals some interesting possibilities: (1) reconstructing clandestine activities after the fact, the Jesuit chronicler was simply confused; (2) Marie Skarichions was only one of several channels by which intelligence reached the Kahnawake devotees; or (3) there was more than one circle of Iroquois penitents in the village.

We need to pause for a moment to consider the third hypothesis. Jesuit writings always speak as though there were one single group, but then their consistent tendency was to downplay any signs of conflict and division in a community they wish to present as perfectly united in a spirit of Christian love. The great schism of 1673, which led to the departure of a large portion of the "Huron" population, is scarcely mentioned in the Jesuit *Relations* or in Chauchetière's history of the mission; the subject arises only obliquely as an occasion to praise the converts for handling a difficult situation without violence or overt displays of anger.[16] Similarly, the Jesuits refrained from dwelling on any tensions within their own ranks or even on their often fierce struggles with rival orders such as the Sulpicians and the Recollets. These missionaries were perfectly well acquainted with factionalism, whether European or Iroquoian, but ecclesiastical etiquette dictated that they avoid such unedifying topics in writings destined for the public.

Undoubtedly there was factionalism at Kahnawake: the various customs and rituals of solidarity mentioned in chapter 4 are evidence of the need to counteract explosive tendencies within this heterogeneous community. There is also every reason to think that a small group, organized on the medicine society model but aiming at the attainment of Christian spiritual power, might generate other, competing groups with similar aims. "Competing" may be too strong a word, since there is no indication that Catholic ascetic circles, any more than traditional medicine societies, sought to injure or defeat others, but when ritual knowledge tended to be guarded within a small clique, sometimes the only way to gain similar benefits was to undertake a separate and parallel initiative. When Chauchetière's two different chronologies of the launching of mystic-ascetic practices at Sault St. Louis— his history of the mission, which says they began in 1676, and his biography of Catherine, which implies that she and her friends initiated them independently in 1678—are juxtaposed, it appears that this intensive version of Iroquois Christianity was invented and reinvented. Catherine Tekakwitha and her associates seem therefore to have embarked on a double "end run": they aimed to bypass both the religious monopoly of the Jesuit missionaries and that of the other native women who had gone before them.

Through Skarichions the women became acquainted with flagellant ascetic practices that French nuns would normally have carried out only in the strictest privacy. They no doubt sifted through whatever hints might be gleaned from the Jesuits' discourse about similar subjects, and gathered whatever they could from "rumors" circulating in the village about the practices of the Iroquois initiates. Then the trio gathered by the riverside and made ready to act.

At this point they consulted Father Jacques Frémin, the mission superior, about their project. That might at first sight seem a puzzling move in what amounted to a spiritual purloining operation, but then Catherine and her companions were never really in revolt against the French and the Jesuits; far from it. Quite apart from the fact that they belonged to an Iroquois community distinguished by its connections through the Jesuits to the French, these women truly valued the access, limited though it might be, which the missionaries gave them to the powers flowing from the Christian god. They faced a delicate dilemma, wanting to probe areas of Christian practice from which the Jesuits evidently wished to exclude them, but needing still to maintain good relations with the priests. As long as it remained a matter of private devotions, they could proceed quietly on their own—as Catherine Tekakwitha and Marie-Thérèse Tegaiaguenta in fact did with their flagellant practices for a full year before the missionaries got wind of it[17]—but a native convent could hardly be concealed. And so they had to take a chance and divulge their plans.

The old superior laughed at the idea of a native convent. You are "too young in the faith," he told them, employing the standard phrase used throughout the Catholic Americas to explain why Indians could not join the clergy.[18] Besides, he added, the Heron Island site is too far from the village; a house of virgins would be an irresistible magnet to young men on their way to and from Montreal, and "disorder" was sure to ensue.[19] Even if Catherine and her friends had been European, any plans they might have entertained to form an all-female association for pious and benevolent purposes would have faced opposition from churchmen. The Catholic Reformation had mobilized the idealism of women to do good "in the world," and many had formed themselves into organizations, such as the Ursulines of northern Italy or the Congrégation de Nôtre-Dame in French Canada, to live and work together, forsaking marriage to devote themselves to works of charity and education. But regardless of how spotless their virtue and meek their demeanor, the all-female independence was profoundly threatening to patriarchal norms. Focusing on the fragility of their chastity as unsupervised women at large in the world, religious and secular authorities pressured these devout groups to transform themselves into conventional religious orders so that, as nuns, they would be safely confined behind impregnable cloister walls.[20] Already suspicious of any such religious initiative on the part of women, Jacques Frémin would have been scandalized at the thought, had he taken it seriously, of Indian women forming a convent. As it was, he chose to regard their proposal as a product of the ludicrous naïveté of unlettered savages whose acquaintance with Catholicism was so superficial that they thought they could set themselves up as a religious order. He knew nothing, at this point, of Catherine's and Marie-Thérèse's flagellant practices. Frémin's own naïveté consisted in assuming that their mimicry was innocent and childlike, thus missing its aggressive edge.

Soon after administering this rebuff sometime in the summer of 1678, Father Frémin departed Kahnawake for France, leaving the women free to ignore most of his instructions. With Claude Chauchetière scarcely pulling his weight, initially through inexperience, later as a consequence of depression, Pierre Cholenec was left to cope with the streams of newcomers arriving from the Mohawk country, as well as attending to a thousand other missionary duties. Thus, the young women faced minimal interference as they continued their quest for sacred knowledge and mystical experience. Carefully avoiding the unacceptable idea of an island retreat, they managed to put into practice most other elements of their original plan. Joining Tekakwitha, Marie-Thérèse, and Marie Skarichions in this endeavor were other village women; the sources give no indication of how many were involved.

"Catherine did not tell me everything on this occasion," Cholenec later admitted, "but in fact she had already chosen her path." Her "overriding passion was to search out that which was most excellent in our religion," since she somehow realized that "there were some who performed extraordinary things which were hidden from her. Conversing with her companion, she complained gently that the missionaries did not tell her all." She and Marie-Thérèse had nevertheless cracked some of the essential secrets of the French spiritual elite. One of these was ascetic penance; the other was a solemn repudiation of sex. Accordingly, "the two of them had agreed between themselves never to marry and to dedicate to God, in one case her virginity, in the other her widowhood, in perpetuity." They did so, he discovered later, "in the strictest secrecy, resolving never to speak of it except in absolute necessity."[21] A complicated game was being played out here, one in which the Indian women and the French priest were simultaneously partners and antagonists. He was their teacher, yet he would not tell them what they wanted to know. They came to him for confession, but they would not tell him exactly how they felt or precisely what they were doing. At Kahnawake, missionaries and converts held their cards tightly to their chests as they scanned the opposite party for clues as to the spiritual assets in play.

Several young women in this devout circle renounced sex and marriage, for their research indicated that such "purity" was a basic qualification for all French religious specialists, even more emphatically so for nuns than for male priests. In a general way, such a notion would have seemed perfectly plausible to people raised in an Iroquois tradition where abstention from sex was a prerequisite for all sorts of undertakings requiring a special spiritual state. Some cut their hair short to make themselves less attractive, another gesture undertaken in imitation of the nuns yet, at the same time, differently meaningful for Iroquoian women, who sometimes cut their hair as an expression of grief over the death of a loved one.[22] Interestingly, Tekakwitha declined to follow the example of the more radical sisters; pursuing the path of moderation, she left her hair long, though she did make a point of avoiding all ornamentation in her attire: "She renounced all the red blankets and the ornaments with which the Indian women adorned one another; she would merely put on a new blue blanket on the days when she received Holy Communion."[23]

According to Pierre Cholenec's account of her life, Catherine's decision to embrace a life of celibacy brought her into conflict, once again, with relatives and friends who wanted her to marry. As she was nearing the age of twenty-three and still single, her "sister" began to wonder how much

Several Persons Embrace Virginity and Continence. Chauchetière depicts seven Iroquois women bowing to a statue of the Virgin and undertaking a life of celibacy. One woman is cutting her hair short, a gesture that had significance in the Christian tradition as a renunciation of female sexuality, while in the Iroquois tradition it was associated with bereavement and grief. © Archives départementales de la Gironde, H Jésuites.

longer she would be eating from the family's pot without bringing a man into its orbit. Translating Catherine's living situation at the Sault into European terms, Chauchetière states that "her brother-in-law took care of her until she died as far as wear and tear and clothing are concerned," meaning presumably that, as part of her sister's family unit, she shared in the fruits of his hunting, which would have included the hides and moose hair she needed for her handiwork, as well as the pelts needed to purchase blankets, needles, and other imported goods. Chauchetière goes on to note that "she easily managed part of her upkeep for she was a good worker and supplied enough to keep herself clothed." He adds, that clothing, or rather the hunter's contribution to clothing manufacture, "is the most difficult part to find, which is why several Indian women have been obliged to marry in spite of their desire to imitate the nuns of France."[24] The importance of the fur trade at Kahnawake put a special premium on bringing husbands into the household, and so the sister's hints became less and less subtle.

Catherine did her best to ignore the hints and evade direct discussion of the issue, but concern about her marital status soon spread from the hearth she shared with her sister to the wider longhouse society. Before long, the clan mother Anastasia Tegonhatsiongo had joined the fray, adding the voice of maternal authority in favor of matrimony. Though the hagiographies insist that the young woman was always meek and mild, there must have been at least one blowup, for Pierre Cholenec received visits in quick succession, first from a distraught Catherine, then from an indignant Anastasia. The two women chose Cholenec as mediator in this family dispute, each of them complaining of the other's stubbornness.

The missionary's main concern was to test and verify Catherine's surprising resolution to remain a virgin. He began by urging her to give careful consideration to the advice of her people. Even in France, a priest would have been careful to avoid encouraging what might well be the passing fancies of young people who thought they had a religious vocation; instead, he would dwell on the advantages of social conformity, trusting that those who were truly inspired would not be swayed. In this case, he was all the more discouraging because he felt that native social organization and mores provided no space for a life outside marriage. He let her think about the issue for a few days, but she seemed determined; "I hate men," she told her confessor, "I have the deepest aversion to marriage." To his great delight, "she renounced marriage in order to have none other than Jesus Christ as her spouse."[25] From that point on, Cholenec claims, he supported her wholeheartedly and, with little difficulty, convinced her sister and her clan mother to do likewise.

As her commitment to celibacy hardened, Tekakwitha's ascetic penances intensified. "She tortured her body in every way she could think of: by toil, by sleepless vigils, by fasting, by cold, by fire, by irons, by belts studded with sharp points, and by harsh disciplines with which she tore her shoulders open several times a week. When in winter she went to the woods with her sister and the other women, she always remained behind, to take off her shoes and walk barefoot in the snow and ice." When people noticed that she ate nothing on Wednesdays and Fridays, they tried to make her take at least take some *sagamite*, but she did her best to destroy any savor by mixing ashes with the food.[26]

Trial by fire became Catherine's specialty. According to Claude Chauchetière, it was the clan mother Anastasia who had initially turned her thoughts in that direction with her talk of the fires of hell: "When everyone was asleep after prayers, she burned herself with brands from the fire, starting at the ends of her toes and continuing up to her knees." On another occasion, she experimented with fire in what amounted to a "dare" with Marie-Thérèse. Her friend proposed to burn herself "like a slave," that is, like a war captive; she intended to place a coal from the fire between her toes and leave it there for the time it took to recite an Ave Maria. Tekakwitha rose to the implied challenge, saying she would do likewise. Each retired to her respective longhouse and waited until the middle of the night to take the test. Marie-Thérèse—once again the Jesuit's witness for deeds he had no inkling of at the time—did her best. Placing the glowing coal between her first and second toes, she felt the pain searing her to the quick and had to relent for fear of fainting before she could make it halfway through the Hail Mary. But she was convinced that Catherine withstood the ordeal, for the next day when she went to see her, there was her friend with a large black hole in the flesh of her foot.[27]

Tekakwitha's frail health could sustain only so much of this punishment. Ever since early childhood, she had been subject to spells of illness, and in the middle of 1679 she suffered a physical breakdown so serious that Marie-Thérèse feared she would die. That fear induced her to tell Pierre Cholenec about the flagellation and the other ascetic practices she and her friend had been carrying on for the past year. Cholenec professed himself shocked and gave Marie-Thérèse a severe scolding for indulging in excessive, unregulated penances. When Catherine recovered her strength and wanted to resume her penances, her confessor insisted on regulating them, introducing her to the sackcloth, iron belt, and disciplinary whip, European devices that seemed more moderate and more susceptible to limitations than some of the dangerous Iroquois techniques. And still she would not stay within the prescribed limitations. In the early months of 1680, as her health went into another decline, Tekakwitha discovered a new technique for making her body suffer. She happened to hear one of the missionaries talking about Aloysius Gonzaga, an Italian Jesuit of the sixteenth century (later canonized as a saint) known for ascetic practices that included sleeping on a bed of thorns. That bit of information on the ways of the saintly Christians was enough to send her to the woods in search of thorny bushes. Already suffering from a fever, she rolled on the prickles for three nights in a row until, once again, her friend intervened with the priest, who then persuaded Catherine to throw them in the fire. "I admired her in my heart, but I did not fail to pretend anger and to reprimand her for her imprudence," wrote Cholenec, expressing an ambivalence that must have been apparent to Tekakwitha throughout.[28]

Though circumstances had forced her to confide more in her Jesuit confessor at this late stage of her life, Tekakwitha's most important relationships were still with other native women. As of February 1680, she was still intimately connected with a circle of female penitents, but in the year and a half since she first became involved in collective devotions, there seems to have been some turnover in the group's membership. The Jesuits did not like to dwell on the instability of personal commitment to the religious life, but it seems clear that many of the women who embarked with Catherine and Marie-Thérèse in the summer of 1678 had either died, moved away from Kahnawake, or simply fallen away, as is perfectly understandable, from the daunting regimen of chastity and flagellation. As of February 1680, the inner circle numbered only five, including an Onondaga woman named Marguerite Gagagouikton, fairly recently baptized as a Christian. There was another Onondaga referred to as "our good Marie" (possibly Marie Skarichions), as well as Tekakwitha herself and two other, unnamed Mohawk women. At least two of them were married, and though they may have maintained a sexless marriage as many pious couples at Kahnawake did, this was no longer a society of virgins and widows. Our source here is a confidential letter from Pierre Cholenec to the Jesuit superior in Quebec, a rare document and the only text dealing with Catherine and her circle to have been written during her lifetime, rather than as a retrospective narrative intended for the edification of a French audience.[29] These women are like sisters, the missionary observed, sharing all their secrets, encouraging one another, and flagellating themselves relentlessly.

But what about Marie-Thérèse? The Oneida widow remained Tekakwitha's dearest friend, but to Catherine's great regret she was no longer a member of her group of devout women. Marie-Thérèse was still a devotee of flagellant Christianity, still firmly attached to her companion, but personal difficulties of some sort seem to have alienated her from the others. Tekakwitha did her best to get her friend reintegrated into the group; on the very point of death in April, she was still begging the other four to accept Marie-Thérèse into their midst. She also had some advice for the latter, in case she was taken back into the group: she should "behave herself and make sure she did not spoil matters which were going so well among the four of them; and, above all, she must be very discrete, as they were."[30]

This cryptic counsel suggests that a certain flamboyance of character may have been at the root of Marie-Thérèse Tegaiaguenta's ostracism. Whatever the particulars may have been—and we can only speculate about these—it is clear that the Catholic sisterhood at Kahnawake, for all its close and intense personal relations, was also riven with jealousy and animosity. Such tensions, almost inevitable under the circumstances and certainly not unknown in the convents and devotional societies of Europe, could lead to schism and migration in the world of the northern Iroquois. Tekakwitha's dying words to her friend were, "If you cannot serve God here, go to the mission of Lorette."[31]

Through all this movement of people, coming to Kahnawake to live and moving away, through the complicated personal dynamics of the women's devotional circle, with its exclusions and defections, Catherine Tekakwitha remained. Confined to the village partly by her physical handicaps and easily accepted by virtue of her placid disposition, she had acquired a certain seniority by the winter of 1679–80. Up until then, she was one among several; neither the first, nor the most extreme in her penances, nor a leader of others, she had never been singled out in any way by missionaries who wrote at the time. In the larger village society, she seems to have been an obscure figure, frequently confined to home by reason of ill health, who went outside only with her head hooded under a blanket that shielded her sensitive eyes from the sun's glare. But then a time came when she began to make an impression on others beyond her little circle. Cholenec's letter of February 1680, referring to her as "the little lame girl," cited her for the first time as "the most fervent" in all the village. Recently, he continued, she reported a great light surrounding her as she was whipping herself. Cholenec and Chauchetière had "looked into the matter" and concluded that the strange light was indeed a sign of divine favor.[32]

In more ways than one, this retiring figure was at last coming into the light. Word spread that the sickly young woman possessed extraordinary spiritual powers, and people began seeking her out (though hardly in great numbers, for she passed her final illness mostly in solitude). Predisposed by what they had heard, no doubt, those who approached her came away with the sense of being warmed by a "sacred fire" that radiated through her eyes, her gestures, and the words she spoke. "Her manner, her reputation, together with a certain indefinable something that both French and Indians noticed in this young virgin," brought many to her doorstep. Mostly they just wanted to be in her presence, but they also asked her to give them guidance. She had never been comfortable speaking out, but the unwonted attention she received during the last phase of her life seems to have loosened her tongue. There was nothing very remarkable in the substance of what visitors heard from Catherine's lips—according to the Jesuits, "virginity, chastity and continence were the subject of her conversations"—but they went away impressed, more by her sincerity and conviction than by the sense of her words.[33]

Though the evidence is utterly inconclusive, it does appear that Tekakwitha had somehow "arrived" by February 1680. We know where she had come from: from the devastating upheavals occasioned by colonization, war, and disease. We have a good basic idea of what she sought: the empowering knowledge that lay deep in the heart of the European supernatural. And we know that her search proceeded through two years of grueling pain and self-denial. We can even say, looking at aspects of her career with a twenty-first-century sensibility, that she was "successful" in gaining notoriety and in outdistancing other Iroquois women engaged in a similar quest. But what exactly was Tekakwitha looking for, and what exactly did she feel she had found at this stage of her life? These are questions that no historian can answer.

Whatever inner serenity and outward fame Catherine may have achieved was short-lived, for already she was beginning to feel the "slow fever" and lassitude that heralded the end. It has to be said that a key to the veneration that would later envelop her memory is to be found in the perfect timing of her death. Of all the Iroquois women who threw themselves into mystic-ascetic Christianity, she was the one whose career was cut short at its peak. As a result, she would forever more be distinguished from those who, over the long run, drifted away, fell in love and married, succumbed to alcohol, or felt the need to consult a shaman. Yet clearly her appeal rested on more than just the circumstances of her death. We have no way of knowing whether Iroquois people might have seen her as a *dehninotaton*, a dangerous/vulnerable child prodigy, signaled at birth by the ominous presence of fetal membrane over the head and valued for her purity after reaching puberty.[34] The Jesuits, for their part, detected a "certain indefinable something," which worked its magic on Claude Chauchetière as he kept watch by her bedside.

We are already acquainted with the profound revolution this experience unleashed in Chauchetière's soul. It led to the long process of prayers, visions, biographical research, and experiments in miraculous healing by which he sought to determine whether he had indeed witnessed the death of a saint. Hagiography would follow, and in time Catherine's virtues would be proclaimed to the world. Almost from the moment she breathed her last on April 17, 1680, the wheels were in motion that would turn an obscure human life into a wonder-working legend.

7

Curing
the
Afflicted

Joseph Kellogg had some serious explaining to do when he returned to New England in 1713. Ten years earlier, at the age of twelve, this son of English colonists had been captured during the Canadian-Indian raid on Deerfield, Massachusetts, and dragged, along with his family and 112 other English-American settlers, across the frozen mountains to Kahnawake. By that time, the mission at Sault St. Louis had been fully integrated into New France's war machine. Men from Catherine's village were in the vanguard of countless expeditions against the vulnerable settlements of New England and New York during the colonial conflicts sometimes known as Queen Anne's War, King George's War, and the French and Indian War. These strikes almost invariably concluded with a procession of frightened English captives stumbling into Kahnawake, where they faced not torture and death but the challenge of adapting to the bewilderingly unfamiliar ways of their captors until such time as they were ransomed and returned to New England or, alternatively, until they blended into the Christian Iroquois community.

Children tended to fit in more easily than their elders, as was the case for Joseph Kellogg. He picked up the Mohawk language, developed skill as a hunter, and accepted Catholicism, an essential feature of community membership. This religious conversion later seemed to him a momentous error when a prisoner repatriation brought him back to his childhood home; only after accounting for his failure to resist the pressures to renounce Protestant

Christianity could the young man expect to be received back into the sternly anti-Papist Puritan fold. And so he recounted his trials, emphasizing, and no doubt exaggerating, the menacing brutality of the Catholic Mohawks and the wily tricks of the Jesuits. Featuring prominently in Joseph Kellogg's self-justifying narrative was the long-dead Catherine Tekakwitha:

> One priest Monsieur Rene [Rémy] told me he had heard of great miracles wrought by Saint Katherine. Here note that this Saint Katherine was a Macqua [Mohawk] squaw, that was dead & sainted. . . . Near a twelve-month after i had lived with them, i was taken sick with the small pox, and when my distemper was at the height, and my sores white and just ready to runt, a Jesuit came to me, and told me my case was very hazardous, and that he had used all ordinary means but without success, but when he was looking over his medicines some of the relick of this saint often came into his hand, but though he knew the great virtue in them, he dare not give them me, because I was not a Roman Catholick in heart, and told me i was near dying, and that if i would now promise that i would confess, & be a Roman Catholick, if upon taking some of these Relicks i should have help, he would give them to me, so i promised him and he gave me something under the name of the relicks of the Rotten wood of the coffin after which i slept better, & grew fatter, & when i was recovered he told me of the promise that i had made, & how angry god would be with me if i did not make good my promise.[1]

There is every possibility that the unnamed Jesuit who cured Joseph Kellogg's smallpox was either Pierre Cholenec or Claude Chauchetière. "Monsieur Rene" was surely Father Pierre Rémy, a Sulpician priest centrally involved in the effort to convert English captives to Catholicism. But the real wonder-worker in this episode was a dead woman now known as "Saint Katherine."

Jesuit writings of the period never referred to her in this way, for it was expressly forbidden to anticipate a papal decision and call anyone a saint who had not been duly canonized (similarly, the terms "martyr" and "miracle" were, in theory, strictly controlled). Yet Kellogg's testimony reveals that the phrase "Saint Catherine" had already found its way into the casual conversation of the clergy by the first decade of the eighteenth century and that Tekakwitha's remains were an ingredient in routine medical miracles. Had he known of it, the pope might have frowned upon the presumptuousness of these priests, but then the latter were only following the example of countless other saint promoters, all of them perfectly aware that no holy person could ever be canonized unless they had already been treated as a saint, with a saintly life story, a shrine, relics, a popular following, and a record of miracles.

In this period of its history, the church bestowed canonization only in the rarest of cases—a grand total of one new saint in the three decades separating Tekakwitha's death and Joseph Kellogg's conversion[2]—where incontrovertible evidence of heroic virtue and miraculous powers existed, and where powerful international political forces backed by vast sums of money could be deployed in support of the case. Nevertheless, indeed partly because of this official stinginess, uncanonized saints with local or even national and international followings continued to spring up across Counter-Reformation Europe. With the religious colonization of the New World, native sacred sites were rededicated (Mexico's Virgin of Guadalupe shrine, to take the most famous example), and new spiritual heroes were added to the colonial pantheon.[3] In Canada, a healing cult developed at the shrine to Saint Anne at Beaupré, near Quebec, and every religious order had its candidates for saintly status. People began to pray to the mystic-ascetic Catherine de St-Augustin, and the pulverized bones of the Jesuit martyr Jean de Brébeuf were used to cure ailments and bring about the conversion of Protestants.[4]

Catherine Tekakwitha, as Joseph Kellogg encountered her, was a miracle worker who helped the ill recover their health. Father Rémy told him that he himself had recovered his hearing, after years of deafness in one ear, when he prayed at the tomb of the "Macqua squaw." Further, Kellogg learned, "A nun at Montreal was very sick and had a grievous pain in her side, sent for a tooth of Saint Katherines, and a dish which she used to use, which she put into her mouth, & drunk in the dish and was cured."[5] Religion, medicine, and a form of magic were indissolubly conjoined in these operations. The Jesuit who came to the aid of the young English Protestant was evidently accustomed to curing bodies as well as souls, as evidenced by his cabinets crammed with medicines and "relicks." In this instance, he must have felt doubly satisfied to have managed, with the help of the saintly Mohawk, to drive out the infection of smallpox, as well as the more fatal virus of heresy.

Christians had been praying to saints and asking for their help since the third century, if not earlier, for the working of wonders was a defining feature of sainthood. Early saints' lives often recounted amazing incidents from the subjects' time on earth—incidents featuring superhuman strength or the ability to be in two places at once—but in the early modern period most miracles were postmortem events, the product of the deceased hero's response to the prayers of the living. Believers turned to saints for a variety of favors, but the curing of bodily ills tended to be their specialty, even their defining ability. After all, saints—both canonized and uncanonized—were seen as the supreme imitators of Christ, and Jesus had manifested his divinity by raising the dead and curing the sick.

Enfeebled and sickly during her lifetime, Tekakwitha had become the restorer of health by Joseph Kellogg's day. The paradox is characteristic of the culture of sainthood: just as the saint represents both death and the denial of death, she also embodies pain and suffering and, at the same time, counteracts the pain and suffering of others. The sickly saint triumphs over illness. In that spirit, people suffering burns prayed for relief to Saint Lawrence, the early Christian martyr who was roasted on a grill; Saint Apolline, a martyr whose teeth were torn out by his torturers, was thought to help with toothache; and those who wanted protection from bubonic plague turned to Saint Sebastian, his skin punctured by arrows so that he looked like a plague sufferer.[6]

But how had this obscure Mohawk woman come to be elevated to the ranks of the wonder-working unofficial saints? A saint, whether canonized or not, was someone who lived on after death as the hero of a particular kind of story: she was at the center of a narrative that recounted her life and death according to the ancient conventions of the hagiographic genre. Furthermore, it was important that her biography be committed to writing. A saint needed a "legend," which implies, in the original sense of the term, "that which is read," and often even the material paper and ink with which it was recorded seemed to be possessed of sacred qualities.[7] The postmodernist literary scholar Edith Wyschogrod insists that "narrativity" and "textuality" are essential attributes of saintliness, to which she adds "corporeality" as a third defining quality. That is to say that the saint's former existence as a living body and the continuing presence of material remains are important to her role as a saint. Whereas a philosopher or military hero might live on as a story and an ideal, the cult of saints requires "relics."[8] To Wyschogrod's saintly qualities of narrativity, textuality, and corporeality, I would add a fourth basic feature: the saint must be a miracle worker; if not endowed with superhuman powers during her lifetime, she should be able to bring about wonders after her death. Memorialized like a saint, prayed to like a saint, the uncanonized spiritual hero was an integral part of the Catholic culture of saintliness.

A saint has to be created after the fact out of the raw material of an admirable life. Only after she dies can the saint's body become a relic and her now-concluded life course the basis of a complete story. From that point on, her fate is in the hands of others, of the living survivors who, convinced of her holiness, will recount her deeds, record the narrative in writing, preserve and venerate her remains, and pray to her for help. "Saints are saints for other people," writes the sociologist Pierre Delooz, "but they are also made saints by other people."[9] Of course, these others are impelled by the belief that they are registering a choice made in heaven and announced in cryptic signs, but even those who see miracles as a tangible reality have to agree that they cannot occur without some prior orchestration; prayers can only be answered if hopeful believers have first been persuaded to ask for help.

✦

In the weeks and months that followed Catherine's death in April 1680, Claude Chauchetière was in a turmoil of grief, ecstasy, and doubt. Praying at her grave, talking with her Mohawk sisters in religion, urging his colleague to bury her in the chapel, experiencing visions of Catherine in heaven, he felt certain that she had been selected by God as one of his emissaries to humanity. And then Cholenec or someone else would throw cold water on his enthusiasm, and he would feel the courage he needed to proclaim the holiness of this *sauvagesse* ebbing away. To conquer his own uncertainty and to convince others, he required divine ratification in the form of miraculous cures. The opportunity to put matters to the test came in January 1681, when Father Chauchetière was summoned to the bedside of a La Prairie settler on the point of death.

Claude Caron, a forty-year-old *habitant* in the parish adjoining Kahnawake, was struggling for breath; for some time he had been troubled by "a great oppression of the chest"—presumably pneumonia or emphysema—but now he was laid low as never before. A surgeon came from Montreal and, after examining the patient, advised his family to fetch a priest to administer the last rites, for no medicine could save him. Claude Chauchetière was the nearest clergyman, and ministering to the flock at La Prairie was one of his duties; most likely he was well aware of Caron's condition when the messenger came for him. Before setting off, he stopped to pray at Tekakwitha's grave, "asking our Lord . . . to show him by healing the sick man if what was said about Catherine was true and if his own feelings came from a good spirit." Proceeding on to La Prairie, he urged the patient to have recourse to the dead Mohawk woman. A desperate Claude Caron readily agreed. Not long after the priest left, they got Caron up to adjust his bed, and he collapsed to the floor. He was lifted back onto the bed and fell into a deep sleep that lasted half an hour, whereupon, feeling that a great stone had been lifted from his chest, he woke up feeling better. He could talk and eat; before long, he had fully recovered his strength.[10]

Chauchetière's doubts were evaporating in view of what seemed to be divine confirmation of his devotion. Meanwhile, word of the "miracle" spread through La Prairie, and volunteers soon came forward offering to try out Catherine's healing powers on their aches and pains and chronic conditions. Claude gave one elderly woman of sixty a little bag of earth from Catherine's grave to wear around her neck when she fell gravely ill with a "grande maladie de rhume" (pneumonia?). She recovered and felt fine as long as she continued to carry the bag close to her body. Then her husband came down with intense back pain caused by rheumatism, and she kindly removed the healing package and placed it around his neck. Result: the husband got better, and the wife suffered a sudden relapse! The two passed the earth back and forth until they were able to procure an additional supply, whereupon both settled into a long and comfortable old age.

From La Prairie, the healing cult soon spread across the river to Lachine, a French-Canadian settlement on the island of Montreal, eight miles west of the city, and just opposite Kahnawake. Word of the Mohawk girl's healing powers was carried by an *habitant* named René Cuillerier, who had heard of her during a visit to La Prairie. Cuillerier had occasion to call on her assistance some months later when his wife was in labor with their child; the delivery was going badly, and so both spouses addressed prayers to Catherine, promising to go to her grave and personally give thanks if she helped bring forth the baby. The delivery was successful in the end, and so the grateful parents duly crossed the St. Lawrence and expressed their gratitude on the site where the virgin lay buried. This seems to have been the first of many cases of women seeking Tekakwitha's help for obstetric and gynecologic problems. It is also the first recorded instance of the practice, common in the saintly healing cults of Europe, of a conditional vow promising a future pilgrimage as "payment" for a specified favor.[11]

Within two years of her death, a regional cult had grown up around "the Good Catherine," as she was coming to be known. It encompassed the rural parishes nearest Kahnawake, particularly La Prairie and Lachine, and it attracted the prayers of what Father Cholenec referred to as "the poor," meaning the ordinary *habitants* who constituted almost the entire population of these communities. By 1682, he continued, "so many miraculous cures had made the name of Catherine so famous people began that summer to ask for masses and novenas to be said in her honor. Cures of this sort became so frequent that we ceased recording them. Not a month, and hardly a week, passed without a significant case; they occurred in all the French settlements."[12]

In the mid-1690s a register was compiled at Lachine of "miraculous cures" wrought on behalf of parishioners by the Good Catherine. It provides names, dates, and surrounding circumstances for twenty-eight such interventions, not a complete record by any means, but still a wonderfully rich source of information, not only on the cult of Tekakwitha but also on the general medical culture of this seventeenth-century settler society.[13] Of course the sample is blatantly "biased" in favor of incidents where saintly intervention "worked" and the surgeon's ministrations failed—selective recording being the very essence of proving miracles—but it still displays something of the range of remedies that people in difficulty tried. We owe this exceptional document to the efforts of the local priest, a Sulpician who had begun as a skeptic but, induced by his parishioners to try praying to Catherine for relief from a stubborn ear infection, was cured and remained a fervent believer from that day forward. This Sulpician later moved to Montreal and acquired a reputation for converting heretics captured in raids on New

England. He was, of course, none other than Pierre Rémy, the instrument of Joseph Kellogg's conversion.

For the settlers of Lachine, this document suggests, Catherine Tekakwitha was mainly a healing saint and, with the exceptions of Father Rémy and one or two others, her devotees were all women. One man felt a special affinity for the Mohawk woman because, like her, he suffered impaired vision, in his case as a result of an eye inflammation. He rubbed his eyes with water impregnated with ashes from the saint's clothes and performed a novena of Hail Marys, and at the end of nine days he was cured. By and large, however, the settlers of Lachine identified with Catherine as a woman, and they invoked her help on their own behalf, as well as for their children.

Frequently, they came to her with specifically female problems: six cases of complications during pregnancy or childbirth (by far the largest single category of miracles), two problems with breast-feeding, and two instances of vaginal bleeding. Here is one example:

> In the year 1694 on the 25th of October, Margueritte Picart, a woman aged 33 years, then seven months pregnant, was injured in the belly when the door of her stable fell on her. She felt compelled to send for Anne Matteau, one of the midwives of this parish, as she feared a premature birth. On examining her, she determined that the child had been displaced, descending into the lower part of the womb. In view of the manifest danger of losing her child or of giving birth before coming to term, she advised her to dedicate herself to Catherine Tegakwita. This she did, promising to have a mass said, and to make a novena of nine Hail Marys for nine days, every day taking some water into which earth from her grave and ashes from her clothes had been dipped. Two days later her baby resumed its place and after two months she came to term and gave birth. This miracle was attested to me by both the mother and the midwife.[14]

Marie-Magdeleine Fortin had a dreadful labor with her third child in March 1695. Married at the age of fourteen, she was only twenty at the time of this ordeal. The baby simply would not be delivered, and as time passed, the increasingly alarmed midwife sent for distant colleagues to come and help. None of their treatments worked, however. Word went through the settlement that the young mother would soon die, and women neighbors gathered round in shared anxiety. One of the latter brought along the inevitable bag of earth and ashes; the bag was dipped in water, which was then given to Marie-Magdeleine to drink. At the urging of the others, she promised to go and pray at Catherine's tomb when she was able and to have a mass said in her honor at the mission chapel. Before long, the baby girl made her way into the world without further difficulty, and the mother recovered and fulfilled her vow.

Striking in both these cases is the all-female cast of characters. Midwives and neighbors helped on the ground, while Catherine, looking down from celestial heights, was asked to do her part in assisting the women in distress. Men were involved in many other cases, most notably Father Rémy himself, apparently the source of the wonder-working bundles of earth from the grave and ashes from the clothes of Tekakwitha, but also surgeons and husbands as well. But women do seem to have gravitated to a local saint who was also a woman, especially when they were troubled by problems connected with reproduction. Just as during her lifetime, Catherine and her companions had tried to bypass the Jesuits in search of the female version of heroic Christianity, now the ordinary Catholic women of Lachine were drawn to a saintly figure of their own sex. Of course the link between supplicants and saint was not a matter of pure and simple correspondence—the female spirit to whom these pregnant wives and nursing mothers addressed their prayers was, after all, famous as a virgin—but then the logic by which early modern Catholics chose their intercessors could work through oppositions as well as resemblances. Moreover, the white settlers of Lachine regarded Catherine Tekakwitha as a "sauvagesse," and though some of them could identify with her as a woman, she still represented cultural and racial difference.

Better than other Euro-Canadians of the time, the French of La Prairie and Lachine were well acquainted with real, living Indians.[15] Situated at the western extremity of the ribbon of French settlement in the St. Lawrence valley, they were close to Kahnawake and other native convert communities. And Indians from the distant west—Ottawas from Lake Huron, Menominees from Green Bay, Illinois people from the Mississippi, to name only a few of the dozens of nations that regularly sent representatives to trade and to negotiate alliances with the French—would have passed by their riverfront houses as their canoes made their way to Montreal. Many would, in fact, have landed at Lachine rather than risk plunging through the rapids; the village was emerging as the terminus of the western fur trade, a spot for natives and French-Canadian fur traders to meet and mingle. While Indian visitors were mostly a source of prosperity for Lachine, there were also dangers inherent in its exposed "frontier" location. When the Five Nations and the French went to war, Lachine absorbed the worst blow of the conflict; on August 5, 1689, an Iroquois force descended on the parish, killing twenty-four, capturing seventy to ninety prisoners, and leaving smoldering ruins in their wake. A smaller number of La Prairie settlers was killed and abducted around this time.[16]

As neighbors, as visitors, and occasionally as enemies, native peoples were familiar to the settlers of Lachine and La Prairie, and yet they remained familiar strangers, a "them" readily distinguishable from "us" by their appearance, their language, and their way of life. Historians are right to emphasize the *métissage* and cultural mixing that occurred in French North America when young white men traveled into the interior, assimilated to native ways, and formed liaisons with native women, but multiculturalism in the St. Lawrence valley took the form more of an archipelago of French, Iroquois, Abenaki, and Huron settlements, all of them comparatively self-contained. In contrast with the *mestizaje* that developed in colonial Latin America, where subjugated Indians tended to be integrated into Spanish society as an inferior servant class, Canadian Indians remained independent and aloof, largely unavailable for sexual exploitation or domestic labor. Métis populations tended to appear only in the west, where it was the Europeans rather than the natives who had to adapt to the ways of the Other.

Though Christian Iroquois were near neighbors and Indians from the west frequent visitors, the Lachine settlers seemed to see them as a people apart, not necessarily despised in the way that nineteenth-century racists despised natives, but clearly and visibly different in their culture. Tekakwitha's people were at once familiar and exotic. And how did these natives view the French Canadians? In some fundamental respects, their attitude mirrored that of the others—the French were known but nonetheless strange—and that very strangeness suggested mysterious medical powers. On both sides, there was a tendency to invest the Other with valuable healing qualities by virtue of its exotic origin. Natives therefore sought out the medicines and arcane religious rituals of the French, while many French turned to Indians when they needed medical assistance. In the Montreal area, settlers frequently visited the old women of Kahnawake for medical treatment, putting their confidence in the healers' skill and knowledge, but also, perhaps, in the mysterious powers attributed to natives as natives.[17] In a similar vein, Rémy reports that the mother of a little Lachine boy, so crippled he was unable to stand, took him across to Kahnawake. After dedicating him to Tekakwitha's care on her grave site, she hired a local "Indian woman" to say a novena for him; at the end of the nine-day cycle of prayers, her son was up and walking again.[18]

Cure by Indian and cure by saint were not necessarily signs of alienation from what might anachronistically be termed "conventional" or "mainstream" medicine. The Rémy accounts suggest that settler folk had recourse to Catherine's intercession as part of a broad array of treatments that included professional medical procedures, home remedies, and magico-religious techniques. "Early modern people were medically promiscuous," writes one historian of medicine,[19] and the case of thirteen-year-old Louis Fortier of Lachine seems to bear this out. Louis's parents came to Father Rémy for help in August 1695 when the boy fell gravely ill with what seems to have been some sort of intestinal blockage. Interestingly, the priest's initial reaction was what might today be called the conventionally medical one: "His father, his mother and I, after having given him several remedies which did nothing for him, sent him to the hospital in Montreal. There he was treated for several days by the doctors and surgeons." The hospital treatments were not specified, but they likely included bleeding, "clysters" (enemas that flushed the intestines with various herbal solutions), and a variety of drugs. To have put young Louis through all this, priest and parents must have thought there were reasonable prospects for recovery in the procedures of the "doctors and surgeons," but as it happens, there was no relief on this occasion: "It was all in vain; they and the hospital nuns despaired of curing him."[20]

If one approach fails, try another. "His mother came to tell me of this with tears in her eyes, begging me to say a mass to obtain from God, through the intercession of Catherine Tegakwita, the cure of her son. This I did willingly, after which the medicines worked effectively and he passed a mass of undigested green fruits. . . . Since that time, he has been well." Whatever may have caused Louis Fortier's distress—and it does seem to have been something more serious than a stomachache occasioned by eating green apples—the eclectic range of treatments he received is what seems most striking. Within the space of a few days, Louis came under the care of, successively, his parents, the priest in his capacity as local healer, the nursing sisters of the *hôtel-dieu*, unnamed "doctors and surgeons," and finally God, through the intercession of Tekakwitha, the latter having been invoked through the good offices of Father Rémy, now acting in his sacred capacity. Note, too, that divine intervention in this case operated as a complement to professional medicine—it allowed the medication to work effectively—rather than as an alternative.

The story of Louis Fortier's blockage also serves to highlight the role of Pierre Rémy as a central figure in Lachine health care generally, a function that overlapped with his role as spiritual shepherd and promoter of the cult of Catherine Tekakwitha. Like other rural priests, in France as well as in Canada, Rémy played the part of local healer and medical consultant, ministering to the physical health of his flock as well as its spiritual well-being. Inevitably people came to him in the direst emergencies, for he alone could administer the last rites to the dying or perform masses imploring God's mercy in times of war or epidemic; in his efforts to comfort and assist, there could be no clear boundary between spiritual and medical succor. Moreover, Father Rémy was required by the twin authorities of church and state to act as a part-time medical practitioner for the people of Lachine. His cupboard contained a jar of all-purpose medicinal "paste" or "unguent" prepared in the city by trained apothecaries to treat injuries and illnesses; the bishop of Quebec sent a supply to every parish priest in his diocese, along with his blessing. It was, however, the colonial government that ordered and financed this public health measure, making use of the clergy's rural network and local knowledge to provide rudimentary medical care to the populace.[21]

In the judgment of Lachine's parish priest, the government-approved, professionally concocted salve was not sufficiently potent for the most serious afflictions, and so he decided to give it a special saintly supercharge. Confirmed in his belief that Catherine Tekakwitha could work curative miracles, Rémy crossed the St. Lawrence and applied to the Jesuits at Kahnawake for a supply of dust from Catherine's grave, as well as some "ashes of her clothes," which together formed a powder impregnated with the Mohawk virgin's presence. Some of this material went into little cloth bags to be dipped in hot water like a modern tea bag; the rest was carefully stirred into the medical unguent, ready to be dispensed to parishioners who called at the rectory with their pains and illnesses. "I do this nearly always before sending my sick and infirm either to the hospital or to the surgeons, because by mixing these powders into the medicines and ointments that I give them, having them make a novena of nine *Ave Marias* per day, and myself offering them to God at the Holy Mass during this novena at the hands and through the intercession of this servant of God, I almost always obtain a cure without the help of the hospital or the surgeons."[22] In the presence of treatments of this sort, distinctions separating "medicine," "religion," and "magic" melt away.

The Tekakwitha curing cult never caught on among the Christian Iroquois of Kahnawake. In spite of the Jesuits' promotional efforts and even though the cult centered on one of their own, the people of Kahnawake showed much less interest in saintly curing than did their French-Canadian neighbors. Iroquois Christians honored the memory of Tekakwitha, but they were not accustomed to seeking cures and other "favors" from the dead.

Claude Chauchetière did manage to persuade a few natives to use earth from Catherine's grave or to hold the crucifix she had worn when asking for help with their afflictions. In one early case, a woman asked Tekakwitha, at Chauchetière's urging, to alleviate chronic and debilitating pain in her arms and legs; not only were her prayers answered but she also lost the passionate addiction to gambling that Catherine and the Jesuits had warned her about during her lifetime. "We have noticed," wrote Cholenec, "that she usually heals the soul as well as the body of those who need such a double cure, even if they do not ask for it."[23]

The Jesuit recounted another "double cure" that saved a man from a characteristically Iroquoian problem. He was, in fact, the son of Anastasia and the brother-in-law of Marie-Thérèse and therefore closely connected with Tekakwitha. One day in the spring of 1682, he had an argument with his mother and received a blunt and severe dressing-down. We do not know what the fight was about, but it is clear that Anastasia overstepped the bounds of Mohawk decorum, which strongly discouraged the open expression of hostility. Violent urges welled up in the young man, but since a direct outward reaction against his mother was inconceivable, these impulses were deflected inward. In this society of severe emotional constraint, suicide had a place among the cultural scripts; it was to be feared whenever a susceptible individual was humiliated and provoked. One Kahnawake missionary wrote about the dangers, in this setting, of the kind of personal criticism that priests commonly indulged in at home in Europe: "Everyone knows how sensitive the Indians ordinarily are to affronts and insults, and that often they go so far as to kill themselves because they cannot brook a word that is somewhat biting."[24] Profoundly wounded by his mother's words, the young man rushed from the cabin and ran toward the river, intending to throw himself in, but as he passed by the tomb of Tekakwitha, he came to a sudden stop, feeling that his feet were rooted to the ground. This break in the action gave him a chance to reflect on what he was doing and recognize it as a sin; and so he repented, turning away from his desperate course.[25]

The Jesuit hagiographers recorded only a handful of miracles wrought through Catherine's intercession for the benefit of native Christians. All of them involved people who had known her in her lifetime, and all the afflictions displayed a characteristically Iroquoian blend of the physical and the moral/psychological. Anthropological studies suggest that Iroquois people have tended to regard good health and its absence, illness, in much broader terms than Europeans; moreover, they do not draw a radical distinction between bodily states and states of mind. Thus, in Iroquoian cultures there was really no such thing as a "double cure"; or, to put the matter in Father Cholenec's terms, all therapeutic procedures aimed at a "double cure" that addressed both the body and the soul. And in those cases where her friends secured healing assistance from Tekakwitha, the problem was conceived and the solution secured in ways that generally ignored any neat distinctions dividing the "mental" and the "physical."

Apart from these few cures, however, the Iroquois Christians of Kahnawake, for all that they may have venerated her memory and drawn strength from her example, do not seem to have found Tekakwitha an effective healer of afflicted bodies. Consequently, Father Chauchetière had to record some cases where God worked for their benefit in truly mysterious ways. François Tsonnatouan had gone with his wife to get advice from Catherine before she died (the two of them had resolved to live together "as brother and sister" after hearing her praise chastity), and after her death he carried her picture with him everywhere and wore her "relics" around his neck. But

François's steady devotion to the saint did nothing to cure him of a debilitating condition Chauchetière describes as "a cold humor which made him so ill on occasion that he could not take a step."[26] Whereas Catherine helped many French-Canadian settlers in relieving their medical problems, she took a different approach with François Tsonnatouan: she sustained his faith and strengthened his patience in affliction as he hobbled along on his stick for fourteen years. Similarly, when babies and small children fell ill at Kahnawake and were treated with earth from Tekakwitha's grave, the same substance that had healed so many French adults only seems to have hastened their deaths. According to the Jesuits, the saint had "drawn them up to Heaven. Thus her grave is surrounded by the children who have died since she has been there, as if this first Iroquois virgin, whom we believe to be in her glory, was pleased to have her chaste body surrounded by these little innocents like so many beautiful lilies."[27]

Iroquois and French Catholics enter the miracle chronicles in very different ways, partly because the missionaries measured success differently for the two categories; it is hard to know how many settlers either died or suffered their maladies with no relief after praying to "the good Catherine," given that such cases would never have been recorded; but the Jesuits counted the resignation of native sufferers and the deaths of native babies—or rather their consequent salvation—as religious victories. Undoubtedly, they would have been pleased to record any straightforward cures among the Iroquois Christians that could have been attributed to Tekakwitha's assistance. The fact that so few appear in the record suggests that, notwithstanding Claude Chauchetière's efforts to promote a healing cult, very few cures occurred.

Why this apparent failure in a community increasingly besieged by pilgrims flocking from across the region to thank their local hero for saving lives and relieving suffering? Saintly healing was one European practice that simply did not mesh easily with Iroquoian traditions. At a time when Tekakwitha was being hailed by white settlers as the source of health-giving magic, she was ill equipped to fill that role for native people, and for one basic reason: she was dead.

The dead were of course very important to the pre-Christian Mohawks; their passing was loudly lamented and marked by elaborate ceremonies. Souls were thought to remain near the death site only for a few days; then they hastened to "the Country of Ancestors," never to be heard from again. Their names were never again spoken until they were resuscitated and reassigned, along with the individual's public personality, to someone else. It would have been unthinkable to communicate with or ask favors of a being whose soul inhabited a remote world and whose name and social personality now belonged to another. Understandings of the relationship between the living and the dead no doubt changed with conversion to Christianity as Jesuits struggled to replace the concept of Eskennanne with that of "heaven," a place where dead humans dwelt with God, the angels, and the saints and where attention was sometimes given to earthly affairs. But it was one thing to gain acceptance for these notions at a theoretical level, quite another to insert them into the Iroquois culture of medicine and healing.

The encounter of native and European medical cultures—their affinities, differences, and exchanges—cannot be usefully summarized as "scientific versus primitive" or "technological versus magical" or "effective versus ineffective." French practitioners could handle some problems much better than any Iroquoian healer: they could, for example, treat syphilis with mercury compounds and remove gallstones surgically. The Iroquois, on the other hand, seem to have done a better job of cleaning wounds, staunching bleeding, and treating a wide range of ailments (scurvy, to name just one example) using herbal medicines.[28] Moreover, they avoided intrusive remedies such as bleedings and purges by which European surgeons of the period inflicted untold damage on their patients. Among the Iroquois and the French, the ill were likely to receive a fundamentally similar range of home remedies and professional therapies that combined drugs, physical interventions, magic, and appeals to spiritual forces. Though they differed in almost every particular, there was a significant degree of commensurability—so much so, indeed, that medical knowledge and healing techniques were readily exchanged in a two-way intercultural trade.

The French, with Jesuit missionaries leading the way, were not slow to recognize native medical expertise, and they borrowed freely from the Iroquoian pharmacopoeia. At the same time, Indian people displayed great eagerness for sampling European cure-alls, such as the sugar and raisins sometimes dispensed by the Jesuits, as well as common drugs such as theriac, a concoction devised in ancient times by Galen and prepared in the seventeenth century with "upwards of seventy ingredients, the chief being viper flesh."[29] What the Jesuits would have regarded as "pagan superstition" pervaded Iroquoian pharmacology—for example, herbs had to be gathered at particular phases of the moon and medicines administered by persons in a specified ritual state—but the missionaries could overlook this spiritual taint when it remained unobtrusive; after all, such superstition was not altogether absent from European pharmacy of the time.[30]

Ethnohistorians have identified as one of the hallmarks of Iroquoian medicine, an integrated understanding of illness and health that incorporates psychological and somatic aspects of the whole person.[31] Listlessness, bodily pain, and melancholy feelings could all be symptomatic of an unfulfilled longing for a person, thing, or place; conversely, good health manifested itself as a subjective state of mind as well as in physical vigor. This important insight about Iroquoian concepts of health and illness should not lead us to exaggerate the divergence between native and European thinking on the subject, however. The intimate connection between body and mind, currently being rediscovered by Western scientific medicine,[32] was by no means foreign to European approaches to illness in the seventeenth century. Descartes's radical separation of the mind and the body was slow to penetrate the medical culture and to drive out the millennia-old Hippocratic/ Galenic tradition, with its emphasis on "humors" (black bile, yellow bile, blood, and phlegm), the fluids that, by their varying balances, determined an individual's personality, predominant mood, and bodily health.[33] When a historian of medicine writes of an early eighteenth-century German physician and his patients, "For them the mental and physical permeated each other, and they viewed the body as easy prey to outside influences," she could just as easily have been referring to Iroquoian people of the same period.[34]

There may have been common ground in the fundamental conception of the ill person as an integrated body-soul, but the Iroquois and the French parted company when it came to treating the "spiritual" aspect of illness. To cure their sick, the Iroquois sometimes had recourse to shamanistic procedures, spectacularly ceremonial and transparently religious, and therefore strongly condemned by the Jesuits. Though they could tolerate a spiritual admixture in cures that seemed to work mainly by chemical means, the missionaries were horrified at rituals that seemed to effect a return to health through the operations of supernatural forces that, because they did not proceed from God, were likely diabolical. "One thing which acts as the greatest obstacle to the conversion of these barbarians," wrote a missionary working among the Oneida in the 1660s, "is what is called among them 'jugglery' [i.e., shamanism] or the art of healing the sick by criminal superstitions."[35]

When a patient was ill with a combination of physical symptoms and bad feelings, it was common to call on a shaman, a healing specialist with privileged access to the sacred, and ask him or her to summon spiritual forces and bring about a cure. Often the shaman was supported by a medicine society entourage. There were likely extensive consultations between patient and healer to establish trust and to gain an understanding of the affliction,[36] but outside observers only described the ceremonial denouement. A Dutch surgeon who visited a Mohawk village in the winter of 1634 wrote the earliest description of an Iroquois shamanistic curing ritual:

> 24 Dec. Since it was Sunday I looked in on a person who was sick. He had invited into his house two of their doctors who were supposed to heal him. They were called SUNACHKOES. As soon as they arrived, they began to sing, and kindled a large fire, sealing the house all around so that no draft could enter. Then both of them put a snakeskin around their heads and laid him before a large fire. Taking a bucket of water in which they had put some medicine, they washed a stick in it ½ ell long. They stuck it down their throats so that the end could not be

seen, and vomited on the patient's head and all over his body. Then they performed many farces with shouting and rapid clapping of hands, as is their custom, with much display, first one thing and then the other, so that the sweat rolled off them everywhere.[37]

European observers ridiculed these procedures, though they frequently had to admit that patients derived benefit from them. Ultimately, Jesuits took native shamanism very seriously, especially when it seemed efficacious, for generally they were convinced that real supernatural forces were at work.

Healing ceremonies could take many forms. Sometimes a shaman would prescribe a feast, alternatively, he might order a game of lacrosse involving the entire village in a great sporting contest. Sometimes a gambling match would be called for, with bets on the patterns formed by dicelike stones spilled from a bowl. Modern Iroquois people have explained the curative powers of games of chance in terms of the warm excitement that accompanies the competition and spreads its effects over the sick person. In medicine as in so many other aspects of life, dreams could play a decisive role. Since a patient's dreams, interpreted perhaps through the intermediary of a shaman, could reveal repressed desires thought to lie at the root of her malady, it was common to enlist kinfolk and neighbors to give the patient whatever objects she wanted or even to act out erotic or violent fantasies, anything to purge the secret wish and the associated illness.[38]

Although this brief sketch can hardly capture the richness and variety of Iroquoian medical culture around the time of European contact, it should be abundantly clear that sick people were consistently treated as members of living collectivities. The assistance of spirits connected with the animal world was invoked, but it was the other people of the longhouse and the village, their actions directed by a shaman, who took the initiative in banishing sickness and distress. The ceremonies of healing fit, in a general way, into what Claude Lévi-Strauss calls the "shamanistic complex," an approach to curing which hinges on a public performance implicating the patient, the shaman, and a broader public. It is "founded on a threefold experience: first, that of the shaman himself, who, if his calling is a true one, . . . undergoes specific states of a psychosomatic nature; second, that of the sick person, who may or may not experience an improvement of his condition; and, finally, that of the public, who also participate in the cure, experiencing an enthusiasm and an intellectual and emotional satisfaction which produce collective support."[39] The ritual of curing was a social event, the act of a living community suffering in one of its constituent parts.

The medico-religious culture of early modern France offered nothing that could take the place of Iroquois shamanism. In so many other respects, there was a basis for exchange, substitution, and fusion—surgery, herbal treatments, magical overtones, the recognition of mind-body connectedness—

but Europeans lacked any equivalent of cure through public performance and collective participation.[40] The white settlers of New France had a different way of enacting illness and health. Their sick were not part of society in the same way that Iroquois sick were; rather, they tended to be socially isolated and their affliction to be understood as a personal and individual problem. This is not to say that sick and injured people were literally shunned and isolated—all the cases from Father Rémy's casebook show patients surrounded by supportive family members, if not crowds of midwives, priests, and surgeons—but once the moment of acute emergency had passed, every effort was made to place the sufferer in quiet seclusion. Missionaries felt that Indians were "cruel" to their own sick because of the way they left them in the midst of the hurly-burly of longhouse life.[41]

Compared with the highly public performances of Iroquois shamanism, the healing treatments of the French tended to be carried out in private. The crucial transactions took place between the patient and the curing specialist, whether a priest, a midwife, or a physician, and if others were present their role was incidental. Drugs were ingested, blood was removed, if not in secret, in an essentially singular relation between the sick person and a succession of healers and celestial helpers. This was not "technological medicine" working on the body as though it were a purely physical object, but it was treatment that addressed a singular corporeal/sentient human being. There was a self-contained quality to the sick person; illness dwelt in that one discrete human entity, and the different European-style therapies all involved interventions from the outside that aimed to drive disease from that bounded individual sphere.[42]

From this point of view, there was a basic similarity, or at least compatibility, in all the various treatments offered to the settlers of Lachine when they were ailing. They might be bled by the surgeon, receive medicines prepared by the apothecary, have Father Rémy's ointment with its saintly additive applied to their wounds, or be offered drinks tinged with traces of Catherine's bodily remains while they promised masses and pilgrimages to her tomb. More likely, as we have seen, they would be subjected to several of these treatments in succession. The main thing is that throughout the ordeal they would remain a patient, one of "the sick," and therefore the object of the therapeutic attentions of "the well." Curing by saint therefore "worked" for the settlers, even in a case where the saint was an Indian, because it fit into their basic understanding of the nature of illness and healing.

Iroquois shamanism proceeded from a different set of assumptions about illness and about the boundaries of the self. The curing ritual was essentially a public performance, one in which the shaman acted as the catalyst in a ceremony implicating the larger society as well as its tutelary spirits. The separation between the sick and the well was less clearly defined than it was among Europeans, both in terms of physical location and conceptually.

Rather than seeing the sick person as a self-contained individual, the Iroquois were more inclined to perceive her as an ailing element within the kin group or village society. It followed that the group as a whole should take part in the curing process. If the high spirits and intense emotions of a lacrosse match or a bowl game gambling session were beneficial, then it made sense to think that the sick member of the group would be helped by the exertions of the well members, since she and her health were not unconnected to that of the whole.[43]

While some healing therapies were transferable from French to Iroquois and from Iroquois to French, some aspects of the respective medical cultures were too deeply rooted in a particular conception of the human self in society to be exchanged. Thus the French were receptive to Iroquois herbal therapies but rejected ceremonies in which the non-Christian spiritual element was too visible; Iroquois showed an interest in some French medicines, as well as some prayers and other religious measures to ward off harm, but they found no acceptable Christian substitute for their shamanistic ceremonies. And so, non-Christian shamanism lived on at Kahnawake generations after the formal adoption of a Catholic identity and in spite of the emergence of a demanding form of Christian asceticism in its midst.[44] Appeals to a saintly Mohawk, revered in memory but remote from the world of the living, were largely unavailing, for they were out of harmony with this community's way of understanding and treating illness.

Though the healing cult of Catherine Tekakwitha had limited purchase with the Indian population, it appealed strongly to the poor white *habitants* of the Montreal area. They turned to her in growing numbers, for medical aid, but also for protection in time of war, for help in resisting vice, and for luck with their crops and livestock. By 1684, the pressure of pilgrimages had won over Claude Chauchetière's colleagues to his plan to honor the Mohawk virgin's body with a church resting place, and so her bones were disinterred and placed within the newly rebuilt mission chapel.[45] A proven miracle worker in heaven, Catherine was represented on earth by tangible remains that were treated increasingly as precious relics. Her profile as an uncanonized saint was almost complete, since she now lived on after death as a story ("narrativity"), as a venerated body ("corporeality"), and as a healing force. Now, all that was missing was a written account of her life and wonders ("textuality"), for a saint was not really a saint without a *vita sanctorum*.

Claude Chauchetière was the first to attempt that literary task, and his efforts were eventually seconded by Pierre Cholenec. Claude was, of course, the more eager Jesuit and completed the first full-length sacred biography, but it was one of Pierre's later accounts that finally appeared in print for the world to read. Yet even Chauchetière, quicker than his colleagues to entertain the idea of Catherine's saintliness, hesitated for a time before committing his views to paper; for even longer, he kept his biographical writings private. Initially, he found it safer to give indirect expression to the hagiographic impulse.

Two Chauchetière texts from the 1680s—though handwritten, they seem to have been semipublic documents intended to circulate widely through French Jesuit networks—focus on native Christianity at Kahnawake. A long letter dated October 1682 brought him considerable notoriety for its glowing portrait of Iroquois piety and heroic asceticism. Though it devotes only a single paragraph to Catherine, there is a sense in which her spirit presides over the entire document. Four years later, Chauchetière wrote a historical chronicle of the La Prairie/Kahnawake mission, illustrated with his own pen-and-ink drawings; it, too, is an idealized account of religious perfection, testimony to the author's transformed attitude toward Christian Indians in general as a consequence of his encounter with one Indian in particular. All his artistic and literary productions from the 1680s read like disguised tributes to Catherine Tekakwitha.[46]

As the years passed and as the healing cult he himself had set in motion gathered force, Chauchetière felt emboldened to take the final step and provide Catherine with the textual qualification needed even by an uncanonized saint. With all his notes before him, together with the fragments of drafts he had begun and then abandoned over the years since her death, Claude sat down sometime in the mid-1680s to compose a proper sacred biography. Having been raised on a diet of saints' lives, he knew just how such a work had to be structured, with its progression through the stages of life, through death, and on to a postmortem glorification. The events of an individual existence had to be arranged in such a way as to highlight the subject's virtues, the signs of divine selection, and the resemblances with the lives of established saints.[47] The basic conventions of the hagiographic genre were familiar enough to anyone in Chauchetière's milieu, particularly to a well-trained Jesuit, but applying them to an Iroquois subject raised daunting literary challenges. There were lives of saints, and there were profiles of pious "savages," but how could the two be reconciled? "The Life of the B[lessed] Catherine Tegakouita, presently called the Holy Indian Woman," which Claude apparently drafted in 1685, bears the marks on almost every one of the 127 manuscript pages of the author's struggles not only to convince European readers but also to overcome his own lingering sense that the terms "holy" and "Indian" belonged to separate, incommensurable universes.[48]

"Participation in the telling of a saint's life," it is said, "was itself an act of faith, an act of witness,"[49] and from the first sentence of the preface, it is clear that this is a work of defiant personal testimony. I feel obliged, Claude states, "to break the silence I have kept for five years concerning the things which occurred at the death and after the burial of the woman whose life I am writing." This silence he attributes to "certain difficulties" on the part of the Jesuit superior of New France and to his own sense that the "marvels" he wished to relate would never be believed when so many French "doubt that there is any faith among the Indians." Now, however, he feels driven by "a powerful inspiration" to bring forth from the shadows "a truth which deserves to be announced across the land, a truth which God himself first made known by the usual signs which he uses to reveal to the living the merits and glories of the dead, which is to say, cures of the sick, revelations, visions, and public approbation."[50]

In addition to highlighting these "usual signs," Chauchetière as biographer molds the raw data of Catherine's life story so as to conform to hagiographic stock plots. Thus the "persecution" she suffered as a convert in her native village is somewhat exaggerated and extracted from its context in Mohawk politics, the better to resemble the familiar contours of martyr narratives set in pre-Constantine Roman times. Thus also, her ascetic practices, as well as her motives for punishing the flesh, are described in terms reminiscent of the lives of the mystic women saints of the late Middle Ages, Catherine of Siena in particular, with no hint that Iroquoian traditions were in any way involved. It was an established tradition in hagiography to place the accent on that which is exemplary rather than that which is peculiar in the saint's life, and so Chauchetière's tendency to assimilate Tekakwitha's story with those of the female saints of Europe is normal enough.[51] And yet there also seems to be something strategic in the way he separated Catherine from her native culture.

Chauchetière was perfectly aware that Catherine's religious development took place in a collective milieu, mainly Iroquois and predominantly female; in other texts composed about this time, he wrote extensively and glowingly of the women's devotional movement that flourished at Kahnawake and that nourished Tekakwitha's ascetic Christianity. In the hagiography, however, she appears as a solitary, alien presence, not only in the "pagan" village of Gandaouagué but even in the godly environment of Sault St. Louis. Aside from the passages on Anastasia and Marie-Thérèse, he reveals very little about her relationship to the larger mystic-ascetic movement. Partly, this reticence can be explained by the demands of the hagiographic genre (or of any biographical project), which require an individual framing of events, but there is also a sense in which the author is trying to imply that his Christian heroine was only superficially and accidentally Indian. Chauchetière himself had come to accept the compatibility of saintliness and a "savage" way of life, but he remained acutely aware that his readers would likely consider these to be contradictory attributes, and so, it seems, he tailored his text to his imagined audience and presented a Catherine whose inner essence belied her outward native identity.

Notwithstanding the compromised form in which he recounted her life, Chauchetière's *Life* of Tekakwitha remains, along with Pierre Cholenec's later texts on the same subject, a unique colonial document: the sacred biography of a New World Catholic who was neither a European missionary celebrated for spiritual conquests nor an assimilated member of the colonized races remembered as an exemplary convert. It was a full-scale *vita sanctorum* dedicated to a woman who remained to the end Mohawk in her appearance, her language, and her way of life.

As of the late 1680s, Tekakwitha possessed the attributes of an uncanonized saint: her bones resided in a shrine of sorts, her life story had been recounted and committed to paper (though never published), and she was the focus of a local healing cult. In the following decade, her reputation took a further leap forward; after fifteen years of curing the ills of the *habitants* of one small region of Canada, she finally came to the attention of the colony's urban elite. Claude Chauchetière, recently transferred to the Jesuit college at Montreal, certainly had a hand in this, using his position as confessor to some of the town's prominent citizens to promote a new round of miracle cures. His autobiography mentions a spectacular case in February 1695 when a sick person was snatched back from the jaws of death through a miraculous intercession.

The circumstances recall those of the Claude Caron cure fourteen years earlier. Chauchetière was mired once again in doubt, wondering whether his feelings about the Mohawk woman, as well as all the other signs of holiness, might be an elaborate trick of the Devil. For five nights running, he had premonitions of a decisive event; and then a call came to administer the last rites to a dying parishioner. Convinced that the moment of truth had arrived, he called upon God to cure the moribund patient in order "to bear witness to the virtue and to the saintliness of Catherine," then set off up the rue Notre-Dame. When he reached the bedside, he was told that all hope had been abandoned, and so he performed the last rites. Then, suddenly, and to the wonderment of all present, the patient recovered. Claude's uncertainties evaporated once more, but more to the point, word of the amazing revitalization spread far and wide. This colonial Lazarus was no mere *habitant*, it appears, but a member of one of Montreal's prominent families, judging by the attention that the case received; according to Chauchetière, "this great miracle . . . created a sensation across Canada."[52]

Soon the merchants, officers, and churchmen who formed the cream of Montreal's little society were being driven across the ice to Sault St. Louis, where they rubbed shoulders with the rough settlers who had long been accustomed to pray at Catherine's tomb. By now, the mission church was a genuine place of pilgrimage, with devotees coming either to submit requests for help or in fulfillment of a vow to thank the Good Catherine for favors received. From town and country they came, among them Daniel Greysolon, Sieur Duluth, a fur trader and military officer well known for his western expeditions. He left a signed attestation thanking Catherine Tekakwitha for ending his attacks of gout.[53] In the spring of 1695 the Jesuits at Kahnawake received a letter from the intendant's palace at Quebec: Madame de Champigny, wife of the highest civilian official in New France, requested help on her husband's behalf for a "gros rhume" (bronchitis?) that had been bothering him for two years. A group of pious Iroquois women accordingly set to work reciting a novena in honor of Tekakwitha; by the time they had finished, the intendant was better. Madame de Champigny later made the five-day journey upriver to Sault St. Louis to give thanks to the Mohawk virgin, returning annually for repeat pilgrimages.[54]

This successful cure at the pinnacle of colonial society unleashed a flood of pilgrimages from within the polite society of the capital. Joining the rush to Kahnawake was Joseph de la Colombière, a canon of the cathedral chapter, incapacitated for some time by fever and diarrhea (dysentery?). Almost from the moment this cleric vowed to thank Catherine personally at her tomb if she cured him, he began to feel better. He therefore set off on a riverboat without delay, and before he had covered one-third of the distance to Montreal, his symptoms had completely disappeared. Needless to say, such high-profile cures spread Tekakwitha's fame abroad; the Jesuit missionaries were thrilled to hear rumors suggesting that, thanks to Madame de Champigny's contacts, members of Louis XIV's court were addressing their prayers to the Mohawk saint.[55]

About the time Catherine's fame as a worker of medical wonders was peaking, she was also coming to be known for miracles of a different sort. Since 1684, the Iroquois of the original Five Nations had been intermittently at war with the French and their native allies, with the Montreal region forming a principal battleground. It was a complicated military-diplomatic struggle with devastating raids such as the 1689 Iroquois assault on Lachine alternating with diplomatic offensives aimed at undermining opposing alliances and establishing partial truces. The Catholic Iroquois of Kahnawake had long dreaded open hostilities between their non-Christian kinfolk in the old Iroquois country and the French with whom they had thrown in their lot; in the event, they felt intense pressure from both sides. Some Kahnawake warriors fought alongside the French; others defected to the Five Nations. Blood was spilled on both sides, including that of a few individuals kidnapped in the vicinity of the Christian village and taken away to be tortured and killed.[56] Yet, on the whole, punches were pulled on both sides; guns aimed high, and threatening war parties turned away at the last moment.

> We have seen these proud Iroquois coming 1500 strong to lay waste the entire settlement of Lachine; they passed by our fields, close enough that they had it in their power to devastate them, but we lost not a single ear of corn. In the seven or eight years that this war has lasted, hardly a year has gone by without them preparing an invasion to destroy the Sault . . . ; every year they set off announcing that this is the Sault's last year. Yet all these plans turn to vapor and the mission survives.[57]

For all their ferocious gestures, the Five Nations Mohawks evidently wanted to intimidate their brothers into returning to the fold or at least into remaining neutral; they never intended to destroy them. In Jesuit eyes, however, the survival of their exposed mission was owing to Catherine's protective presence. About the time Pierre Cholenec penned these words (1696), the tide of war turned against the Five Nations, and as the whole colony breathed more easily, there was some tendency to credit the saintly virgin's influence with saving New France as a whole from its enemies. When the bishop of Quebec came to pray at her tomb, he praised Catherine as "the Geneviève of Canada," linking her memory with that of the girl whose penances were supposed to have saved Paris when Attila the Hun was sweeping across Gaul in A.D. 451.[58]

Somehow, Chauchetière's manuscript biography made its way to France, where it languished, unpublished, for almost two hundred years. A copy was eventually printed in the United States in 1887,[59] but the work seems to have had little impact during the Jesuit's lifetime or after his death. And yet, the act of composing the life of the blessed Catherine Tegakouita was a gesture of the utmost personal importance to Claude, for it capped his long effort to recognize and fully accept the astonishing fact of Tekakwitha's holiness.

Of all the cures the missionary credited to the Mohawk saint, none was more striking than the healing of his own troubled soul. His whole life, as he saw it, had been punctuated by recurrent religious crises, the blackest of them all beginning not long after his arrival at Sault St. Louis. Earlier, I attributed this spiritual malaise to the collision between noble savage fantasies nourished by the French mystical movement of the time and the concrete realities of native life in an Iroquois mission. Witnessing Catherine's serene and beautiful death had saved him, he later claimed, and set him on the road to recovery. The cure was prolonged, proceeding through stages that culminated in miracles and hagiography, but it was all set in motion at that moment of recognition when the strangeness of the Other was acknowledged, accepted, and prized.

Chauchetière's "illness of the soul" might be seen as symptomatic of the divisions and contradictions inherent in the missionary enterprise. From that point of view, I would suggest that this one, rather sensitive missionary experienced as personal suffering a conflict that was not his alone: the clash of Christianity's aspirations to universalism and its tendency to treat "pagans" as an inferior form of humanity. The idealization of "savagery" as the antithesis of "civilization" without any conceptual space for a genuine multiplicity of cultural norms was another, related, source of inner tension. Then, at a concrete experiential level, there was the anomalous situation of the missionary: in but not of the native community; offering friendship and respect but striving to assimilate; proclaiming love but rejoicing in death and adversity. Claude attributed his cure to divine Providence acting through the agency of the saintly Mohawk, which is one way of putting it. In the Jesuit's mind, however, "Catherine" was both a flesh-and-blood individual and the personification of Indians generally, and so his recovery stemmed from a transformation in his view of her and of her native culture. Conflicted at first by his preconceived notions about "savagery," close and prolonged contact with the Iroquois of Kahnawake eventually opened him to a broader, more complex understanding of human difference. His epiphany came in April 1680 as he sat watching a young woman die; then two years spent struggling to reconcile European abstractions with North American cultural realities crystallized in a sudden shift of perspective.

Claude Chauchetière's afflicted soul was beginning to heal.

8

Virgins
and
Cannibals

ABOUT THE TIME CHAUCHETIÈRE WROTE HIS BIOGRAPHY OF CATHERINE TEKAKWITHA, Pierre Cholenec was at work on his own hagiographic project. This was in 1696, when excitement about miraculous cures was running high and pilgrims were flocking to Sault St. Louis. "Wherever we went, we missionaries from the Sault encountered nothing but talk of Catherine Tegakouita, of the marvels that she performs, of the pilgrimages that will be made to her tomb, of the masses and novenas said in her honor. And always people ask insistently to see her Life." It is not even certain that the faithful wanted to read her life story, but they do seem to have felt that their visit to the makeshift shrine was incomplete unless they had come into contact with both the saint's relics and her text. "In the end," Cholenec modestly observed, "I felt obliged to satisfy the public on that head to the best of my limited ability."[1]

It was as if there were no Claude Chauchetière, just across the river at Montreal and already hard at work on his expanded life narrative designed to tell the world about the Mohawk saint. The manuscript may even have been finished by the time Cholenec took up his pen. Why, then, this duplicate effort? It is hard to escape the conclusion that Pierre distrusted his impassioned colleague; indeed, it appears that, right up through the Canadian Jesuit hierarchy, there was a distinct lack of confidence in Claude Chauchetière's judgment. The mystic's intuitive sense that God had specially marked this Indian girl seemed at last to have been vindicated by the popular cult and the accompanying miracles, and though the Jesuits

171

finally bowed before this evidence of divine election, they were far from hailing Claude as a prophet. Not that he was muzzled or disgraced in any overt way, but he was quietly moved into the Montreal college and found himself passed over when it came to public pronouncements about the life and wonders of the Good Catherine. Thus Cholenec was encouraged to compose a book-length manuscript biography that paralleled Claude's hagiography; any plans to publish her life story were postponed until after Chauchetière died.

This is perhaps an overly conspiratorial interpretation of events. Although Claude Chauchetière had for fifteen years provided the impulse that led to recognition of Catherine as an uncanonized saint, Cholenec was eminently qualified to act as her hagiographer. He had been her confessor, and during her years at Kahnawake, he knew her much better than Claude ever did; in his detached and tentative fashion, he seems to have recognized her extraordinary qualities. Moreover, he was a more disciplined writer than his colleague; his texts on Tekakwitha are more carefully organized, with few of the opinionated asides and long digressions that characterize Chauchetière's Life. It is easy to understand why the Society of Jesus would have chosen Pierre as their spokesman on the Mohawk saint. He seems to have been a solid and reliable Jesuit with a much more confidence-inspiring profile than Claude's.

It is difficult to get to know Pierre Cholenec, for he left no autobiographical texts or personal letters, and his writings on Catherine contain few of the personal observations that enliven Chauchetière's Life. We know a little about his background. Pierre was a Breton from the old river port of Landerneau, not far from the farthest tip of France's northwestern peninsula. His father, "noble homme Jan Le Cholenec, Sieur d'Egourion," was probably not a noble, in spite of his impressive titles; he does seem to have been a prominent townsman, however, since he served a term on the city council.[2] Brittany had never been strongly affected by Protestantism, and so Catholicism here was not marked with quite the same crusading Counter-Reformation zeal that it possessed in Chauchetière's Poitou. Here the church worried less about combating heresy than about instilling a basic sense of Christianity in the "primitive" Breton peasantry, judged every bit as benighted, from a religious and cultural point of view, as the Indians of New France. Like Canada, Brittany was prime missionary territory, and Landerneau frequently served as a base from which the most famous preachers, Michel Le Nobletz and Julien Maunoir, launched their forays into the pagan countryside.[3] Intensive missionary campaigns were part of the atmosphere in which Pierre Cholenec grew up, and it seems likely that they played a part in shaping the boy's outlook and plans.

It was in Paris that Cholenec entered the Society of Jesus in 1659, at the age of eighteen. He followed the usual pattern of alternating course work and teaching assignments in different Jesuit colleges across Normandy and the Paris region, ending his studies with four years of theology at Paris's prestigious Collège Clermont. Before departing for New France in 1674, he had accumulated more impressive academic credentials than Chauchetière's (another reason to favor him as official hagiographer), and before his missionary career was three years old, he was admitted to the top rank of Jesuits as a "professed father." In general, he seems to have been a competent, stable, and controlled individual, though it must be said that most Jesuits appear comparatively staid when their writings are placed next to Claude Chauchetière's.[4]

Cholenec's manuscript biography of 1696, as well as a more compressed text that was published in 1717, follow the same basic plot line as Chauchetière's hagiographic narrative. Although the two Jesuits were, at a certain level, rival custodians of the Catherine story, they were also collaborators; Claude had drawn on his colleague's memories as part of his biographical researches, and Pierre seems to have benefited from the other's interviews with Anastasia Tegonhatsiongo and other Iroquois Christians. The parallel biographies are similar in their essential features, but with just enough divergence in emphasis, as well as some minor and perfectly understandable discrepancies about dates and names, to suggest that these were independently authored documents, not just an original text and an adaptation. The two Jesuits constructed Tekakwitha's life story in different, though basically complementary, terms; apart from one flagrant contradiction, they tend to be mutually reinforcing.

It is particularly in the area of sexuality that the two accounts diverge. Both Jesuits insist on Catherine's chastity, as well they might, for sexual purity was a prime religious virtue in the Catholic tradition and one that was considered especially crucial where saintly women were concerned. Even more than the medieval church, "the Counter-Reformation Church placed chastity above all other attributes for female religiosity."[5] Chauchetière's account certainly acknowledges Tekakwitha's "purity," but it also celebrates other virtues, her heroic "austerities," her charity and industry, as well as her strength of character in withstanding slanderous rumors of adultery; Chauchetière the mystic also emphasizes a certain ineffable holy quality in his subject. In Pierre Cholenec's biography, on the other hand, the triumph of the spirit over bodily impurity is a central theme, one that threatens to overwhelm all others.

Catherine was not simply a woman who decided to forgo sexual relations; she was someone who had never since birth been "tainted" by carnality. For Cholenec, her virginity was of paramount importance. More emphatically than Chauchetière, he argued the case for sainthood in the arena of sexuality. He even went so far as to attach the subtitle "The First Iroquois Virgin" to his 1696 manuscript "Life of Catherine Tegakouita," staking a claim to absolute priority that seems rather puzzling at first glance. Behind this seemingly absurd claim—as though no Iroquois had ever before been a virgin!—lies a complex set of religious distinctions and moral gradations in the Catholic understanding of sexual virtue. Cholenec wished to highlight this special virginal quality and even to distinguish her virginity from other, less religiously exalted, virginal states.

In many cultures around the world, sexuality is enmeshed in ideas of pollution and purity.[6] Commonly, erotic activity is considered polluting for certain individuals within a society or in specified circumstances, whereas abstinence can have a spiritually empowering effect. For example, among the Iroquois of the early colonial period, hunters and warriors habitually shunned sex to maintain their strength and enhance their luck, while certain medicinal plants were efficacious only when "put to work by chaste hands." According to Lafitau, "They attribute to virginity and chastity certain particular qualities and virtues and it is certain that, if continence appears to them an essential condition for gaining success, as their superstition suggests to them, they will guard it with scrupulous care and not dare to violate it the least bit in the world for fear that their fasts and everything that they could do besides would be rendered useless by this non-observance."[7]

In European Catholicism, there was a tendency, dating back to Saint Augustine according to one scholar, to link sexuality with original sin and therefore to consider it polluting in a general and pervasive sense.[8] While orthodox churchmen always maintained that sexual enjoyment within marriage was perfectly legitimate, there was much anxiety in the early modern period about the dangers posed by lustful impulses, even when those urges were directed toward a spouse.[9] Sex was never considered "bad" in an absolute sense (except by heretics), but it did carry a vague taint associated with human weakness and mortality. Chastity, by contrast, was a virtue, symbolized by the "pure" color white and required of all priests, nuns, and monks. The Protestant assault on clerical celibacy only served to reinforce Catholic insistence on this as a prime requisite for the dedicated religious life.

It is not surprising that celibacy emerged as a central component of the women's religious circle that Catherine belonged to at Kahnawake. Aiming as they did to appropriate French spiritual power by emulating the ways of the most religiously potent French women, they could not help noticing how much store the European nuns set by their nonmarital, asexual regimen. Even though the Iroquois tended to value abstinence in situational terms—it was a requirement of certain functions and situations rather than an attribute essential to an elevated state of existence—the spiritual seekers of Kahnawake would have been prepared to accept the basic notion of a connection between sexual abstinence and spiritual empowerment. This fundamental correspondence encouraged a cross-cultural reading of religious celibacy in spite of the untranslatability of Christian concepts such as "sin," "virtue," and "concupiscence."

Sex for the Iroquois was not "bad," and for most purposes sexual activity did not leave any lasting contamination: it was simply incompatible with certain states and activities. Virginity was characteristic of a particular life stage, and celibacy was usually a temporary state; lifelong renunciation of sex not only was a potential health hazard but also could be hard to square with an individual's responsibilities to others. The conflict between celibacy and family obligations was precisely what had long recommended that state to Old World Christians seeking religious perfection. Alongside shifting attitudes toward sexual purity and pollution ran an enduring distrust of "worldly ties" that harked back to Saint Paul's advice to the unmarried in 1 Corinthians 7: marry if you must, but stay single if you can, "that ye may attend upon the Lord without distraction." According to some interpretations, Christian celibacy was, in its origins, not so much about condemning "the flesh" as about emancipating individual believers from the constraining bonds of matrimony and kin. To return to the words of Paul's epistle, "He that is unmarried careth for the things that belong to the Lord, how he may please the Lord. But he that is married careth for the things that are of the world, how he may please his wife."[10]

This antifamily dimension of Catholic celibacy was what Iroquois people had difficulty contemplating. Self-control and the subordination of erotic urges for spiritual purposes were a part of their culture no less than that of the Europeans, but an individual existence outside the framework of clan and longhouse, and free from the marital ties that constituted these units, was harder to fathom. Men normally needed to marry in order to gain entry to a nourishing and sheltering longhouse society, and women had need of a husband for a variety of reasons; prominent among the latter was the necessity of securing the skins and meat that only a hunter could supply. Accordingly, many of the most pious Christian Iroquois seem to have found it easier to renounce sex within marriage than to forgo the social and economic dimensions of matrimony; the Jesuits mention several couples living together at the Sault "as brother and sister."[11]

Catherine was one of the few who avoided sexual and domestic entanglements with men to the end of her life. To do so, she had to resist pressures to marry, both before her conversion to Christianity and after her move to Kahnawake. Pierre Cholenec recounts the later challenges to her virginal vocation in great detail, for he considered this "one of the most beautiful passages in the story of her life,"[12] no doubt because it revolved around his favorite theme and because, in his telling, it recalled the heroic struggles of saintly European girls such as Catherine of Siena to resist parental attempts to force them into wedlock. Chauchetière makes no mention of any of this in his biography. His silence does not necessarily mean that the other Jesuit fabricated the whole story, though that is a possibility. But regardless of discrepancies over plot details, it does appear that Catherine shunned marriage and thus gained credit, from Cholenec's standpoint, for choosing the Lord in preference to any flesh-and-blood husband.

More was at stake, however, than strength of character and the renunciation of worldly ties: in proclaiming her a virgin, Cholenec surrounded his heroine with a quasi-magical quality. Anthropologists tell us that, in many cultures where purity anxieties prevail, sex is seen as a threat to the impermeability of the body; conversely, the unpenetrated body of the female virgin is especially venerated.[13] Father Lafitau reports that several native nations of the Americas accorded special status to virginal young women:

> As regards the Iroquois, whom I know a little better, they have certainly had their virgins who are so by status, whom they called Ieouinnon. I cannot possibly say what their religious functions properly were. All that I have been able to get out of the Iroquois is that they never left their cabins, that they were occupied in small tasks purely to keep busy. The people held them in respect and left them in peace.

European traders debauched these "vestal virgins" with brandy, continues Lafitau, and so their special status dissolved at an early stage of colonial contact.[14] Catholic Christendom was another culture in which female virgins enjoyed quasi-sacred status. From the fourth century, writes Peter Brown, "Dedicated women came to be thought of as harboring a deposit of values that were prized by their male spokesmen, as peculiarly precious to the Christian community."[15] Through the Middle Ages and the early modern period, when clergymen were expected to cultivate celibacy as one virtue among many, virginal "brides of Christ" (nuns) seemed to radiate a spiritual potency from the core of their untainted beings.

But what should we make of Father Cholenec's designation of Catherine as "the first Iroquois virgin"? Never mind Lafitau's observations about the "vestal virgins" of ancient times: there were cases in the Jesuit record from Cholenec's own time citing Iroquois, "pagans" as well as converts, who shunned sex and marriage to the end of their days.[16] In claiming this unique priority for his heroine, the Jesuit clearly has in mind factors other than simple abstinence from a physical act. The author explains in his biography:

> But what made our Catherine more blessed than all the rest and placed her in a higher rank, not only than the other Indians of the Sault, but than all the Indians who have embraced the faith throughout New France, was this great and glorious title of virgin. It was to have been the first in this new world who, by a special inspiration of the Holy Ghost, consecrated her virginity to Our Lord.[17]

Though we might think of virginity as an all-or-nothing condition, comparable in that respect to pregnancy, it turns out that for a sophisticated cleric of the seventeenth century, there were degrees and varieties of virginity.

Virginity as a Christian virtue required complete abstention from coitus, but that physical state counted for little if it was merely accidental; to merit the virgin's halo, abstention had to be intentional and religiously motivated. As a graduate in theology, the Jesuit hagiographer would surely have been aware of Thomas Aquinas's writings on the "special crown called the aureole," that "is due virginity." The philosopher insists that the aureole is not "due to the act . . . because in this case those who have the will to marry and nevertheless die before marrying would have the aureole." Instead, "virginity comes under the genus of virtue in so far as perpetual incorruption of mind and body is an object of choice. . . . Consequently the aureole is due to those virgins alone, who had the purpose of observing perpetual virginity, whether or not they have confirmed this purpose by vow—and this I say with reference to the aureole in its proper signification of a reward due to merit." "Integrity of the flesh" remains the sine qua non, but religious significance depends on the state of mind and intention for the future.[18]

To the degree that Cholenec was writing with an audience of theological experts in mind, he clearly wished to establish a claim on Catherine's behalf to that virginal crown: hence his emphasis on her struggles to avoid marriage and maintain her sexual purity. He would have been aware of the skepticism such a proposition was bound to provoke, and he presumably felt that a dramatic event was needed to distinguish Tekakwitha's story from those of other pious Indian converts. Accordingly, he consolidates and reinforces his claim by declaring that, in addition to preserving her purity, she actually took a solemn vow of perpetual virginity.

After triumphing over the pressures to marry, and after pursuing ever more painful penitential practices, Cholenec's Catherine formed a desire to "give herself entirely to the Lord by an irrevocable pledge." Such a momentous gesture was unheard of for Indians, and so, as a prudent spiritual director, he made her wait, pending additional proof of her unflagging constancy. She was overjoyed when the priest finally gave permission. Then, "on the Feast of the Annunciation, 25 March 1679, about eight in the morning," Catherine Tekakwitha took communion and promised Jesus Christ "perpetual virginity," asking him "to be her only spouse." In the same ceremony, she solemnly dedicated her virginity to Mary as well as to her son. Cholenec considered this nunlike vow "her greatest glory before God."[19]

So writes Pierre Cholenec. But what about Tekakwitha's other biographer? How does Chauchetière treat this crucial incident? Under the heading "Her Chastity" appears the following passage:

It is the most beautiful jewel in her crown. . . . Men, God and conscience have given witness to the truth that Catherine never committed a single sin of the flesh. . . . If it had occurred to anyone to have
her take a vow, the vow of chastity would not have been wanting,
though she did not fail to live up to such a vow, which makes me
believe that she received the merit of it. The priest was sorry after her
death not to have let her make it.[20]

The wording is rather awkward, as no doubt were Claude's sentiments on
the subject, but the contradiction is clear enough: Pierre Cholenec himself
had declined to administer the vow of chastity while Catherine was alive,
and, regretting his decision afterward, he revised the record of events.

It is apparent that the Jesuits, Claude and Pierre at least, but perhaps others
as well, had argued among themselves about what to make of Tekakwitha's
virginity and how to present their case to a skeptical audience of European
Catholics. There are hints in Cholenec's manuscript that one missionary at
the Sault (Chauchetière?) had harbored doubts shortly after the death about
whether Catherine had even been a genuine virgin in the minimal, biological,
sense. There had, after all, been rumors of illicit liaisons.[21] But all uncertainty had been laid to rest by the miraculous cures that God had presumably sent to signal her saintliness and thus, by implication, to verify her sexual
purity. Because prayers in her name were efficacious, she must have been a
virgin. This established fact, joined to all the other evidence of holiness in
her life story, indicated that she possessed as much religious merit as any
nun who may have dedicated her chastity to God through the holiest of vows.
This is what Chauchetière means when he avers that she "received the merit"
of a vow she would have taken had she been given the opportunity and whose
terms she did in fact adhere to. And his colleague, following the example of
innumerable hagiographers in adjusting raw historical data to the demands
of religiously meaningful discourse, simply translated this virtual vow into
a literal event.

The story of the fictive vow, repeated in most subsequent retellings of
the Catherine Tekakwitha narrative, seems designed both to bring the larger
narrative into closer conformity with standard hagiographic plots for women
saints and to shore up the claim to virginal status. The emphasis on holy
virginity, so much more insistent in Cholenec's shrewd writings than in
Claude's more naïve biography, has to be understood in light of prevailing
European views of native women's sexuality. One early vulgarizer of the
Tekakwitha story, a military officer who had served many years in Canada,
suggested that Catherine could only have had a confused idea of what virginity was when she first came to the Sault, as "this state was too elevated to
be proposed to Indians, the latter being so carnal by nature."[22] Against the
backdrop of this underlying suspicion—the sense that the sexual propriety

of Indians women was always in question, even when there was no particular evidence of vice—Pierre Cholenec penned his overstated defense of Catherine's virginal purity.

When Europeans and Euro-Americans of the early modern period thought about *inidas, indiennes,* or "Indian women," their views were shaped by a number of assumptions about culture, race, and sexuality. More important than any propositions consciously agreed upon were the basic mental structures—built into language and prior to reflection—by which people organized information about the world. There was a tendency, for example, to consider natives under the heading of "savages," a category that suggested an absence of effective government and personal restraint. The concept of savagery had ancient antecedents leading back to Greek views of the "barbarians,"[23] but centuries of conquest and colonization in the Americas had shaped and modified the sense of basic difference between the "civilized" and the "savage" state. Thus, Europeans of the time generally expected to find poverty, violence, and unconstrained lust among the indigenous peoples they encountered, because these were understood to be essential features that identified them as savages. (Explorers and missionaries kept coming across contrary evidence, but such puzzling anomalies were slow to affect the architecture of the imperial mind.) Certainly there was room for considerable variation in the way the savage/civilized dichotomy was deployed—in the hands of Claude Chauchetière, for one, its values were inverted to the advantage of the natives—but the sense of fundamental difference was a constant. The fact that it tended to accompany, and serve as justification for, the dehumanizing processes of colonization, conquest, and enslavement does not mean that it was simply an ideology, cynically constructed with a practical purpose in mind; rather, it represented a deeper level of mental operations.

The male/female dichotomy was another deep organizing principle that conditioned the way Europeans of the seventeenth century made sense of the world. Like the savage/civilized polarity, it was rich in overtones and adaptable, but as with the discourse on the savage, it also tended to define one element, in this case the female, as a deficient version of the other. Women had many admirable qualities, it was thought, but as a species they were less strong, less courageous, less governed by rational constraint than were men. Closer to nature and more subject to bodily appetites, they were more likely to succumb to sexual urges if they were not properly supervised.

Native women therefore seemed doubly savage in their essential nature, for they stood at the wild end of two basic polarities of European thinking. Moreover, when we remember that the moral evaluation of women in this period was primarily sexual—"vice" and "virtue" had connotations that were specific to one gender or the other—then it becomes clear that to refer to someone as an Indian in the feminine form (indienne, iroquoise) was to situate her in the realm of sexual disorder. Prior to anything specific that might be said was an ontological starting point suggestive of impurity. It was still possible to speak of native women as virgins or as virtuous wives—and of course the French Jesuits often did just that—but the assertion could not help conveying a sense of internal contradiction, since the manifest content of the message was at odds with the overtones of the language in which it was expressed.

The image of the native woman as it developed through centuries of European conquest and colonization in the New World tended to reflect the brutally exploitive race relations that characterized the Spanish and Portuguese empires. In the Ibero-American colonies, "white" men frequently enjoyed power over the bodies of servant women of other races. French men in seventeenth-century Canada rarely confronted indigenous women in such starkly asymmetrical power relations, but many of them did take advantage of differences in native and European customs regulating extramarital sex, reinforcing in the process the notion that Indian women were inherently promiscuous. Experience thus seemed to "prove" what racial ontology suggested: that indigenous women were more readily available to white men than were women of European origin.

Europeans also encountered sexualized images of native women in the discourses and iconography of colonialism. Once again, these tendencies were most apparent where the older empires of the Iberian powers are concerned. The stories of discovery, conquest, and colonization of the New World were rife with sexual metaphors. In what the literary scholar Anne McClintock calls "the erotics of imperial conquest," Europeans were depicted entering, possessing, and ravishing a feminized America.[24] Texts and visual images frequently used women's bodies as "the boundary markers of empire." The New World's women, like its other treasures and allurements, were there to be taken by the men from Europe; consequently, even if an individual indienne led a life of blameless chastity, she would still be ascribed a species identity suggestive of sexual availability.[25]

It was against this background that two New France Jesuits struggled to gain acceptance for the view that a Mohawk woman stood out as a radiant example of holiness, virtue, and—of necessity—virginal purity. Pierre Cholenec seems to have grasped the importance of this last quality better than his colleague, and so he crafted his hagiography in counterpoint: difference within difference, purity in an ambience of savage impurity. In his hagiography, Catherine's virginity, certified in and through the church, was the crucial quality that served to lift her out of the native society that had nourished and raised her. She was unique, even in the pious atmosphere of Iroquois-Catholic Kahnawake, and even among the zealous ascetics whose feats of penitence were at least as amazing as her own, even among women so devoted to religious celibacy that they cut their hair as a sign of chastity. The quality of undefiled purity distinguished her in particularly striking fashion from her bosom companion, Marie-Thérèse Tegaiaguenta, a fervent Catholic who shared many of Tekakwitha's other saintly virtues.

As a widow, Marie-Thérèse suffered from the disability of sexual experience prior to her commitment to celibacy and asceticism. Moreover, both Jesuit hagiographers imply that she had wavered between "sin" and repentance over the years following her baptism (the nature of the sin is not specified, though that term, applied to a woman, suggested sexual misconduct). Married to a non-Christian, she remained strongly affected by "the disorders of her country" even after migrating to Kentake (La Prairie), but eventually she experienced what the writers considered a true conversion about the time she encountered Tekakwitha in the spring of 1678. Their first meeting occurred not long after Catherine returned from a winter hunt, the one on which the saintly Mohawk had spent her time praying at her little oratory and imaginatively projecting her soul back to its proper home in the mission chapel. In introducing this new character to their story, the Jesuit hagiographers flash back to a hunting expedition Marie-Thérèse had participated in two years earlier, in the winter of 1675–76. This juxtaposition of two different hunt subplots, parallel stories featuring young women who were Indians but also Christians and who had to negotiate the tensions between these two aspects of their identity in the "savage" environment of the forest hunting camp, seems designed to highlight Catherine's unique excellence through contrast with another worthy, but not saintly, convert.

Chauchetière includes a brief version of Tegaiaguenta's hunt in his Life of Catherine, but Cholenec develops the subplot much more fully in his two hagiographic texts. It constitutes a long digression from the main story of Tekakwitha's life. This is how it goes:

> In the early autumn [of 1675], she had embarked with her husband and a small child, the son of her sister, to go hunting on the Ottawa River. En route, they fell in with some other Iroquois, forming a party of eleven persons, four men, four women and three children. Unfortunately for them, the snows came very late that year, so that they were unable to hunt. Consequently, after having eaten all their provisions, as well as the meat of a moose her husband killed, they faced starvation. First they ate some bits of rawhide they had brought with them to make shoes [moccasins], then they ate their own shoes [possibly

their moccasins, possibly the sinews of their snowshoes], and finally they were reduced to eating grasses and the bark of trees, like animals.

Starvation in the winter forests was a danger that constantly stalked hunting-gathering peoples of the northern woodlands. With fishing streams frozen hard and roots and berries no longer available, survival hinged on the hunt for mammals, particularly large animals such as moose and caribou, whose carcasses would sustain a band for some time. Proper snow conditions were critical to hunting success, not only because animals left tracks for human predators to follow but also because animals could become bogged down in deep, crusty snow when snowshoed hunters closed in for the kill. If the weather failed to cooperate for extended periods, disaster could ensue, even for the Algonquin bands who knew the land best and whose way of life revolved around finely tuned seasonal migrations in pursuit of shifting food resources.[26] Iroquois existence was usually less tenuous, for Tekakwitha's people could depend on their corn and other field crops for easily stored provisions. However, the fur trade boom and the migration to the St. Lawrence, where agricultural conditions were marginal, had given hunting a more central place in the economy of the northern Iroquois, with the result that women and children, as well as men, were embarking on long expeditions from Kentake/Kahnawake. Marie-Thérèse's party may have been at greater risk than a more experienced Algonquin band would have been under the same conditions; certainly the Iroquois people would have been comparatively ill equipped to face the terrifying prospect of winter starvation.

In every respect, Tegaiaguenta's experience was exceptional, and as the days of relentless hunger succeeded one another, desperation set in.

Meanwhile, the husband of the woman in question [since she was still alive at the time of writing, Cholenec leaves her unnamed] fell ill and two of the party, a Mohawk and a Seneca, went off in search of game, promising to return within ten days. The Mohawk returned on the appointed day, but he came alone, assuring the others that his comrade had died of want, but it was not without reason that they suspected him of having killed him and subsisted on his flesh while he was away. They doubted him all the more because he seemed healthy though he admitted he had taken no animals. Since it was clear that the hunting there was hopeless, they decided to leave that place, urging our Christian to abandon her husband to death, since he could no longer travel, and to save herself and her nephew. But she would never consent and, resisting bravely, she was left behind with her husband and the nephew.

Two days later, the sick man died, greatly regretting he had never been baptized. She buried him and then set off after the others, carrying her nephew on her shoulders. After several days walking, she caught up with the party then making its way down the river in an effort to reach the French settlements. However, they were so weak and exhausted that, after twenty days march, they could go no further.

In the fall, they would have all traveled from Kentake by canoe, a comparatively easy mode of transport, even if they did have to toil against the current of the Ottawa River. But in this midwinter evacuation, there was no choice but to trudge over those same waters, now windswept and rock hard, the adults carrying the smaller children on their backs. Under normal circumstances, a well-fed, properly clothed native party could make excellent time traveling on foot in the winter and using snowshoes wherever the snow was deep, but this bedraggled and famished band, their feet wrapped in whatever covering they were able to improvise, must have been inching along, step by painful step.

> It was then, facing starvation, that their desperation led them to a strange resolution: they would kill one of their number to sustain the others. They cast their eyes on the widow of the Seneca and her two children and they asked [Marie-Thérèse] if it was permissible to kill them, and what the law of the Christians said on that point, for she was the only one of the party who had been baptized. She did not dare reply as she did not know enough about this important question and she was afraid of contributing to a homicide. More to the point, she quite naturally felt that her own life depended on the answer, for she believed that, after they had eaten the woman and her two children, as they did in fact do, she herself would then be killed.
>   As her eyes were opened to the danger to her body, [Marie-Thérèse] also began to realize that the deplorable state of her soul was infinitely more pitiable than that of her body. She felt great horror for the disorders of her past life and the fault she had committed in going on a hunting trip without first going to confession. Asking God's pardon with all her heart, she promised that if He delivered her from this danger and returned her safely to the village, she would not only confess herself immediately, but reform her life and do penance. God wished to use this woman to make Catherine known, and so He answered her prayer and after incredible pains and exertions, five of the twelve [sic] returned to La Prairie toward the middle of the winter. Among them were this woman and her little nephew.[27]

And so Tegaiaguenta survived that ordeal of starvation and anthropophagy. Did she herself taste the flesh of the unfortunate widow or her children? Cholenec does not say one way or the other, but the anecdote about the suspiciously healthy Mohawk hunter and the obvious parallel to Marie-Thérèse's situation at the journey's end constitute a broad enough hint to the reader. In any case, as a character in the life narrative of Catherine Tekakwitha, she is, to say the least, strongly associated with cannibalism, for this long digression on the ill-fated hunting expedition is almost all that we are told about her personal background. Present in all versions of the hagiography, it is one of the most vivid passages in Cholenec's 1696 manuscript and of his later published biography, even though it is quite tangential to the main plot. Evidently it was important to the Jesuit.

"Survival cannibalism" of the sort Tegaiaguenta was involved in can occur in any society, though it may be especially common among hunting peoples living in inhospitable environments.[28] If pressed, Pierre Cholenec might well have admitted that human flesh had been eaten in his own country, and in the comparatively recent past. Indeed, he does present Tegaiaguenta's "crime" as a regrettable response to extreme circumstances rather than as normal or approved Iroquois practice.

And yet, a story recounted to European readers of Indians eating human flesh could only be read as a comment on savagery, so powerful and pervasive were the ideological effects of almost two centuries of European colonization. "Man-eater" is the epithet leveled in a multitude of societies against enemy outsiders—the term "Mohawk," for example, derives from the Algonquian word for "eater of human flesh"—and in medieval Europe, "internal outsiders" such as heretics, Jews, and witches were often accused of ritual murder and the eating of Christians. Ever since 1492, however, cannibalism and American savagery had become indissolubly linked in Europe's colonial imagination. Columbus himself introduced the word "cannibal" into Spanish, and thence into other European tongues, when he adopted the Arawaks' designation of their supposedly ferocious enemies from the Lesser Antilles: Carib/Caribal/Cannibal. What had previously been seen as a sin tended to become, with this new linguistic coinage, the defining feature of an entire sector of humanity. "Cannibals" were not simply people with a strange offensive custom; they became the quintessence of savagery, a species of humanity classified under the insignia of a monstrous crime. There were indeed countercurrents in the European cannibal discourse, critics such as Michel de Montaigne and Jean de Léry, who insisted that Brazilian cannibals possessed redeeming qualities and that European civilization was, on balance, no less cruel in its customs. But even in these relativist accounts, anthopophagy still stamped whole nations with a complete, and a fundamentally alien, identity.[29]

When Europeans of the early modern period read or heard about the Caribs of the West Indies or the Tupinambá of coastal Brazil and when they viewed woodcut images supposedly depicting their cannibal feasts, a varied blend of savage excesses enriched the scene of barbarity. The guiding assumption was that eating humans betokened a complete breakdown of civility and constraint, and so cannibalism and sexual license always seemed to go together.[30] Theodore de Bry's influential prints of sixteenth-century Brazil showed the cannibals as naked and sexualized, with women portrayed as the most forward in indulging their lusts and appetites.[31]

Pierre Cholenec made no such explicit denunciations of Marie-Thérèse, nor did he even apply the "cannibal" label to the winter incidents of 1676. But when the colonialist images and assumptions lurking in the background and conditioning the outlooks of author and reader are borne in mind, this episode in the biography of Tekakwitha seems laden with meaning. A young woman, raised as a savage, finds herself deep in the forest, a "savage" location, engaged in hunting, a "savage" pursuit. She is sexually experienced

An early modern depiction of a cannibal feast, in this case featuring the Tupinamba of coastal Brazil. The artist, Theodore de Bry, never set foot in America and is therefore imagining the scene rather than recording it. The naked, ravenous women, one of them apparently touching her genitals, illustrate the European tendency to sexualize female anthropophagy. Theodor de Bry, *Dritte Buch Americae* (Frankfurt am Main, 1593), vol. 3, plate 24. Reproduction courtesy University of Toronto digital studio.

and, though baptized, still attached to the sinful customs of her people. When circumstances force her to eat human flesh (whether or not she actually indulged in cannibalism, Cholenec leaves at least a suspicion hanging in the air), that act conclusively identifies her as a tainted being, notwithstanding her later piety. All these evil associations operate as so many points of contrast that serve to highlight Catherine's fundamental purity. Entirely free of sexual contamination, the younger woman had grown up among pagan Indians without her inner nature having been affected by Iroquois "savagery." Moreover, when she went off to the forest with a winter hunting party, far from surrendering to evil, she remained immune to the savage influences of that locale and of that bloody endeavor.

Thus the story of Catherine's vow of virginity and the digression on Marie-Thérèse's cannibal adventure have a convergent tendency, both serving to dissociate the holy girl from the polluting effects of sexuality and savagery. Together they have the calculated effect of assuring the European reader that this *indienne* was not what she seemed. On the surface an Indian woman, with all that that phrase stood for at the time, she was still a saint in her essential inner being.

As the seventeenth century drew to a close, Catherine Tekakwitha's fame was spreading through the Jesuits' transatlantic network of correspondence. Versions of Chauchetière's and Cholenec's manuscript hagiographies were read in France and in the French West Indies, while Claude dispatched drawings of the Mohawk saint to acquaintances overseas. (These pictures reportedly brought relief to headache sufferers when pressed against the forehead.)[32] However, the time was not considered right to publish the astonishing news of Indian saintliness.

This was the era of the "Chinese Rites" controversy, when the Society of Jesus was under attack for compromising Catholic orthodoxy by adapting to the local culture in its missionary efforts in China. Enemies within the church had seized the opportunity to accuse the Jesuits of heterodoxy, and the once-mighty order was on the defensive, afraid to make any extravagant claims, especially in the area of overseas missions. The Jesuit *Relations* had long since been suppressed by a papacy alarmed at the dangers inherent in public discussion of Jesuit experiments in cross-cultural religion, but restrictions eased somewhat after the acute phase of the Chinese Rites controversy died down. In the early eighteenth century, French Jesuits ventured to resurrect an annual mission publication, though this time it was global in scope and not restricted, as the *Relations* had been, to New France. The *Lettres édifiantes et curieuses* took the form of reports from Jesuits (mainly French) working in Vietnam, China, California, Africa, the West Indies, and other distant lands. In the Francis Xavier tradition, they were crammed with interesting information about the flora, fauna, landscape, and human customs of exotic lands, as well as with inspiring tales of conversion; in fact, "curious" content rather outweighed "edifying" material, thus ensuring a wide readership among the secular minded. It was in the pages of the Lettres édifiantes et curieuses that a reworked version of Pierre Cholenec's life of Catherine Tekakwitha was published in 1717.[33]

At this point in the eighteenth century, French Jesuits were among those most closely engaged in the intellectual ferment of the time, as churchmen and early Enlightenment philosophers reassessed basic questions about human nature, the truths of religion, and the diversity of cultures.[34] Regardless of the considerations that drove Cholenec and Chauchetière to proclaim the holiness of the saintly Mohawk, the editors of the Lettres édifiantes likely had European philosophical issues of the day in mind when they decided to print this ninety-two-page tale of virginal perfection and wondrous cures. "Pagans" and "savages" had long played a prominent part in Western discussions of fundamental questions about what it means to be human, and in the hands of thinkers such as Rousseau and Diderot, they would continue to be called upon for that purpose down through the century.

Around 1717, Jesuit intellectuals tended to be preoccupied with the struggle against Augustinian tendencies within the church and secular deist tendencies outside it. To summarize, briefly and crudely, the way in which larger debates were played out in discussions of overseas missions, Augustinians were inclined to attribute paganism to sin and to hold out little hope for the genuine conversion of peoples outside the European cultural sphere. Whereas Augustinians would see natives as depraved and largely irredeemable, secular deists regarded them as people without religion, guided by natural reason; this view reinforced skepticism as to the universal applicability and absolute truth of Christian revelation. The Jesuits challenged both these views with a theory of universal theism that found inklings of Christian faith and instances of Christian virtue spread among the cultures of the globe; conversion therefore was only a matter of bringing to the fore a latent Christianity that was already present among pagans and savages. A comparatively favorable view of Indians, of their indigenous culture, and of their potential for Christian sanctity thus formed an integral element of Jesuit debates with opponents both within and beyond the Catholic fold.[35] The story of the Mohawk Virgin would have served the polemical purpose of demonstrating the unlimited spiritual potential even of natives raised in paganism. Since deists denied the possibility of God working outside the laws of nature, it may also have served the secondary purpose of asserting the reality of miracles.

Whatever philosophical agenda may have led to the publication of Cholenec's hagiography, it had now been published and widely disseminated. In place of the many drafts and manuscript biographies that Cholenec and Chauchetière had labored over through the previous decades—divergent, constantly under revision, limited in their circulation—there was now a printed text: permanent, authoritative, mass-produced. For almost two centuries, until Chauchetière's hagiography was retrieved from obscurity and printed in 1887, Cholenec's account defined the Tekakwitha story and served as the source for hundreds of subsequent versions of the narrative.

Seven years after the initial *Lettres édifiantes* article, the story first appeared as a freestanding book; moreover, this was a Spanish translation of Cholenec's biography, and it was published not in Europe but in the New World. *La gracia triunfante en la vida de Catharina Tegakovita, india iroquesa*, appeared in 1724 in Mexico City, capital of the viceroyalty of New Spain, a city far older, richer, and more impressive than any of the little settlements then established in French or British North America.[36] So remote from Mexico were New France and the lands of the Iroquois that hardly anyone there had heard of such places. The translator located them just east of New Mexico and the Apaches.[37] It seems that the international Jesuit network had delivered the French publication to residents of one of the order's colleges in Mexico City just at a moment when issues surrounding native women, religion, and chastity were agitating local spirits.

A convent was about to open, specially endowed for Indian nuns, and the municipal authorities were attempting to block it. *Indias* were unsuited to the religious life, according to expert witnesses testifying before the city council, because they could not be trusted to "mortify their disorderly appetites" and observe the vow of chastity. Proponents of the convent had to counter a colonialist mentality, much more pronounced in New Spain than in New France, that associated indigenous women and sexual promiscuity. Whereas natives enjoyed a high degree of cultural and economic autonomy in the Canadian setting, they were very much a subjugated people in Mexico City. Subjugated but omnipresent, they outnumbered "white" residents in the region and played a vital role in the city's labor market. As domestic servants, Indians—especially Indian women—entered the households of the urban elite, where they faced sexual and economic exploitation. With servants giving birth to mixed-race babies and with Spanish tastes being affected by Nahua aesthetics, cuisine, and child-rearing practices, anxieties about preserving boundaries between the colonizers and the colonized were bound to intensify. Hence the long tradition in New Spain of attempting to legislate racial divisions, with laws prohibiting Indians and other members of inferior races from carrying swords, taking university degrees, or entering the clergy. Honor and prestige were reserved to Spaniards of "pure blood," and that included access to religious orders.

For Indians to be accepted as nuns was particularly objectionable to colonial opinion in Mexico, for convents had a special symbolic role as reservoirs of white female sexuality and reserved procreative power. Often referred to as "virgins" (even though some were widows and therefore honorary virgins), nuns were women with a unique claim to perfect purity on both racial and sexual grounds. In theory, every postulant in New Spain had to produce a certificate of *limpieza de sangre* guaranteeing that her blood was untainted by Jewish, Muslim, or Indian ancestry before she could take her oath of chastity.[38] The fact that Indian women did actually gain entry to nunneries as religious women of uncertain status did not alter the basic image of the convent as an island of purity radiating spiritual power over a colonial society threatened by the menace of hybridity.

In this context, *La gracia triunfante en la vida de Catharina Tegakovita, india iroquesa*, was presented as a political pamphlet in hagiographic form, and it was meant, as the preface states quite explicitly, to prove that Indian women really were capable of lifelong virginity for religious purposes. Some biographical sketches of exemplary piety on the part of Mexican native women were appended, but Cholenec's life of Tekakwitha was the central document in the volume. In a Catholic society, the sacred biography genre carried a weight and an authority that made it an ideal instrument for reconfiguring ontological assumptions about the nature of Indian women. There may have been saintly women in Spanish America whose life stories could have been recounted for this purpose, but no white clergyman had ever thought to research and record a native biography in any detail. Consequently, when the Jesuit defenders of the new convent went looking for material to fuel their polemics, they were forced to turn to the religious literature of New France, where a Catholic empire had been built upon alliance rather than conquest and where the conventions of colonial hagiography had been turned upside down.[39]

Given that it is a biography of a virgin written by a celibate Jesuit priest, sexuality forms a surprisingly prominent theme in Pierre Cholenec's account of the life of Tekakwitha. But, of course, how could the subject be avoided in a hagiographic work, when hagiography is a catalog of Christian virtues and when virtue in a woman was understood to be fundamentally sexual virtue? The special veneration long accorded to female virgins in the European Catholic tradition was another dimension of the mentality of the period that led the hagiographer to bolster his case by dwelling on Catherine's exceptional "purity." The fact that she was a "savage," a woman raised outside the constraining influence of civilization, meant that her sexual virtue was doubly uncertain and therefore doubly in need of verification and emphasis. As Indian and as woman she tended to be associated with nature, a wild, unregulated, and therefore dangerous domain in the eyes of many Europeans of the seventeenth century.

Over the course of the eighteenth century, and under the influence of intellectual and artistic currents conventionally labeled "the Enlightenment" and "Romanticism," the idea of nature acquired new and generally more positive connotations. And even as settler regimes continued to subjugate or marginalize native peoples in the Americas, artists and philosophers were increasingly inclined to idealize Indians as the embodiment of simplicity, transparency, and stoic fortitude.[40] In this altered intellectual atmosphere, the story of the Mohawk saint continued to find an audience. The various poles of opposition that structured the original biography—nature/culture, savage/civilized, female/male, polluted/pure—had shifted significantly in their meaning and valence, but Tekakwitha continued to represent basic difference: she was the exotic figure onto which writer and reader projected fantasies. And in the hands of a series of novelists, these fantasies carried a barely concealed erotic charge.

François-René de Chateaubriand, a major early Romantic writer, inserted Catherine Tekakwitha into his sprawling and never completely finished novel, Les Natchez. Published in 1826, the work had been written in the 1790s when Chateaubriand was a Royalist exile from the French Revolution living in London. Set in the North American forests, Les Natchez was inspired partly by the writer's tour through the young United States, from Baltimore to Niagara Falls, and partly by his readings on France's now shattered colonial empire. His favorite source was the works of the Jesuit traveler and historian Pierre-François-Xavier de Charlevoix. In the mid–eighteenth century, Charlevoix had published massive, multivolume histories of Canada, Louisiana, other distant lands; one long chapter in the History and General Description of New France[41] consisted of a paraphrased version of Cholenec's 1717 sacred biography of Catherine Tekakwitha.

Chateaubriand's central theme was love and sex in the natural world of America, with the encounter of European civilization and savage North America providing the tension to his narrative. Set on the frontiers of French Louisiana and Spanish Florida, the novel contains an extended subplot about the passion of the Natchez chief Chactas for the beautiful Atala, a Catholic convert who had pledged to preserve her virginity. Another part of the narrative takes the form of a colonial love story featuring the solitary French explorer, René, who arrives in the Natchez village years later, when Chactas is an old man. The chief's lovely daughter, Céluta, is assigned to cook for the white stranger, and she instantly falls in love with him. René responds to her naïve and artless devotion, but there can be no happiness for the young couple, since the native enemies of the Natchez have enlisted the aid of a French army to attack and destroy Céluta's doomed people.

On the verge of the looming holocaust, Chateaubriand shifts the scene to heaven, where saintly figures are about to implore divine intervention. A strange amalgam of Greek mythology and Catholic mysticism, all wrapped in a style derived from Milton, this celestial interlude also seems morally confused, since the object of concern slides from an imperiled "America"—apparently represented by the Natchez town about to be immolated—to "la France," the imperial power whose troops are preparing the attack. It is in the midst of this contradictory thrust that Catherine Tekakwitha makes her appearance as, at once, the personification of native North America and the guardian spirit of France. Along with Saintè Genevieve, the shepherd girl who mobilized Paris to defend itself against the barbarian Huns, Catherine appears at the head of a delegation of saints—including the Jesuit martyr Jean de Brébeuf and the medieval crusader-king, Saint Louis—to petition the Virgin Mary:

> People of France: warlike nation, nation of genius! Is it some famous conqueror whose spirit looks down from on high and protects your double empire? No, it is a shepherdess in Europe and an Indian girl in America! Geneviève, from the village of Nanterre, and you, Catherine of the Canadian forests, hold out your crook and your beech cross above my homeland. Preserve that naiveté and that natural charm which it surely draws from its patronesses!

The two female saints both strengthen France through their natural innocence, but thanks to her origins in the American wilds, Catherine possesses a distilled version of this quality. "Perhaps more simple even than the patron of civilized and regulated France is the patron of savage France."[42] One might well argue that the original Jesuit biographers of Tekakwitha tended to indulge in a form of spiritual appropriation, assimilating her specifically "savage" virtues to the cause of European Christendom, but Chateaubriand is much more direct, and quite explicit. Moreover, the appropriation he performs is in the interests of the French nation, not of the Catholic Church. A nationalist as well as a Romantic (and a contemporary of Herder's), the novelist had no hesitation in incorporating the qualities associated with the Mohawk maiden—naturalness, transparent sincerity, savage freedom—directly into the French national character. He was by no means the last to enlist the figure of Catherine Tekakwitha in the service of an improbable nationalist cause.

Though Tekakwitha herself is not sexualized in Les Natchez, she is placed in the midst of a highly eroticized story of colonial desire. In this respect, Chateaubriand's novel is at once archetypical and characteristic of its time. Almost from the beginning of American colonization, stories of love—invariably ill-fated—between a native woman and a man from Europe form a staple of the literature of travel and encounter. Typically, the Indian maiden is spontaneously and immediately attracted to the white stranger. She gives of herself with generosity and naïveté, providing food and other assistance as well as uncomplicated sex. The Pocahontas legend is only the best known of these colonial narratives. "The major feature of this myth," writes the literary critic Peter Hulme, "is the ideal of cultural harmony through romance." The relationship between colonizers and indigenous people, marked in historical reality by violence and exploitation, is transformed into a redeeming story of interracial love. Why Pocahontas, like Céluta, falls for a white stranger is never explained, but the implications are clear enough according to Hulme: "Inseparable from Pocahontas's love for Smith is her recognition of the superiority of English culture."[43]

Though built around the venerable colonial fantasy of the redeeming romance, Chateaubriand's novel is also a characteristic creation of the Romantic age. America and its indigenous inhabitants represent heightened passion and an authenticity that was felt to be lacking in Europe.[44] While one Indian maid, Céluta, serves as the object of French lust, another Indian girl, Tekakwitha, contributes the natural force of savagery—in a spiritualized form—to the French national character. As in Cholenec's hagiographies, a figure of savage purity appears in the company of a contrasting figure of savage passion. Chateaubriand may well have injected Catholic saints into his novel, and he may well have won fame as an opponent of de-Christianization campaigns of the French Revolution, but Les Natchez is still the product of a secular mind. Eroticism supplies the main vehicle for the exploration of human relations, while race and nationality serve as fundamental lines of division.

Chateaubriand was not the last writer to entangle Tekakwitha in stories of sexual conquest. Beautiful Losers, a postmodernist novel published in 1966 by a young Leonard Cohen, before he became famous as a singer and songwriter, takes the form of an extended—and quite obscene—riff on the hagiography.[45] Comparing Tekakwitha to the recently martyred Marilyn Monroe, Cohen concocts lurid fantasies for his narrator and has him coupling in a variety of ways with the nubile virgin. Critics have commented on the carnivalesque strategy at work here, the author's use of obscenity for the traditional purpose of shocking the reader and undermining authority.[46] Equally striking, however, is Cohen's shrewdness—and he seems to have had before him nothing more than one Cholenec-inspired hagiography from the 1920s—in picking up on and caricaturing the exotic/erotic theme that runs through the writings of Cholenec, Chateaubriand, and their imitators.

9

Epilogue: "Our Catherine"

FATHERS CHAUCHETIÈRE AND CHOLENEC MAY HAVE HOPED THAT THEIR HAGIOGRAPHIC efforts would lead to Catherine taking her place in the pantheon of official Catholic saints, but for two centuries there was no serious effort to secure papal canonization. Canonizations were, in fact, extremely rare in the seventeenth and eighteenth centuries; only thirty-two new saints were named between 1540 and 1770, the majority of these Italian or Spanish.[1] More than verified miracles were required. It took an extended and hugely expensive campaign to bring these to the attention of the Vatican, and so it is hardly surprising that the Mohawk virgin remained an unofficial cult figure. As such, she was remembered in the Kahnawake/Montreal region, while occasional reeditions of her life story brought her to the attention of succeeding generations of European Catholic readers. Then, toward the end of the nineteenth century, Tekakwitha suddenly became known in the United States, and with her chariot hitched to the powerful engines of American nationalism, papal recognition began to seem a real possibility.

In 1884, the Catholic bishops of the United States were preparing to meet at Baltimore for a great plenary council that would reorganize and reinvigorate the American church. One of their goals was to solidify the church's position in a predominantly Protestant society with pronounced anti-Papist traditions. Waves of immigration from Ireland, Italy, French Canada, and other countries had bolstered the Catholic population enormously but had done nothing to allay the suspicions of old-stock Americans, quite the reverse. This was a time of disturbing change: rapid industrialization, burgeoning cities with teeming slums, strikes, and violent labor strife all appeared profoundly threatening to many Americans, and the "foreign laborer," economically degraded and politically radical, seemed to embody all the "alien" forces that were transforming the country and subverting its traditional self-image. Since so many immigrant workers were Catholic, xenophobia united with traditional religious prejudice to produce an upsurge of anti-Papist nativism.[2] Alarmed by the hostile atmosphere they faced, leaders of the church had strong motives to establish an American profile for Catholicism. So began the search for an American saint that could symbolically root the church in America soil. By the time the bishops gathered at Baltimore, they had identified a perfect candidate: an innocent Indian from the distant colonial past, the embodiment of nature and the land, and the antithesis of immigration, urban grime, and industrial conflict.

What made Tekakwitha doubly attractive as a nationalist icon for American Catholics was her status as both noble savage and woman/girl. Nations were frequently personified in the nineteenth century through female figures—Britannia, Marianne, the Virgin of Guadalupe—who symbolized not only fecundity but also continuity with the past. In the rhetorical gender division of labor, these feminine symbols of the nation's conservative aspect found their complement in masculine military and industrial motifs symbolizing the nation's power and progressive stance.[3] Energetic, forward-looking qualities also tended to be associated with the white race, whereas subjugated peoples with darker complexions were seen as atavistic. Thus the fin de siècle cult of Tekakwitha, like the contemporary cult of Pocahontas, should be seen in the context of a general tendency for nationalist discourse to operate through the interplay of racial and gender oppositions: masculine/feminine, white/colored, civilized/savage, progressive/atavistic.

In this age of nationalism, a figure who had once been portrayed as a spiritual exile in the pagan land of her birth now became, for American Catholics, "our Katherine." Such an appropriation naturally provoked a nationalist reaction on the part of the French-Canadian church, which initiated its own campaign to stimulate devotion to Tekakwitha and to secure official recognition of her holiness. Soon there were two major shrines devoted to her, one at Auriesville, New York, the site of her birth, and another at Kahnawake, where her body was interred. Moreover, there have long been two parallel vice-postulators orchestrating the canonization campaign, one in the United States and one in Quebec.

It was the Americans who took the first step, wisely setting their sights on beatification, a preliminary stage that typically precedes canonization. The Baltimore Council approved a petition calling on the Holy See to institute a cause for Tekakwitha's beatification. Her case was suspended for many decades in order to give priority to the Jesuit martyrs of New France, and so

it was only in 1932 that her formal process got under way. It proved difficult to verify any of the hundreds of miracles attributed to the Mohawk
Virgin, but finally Pope John Paul II, unusually generous in such matters
and anxious to recognize and affirm the global and multiracial nature of the
church, pronounced her numerous unverified miracles equivalent to one
certified miracle. And so she was beatified, in 1980, three hundred years
after her death. Now officially the "Blessed Catherine Tekakwitha," she remains a candidate for canonization.

A central figure in the original American campaign to secure recognition
for Catherine Tekakwitha was Father Clarence Walworth, a native of New
York who grew up in Saratoga Springs, not far from Tekakwitha's birth-
place in the old Mohawk country. Aided by his schoolteacher niece, Ellen
(Nelly) Walworth, he traveled to Kahnawake and Montreal to gather docu-
mentary evidence and to consult with French-Canadian churchmen. The
research was a source of pleasure, for both uncle and niece were fascinated
with native archaeology, native ethnography, native artifacts, and everything
else relating to Indians. Like other white North Americans of the time, they
tended to harbor sentimental attitudes toward natives, associating them with
nature and with the picturesque and the exotic.

Images of "bloodthirsty savagery" were fading in the late nineteenth
century, a time when the West had been "won" following the defeat of the
Plains Indians' military resistance. Government agencies were busy doing
their best to assimilate surviving Indians to the American mainstream, and
native cultures seemed increasingly out of place in the modern world.
Marginalized in real life, Indians exercised a powerful attraction over the
national, and international, imagination: Wild West shows toured the land,
children learned native crafts at summer camps, tourists purchased Indian
souvenirs, and the Mohawk Virgin became the darling of the American
Catholic Church. This was an age of self-conscious modernity when indigenous peoples were regarded as "primitive," which is to say, belonging to
another age, outside the forward march of history. The "primitive" was
fascinating not because it negated modernity but because it gave definition
through contrast to the progressive and the modern, while providing a focus
for nostalgic fantasies generated by the anxieties inherent in modern life.[4]
The updated and Americanized cult of Tekakwitha emerged under the sign
of primitivism.

When Clarence Walworth's priestly attention shifted to other subjects,
his niece Nelly remained focused on the Mohawk saint, and her research
over the years was prodigious. She discovered Claude Chauchetière's hagiographic manuscript, made a careful copy, and prepared it for its first-ever

publication.[5] Then, in 1891, she published *The Life and Times of Kateri Tekakwitha*, a watershed work that dramatically refashioned her heroine's story.[6]

Though written by a Catholic and suffused with pious sentiments, Walworth's *Life and Times* is no hagiography. It is an essentially modern work—part rigorously researched historical biography, part sentimental novel complete with imagined dialogue—and it bears the marks of the feminist movement of the late Victorian period. Her biography concentrates on sentiment and emotions, especially feelings concerning personal relations with family and friends. Tekakwitha's "pangs of regret" on quitting the country of her birth, her joy on meeting with a warm welcome at Kahnawake, her wounded feelings on being falsely accused of adultery are all recounted in poignant detail. In this telling, God plays an unobtrusive part in Tekakwitha's emotional life.

Certainly Walworth's treatment of Tekakwitha tends to center on the adolescent girl's struggle to discover and assert her identity. When her aunts try to pressure her into marriage, the docile child "showed at this time a sudden development of will, with inherent force to mould its own fate, and a strength of character that had not before asserted itself." On the trail to Kahnawake, after the pangs of separation had passed, she experiences the thrill of "sudden freedom, then, from all the bonds that bound her to her lodge and tribe." Finally, she takes the vow of perpetual virginity, and this, too, becomes an assertion of autonomy: "However others might look upon her act, this solemn engagement with God gave her a feeling of freedom rather than of thralldom. At last she had an acknowledged right to live her own life in her own way."[7] Since the time of Chauchetière, the story of the Mohawk Virgin had always been constructed around clashes between an emergent self and (mostly hostile) others, but it took a "New Woman" of the late nineteenth century to reshape the narrative into a psychological drama in which the thoroughly modern quest for personal autonomy provided a central dynamic.[8]

Projecting her own generation's quest for independence onto Tekakwitha, Nelly Walworth distanced herself from her own creation by stressing racial difference. The biography is packed with details about moccasins and longhouses, songs, crafts, and customs: ethnographic verisimilitude that adds interest to the narrative while underlining the subject's fundamental Indianness. Some of these touches are specifically Mohawk, but many signify a generic Indian identity: women are "squaws," men are "braves," hunting is the main economic pursuit, and people are most at home in the forest. Tekakwitha, says Walworth, was "an untamed Indian. . . . She was still a child of the woods, and out of her element elsewhere."[9] Whereas Cholenec and Chauchetière had considered Catherine's proper environment to be the agricultural village and the chapel, and had treated her hunting expedition into the wilderness as an exile, Nelly Walworth takes the opposite view. Of course, she meant this in the nicest way—"nature" having acquired more positive connotations since the time the Jesuits wrote[10]—but Walworth's heroine nevertheless carried markers of an essentialized Indian identity: pure otherness beyond the reach of historical progress.

Walworth was at pains to maintain her subject's native identity undefiled, and to that end, she went so far as to give her a new name. Until this book appeared, writers had always referred to the Mohawk Virgin as "Catherine Tekakwitha," with some variations in spelling. As noted earlier, the double name reflected a layered identity that included Christian as well as Mohawk elements. Such a complicated badge of colonial hybridity would hardly do for a portrait of unadulterated Indianness, however, and so Walworth rechristened her subject "Kateri Tekakwitha." Where did the name "Kateri" come from? The author explains in a footnote that this is "the Iroquois form of the Christian name Katherine."[11] In other words, if you take the French sound of "Catherine" and try to pronounce it with an Iroquois accent, you end up with something that might well be rendered "Kateri" by an English speaker. Jesuits no doubt mispronounced "Tekakwitha," and Mohawks presumably mispronounced "Catherine"; the result is a local usage formed through long years of linguistic interpenetration involving several native languages and two European languages. Nelly Walworth, anxious to eliminate the blatantly European "Catherine" from her title, was using a Mohawk mispronunciation of an Italian saint's name, linked to a French approximation of a Mohawk name, to clothe her heroine in an identity designed to look immaculately aboriginal. The gambit was a complete success; ever since, Tekakwitha/Catherine has been known around the world as "Kateri Tekakwitha."

Walworth's humanizing biography was bound to provoke reactions from Catholic traditionalists utterly out of sympathy with the attempt to bring even an uncanonized saint down from the clouds. Add to that the fact that her book was linked to the American appropriation of Catherine's memory, and it is no wonder that elements within the French-Canadian church were quick to react to this double assault on "notre Catherine." Accordingly, Father Nicholas Burtin, the parish priest at Kahnawake, paused in his efforts to fend off the influence of Protestant evangelists among his Iroquois flock and rushed to compose a new Life of Tekakwitha, one designed to reposition her story, placing it back firmly within a classical hagiographic frame. Familiar with the Jesuit sources, knowledgeable about the history of the Sault St. Louis mission, and fluent in the Mohawk language, Burtin had been a major source of information and guidance to Clarence and Nelly Walworth, but he clearly felt that the latter's literary flights of fancy called out for a corrective. Published in French in 1894, Burtin's Life of Catherine Tekakwitha,

Iroquois Virgin, presents itself as a scholarly work, carefully grounded in the original Jesuit sources.[12] Walworth's *Life and Times of Kateri Tekakwitha* was declared "fresh" and "interesting" by the author, but his work was about virtue, virginity, and miracles. "Our aim in publishing these edifying details is to restore the confidence of the faithful in the woman once known as 'the thaumaturge [miracle worker] of Canada,' 'the Geneviève of New France.'"[13] Burtin's attempt to maintain the purity of the hagiographic genre and to eliminate historicist and novelistic impurities was not entirely successful, though a "sacred biography" tradition of writings about Tekakwitha did continue through much of the twentieth century, especially in French-language works.[14]

The last hundred years have seen a growing stream of stories and images about the "Lily of the Mohawks." Books, pictures, statues, children's stories, films, and Web sites combine to bring Tekakwitha to the attention of millions of Catholics and non-Catholics around the world.[15] Genre traditions blur and interpenetrate as even the most conventionally hagiographic works adjust their narratives to better harmonize with contemporary sensibilities: borrowing from Walworth, they play down the troubling theme of Catherine's radical asceticism, even as they incorporate humanizing touches and modern conceptions of personality development and social relations. And as in all the writings and images from the time of Chauchetière on, Tekakwitha's identity as an "Indian" is a central concern.

Nelly Walworth's view of Kateri as a child of nature and the embodiment of a Native American essence has become increasingly pronounced with the passage of time. References to uncultivated nature abound: the rushing streams, the lonely forest, the call of the loon. Natural man is present, too, in the form of brave warriors with evocative (invented) names such as "the Eagle" or "the Fox."[16] Illustrations generally emphasize the young woman's dark complexion, as Claude Chauchetière's oil portrait, the one surviving depiction by someone who actually saw Tekakwitha, does not. And whereas Chauchetière shows her dressed in a cloth tunic, modern images invariably outfit her in fringed buckskin and feathers. The backgrounds also differ strikingly: she appears in the seventeenth-century painting in a basically agricultural landscape with a church as its most prominent feature, but contemporary iconography always places her in a sylvan setting. One Italian *Life* of Tekakwitha includes a tourist album of Canadian wilderness scenes featuring waterfalls and birch groves; there is also a handsome portrait of "un guerriero pellirossa" in what appears to be the costume of a Sioux warrior of the late nineteenth century.[17] In recent years, Tekakwitha has become known as the patron (almost) saint of ecology, sharing that billing with Francis of Assisi. One children's book presents Kateri's people as primitive environmentalists: "The Iroquois, who depended more on hunting and gathering than on farming, . . . took care of the land, being careful to keep the lakes and rivers pure."[18]

Cover illustration of a modern children's book. The feathers, beadwork, and fringed buckskin identify Tekakwitha as a generic Indian, while the bunch of wildflowers in her hands serves to situate her in the realm of a benign nature. Reproduced with permission from *Blessed Kateri Tekakwitha*. Copyright © 1981, Catholic Book Publishing Co., New York, NY. All rights reserved.

The "nature" associated with this updated version of the noble savage is a benign and generally attractive environment of birds and flowers. It is a far cry from the dark and menacing wilderness of dangerous savagery that haunted the imagination of a young Jesuit student from Poitiers three and a half centuries ago. But then, Claude Chauchetière also constructed fantasy images of "Indians" as an inversion of and antidote to his own angst-filled situation. Only sustained exposure to actual native people in their own setting, in their language, and, at least to some degree, on their terms enabled him to come to grips with their human reality. Forced to confront some flesh-and-blood Iroquois and watching them pursue diverse and complex individual destinies, he began to see that they were not all the same and that one of them might indeed be a saint. But as we have seen, Chauchetière's self-emancipation from colonialist stereotypes was provisional and incomplete. And the greatest irony of his career is the fact that his crowning literary creation, the "Life of the Blessed Catherine Tegakouita," became grist for the discursive mills of countless tales of savagery and civilization.

For three hundred years Catherine/Kateri has served as a symbol, rich in exotic overtones, to be incorporated into the identities of European Catholics, conservative French nationalists, and Americanizing Catholic immigrants; she has been assimilated into these various identities, even as she has been made to stand for the antithesis of modernity. Her basic muteness in the hagiographical/historical record made her all the more adaptable to the needs of writers and artists working in different settings around the

Atlantic world. For centuries, it was Europeans and Euro-Americans who invoked and reshaped her story, always as a tale of the Indian Other recounted in counterpoint to the author's own situation. But what has Tekakwitha meant to the original inhabitants of North America and their descendants?

When I first visited Kahnawake in 1993, I had difficulty finding anyone interested in talking about Catherine Tekakwitha. I had approached through ranks of raw subdivisions, which finally opened out into some abandoned farm fields, at which point a sign announced that I was entering the territory of the Mohawk nation. A little farther on, I had to slow for a makeshift guard post where a Mohawk Warrior waved me through. Soon I arrived at the village center, a collection of closely packed frame houses, with shops, schools, a hospital, and, at its core, an attractive stone church and attached rectory in the style of the eighteenth century. A few miles west of the site where Tekakwitha lived and died, the village has been here since the last relocation in 1716, and the visitor has the sense of a strongly rooted human community. At the same time, signs of a transformed environment are highly visible: high overhead, the Mercier Bridge carries a stream of commuters to jobs in Montreal; and the banks of the St. Lawrence Seaway rise up in front of the village, cutting off access to the river and bringing oceangoing freighters past residents' windows.

The Warrior's guard post is gone now, but at the time of my first visit, tensions still ran high in the wake of the "Oka Crisis," a prolonged confrontation in the summer of 1990 when native militants had blocked roads in solidarity with the embattled Iroquois of nearby Kanesatake. There had been talk then of destroying Kahnawake's Tekakwitha shrine as a symbol of spiritual conquest and oppression.[19] But the suggestion was rebuffed; the shrine, with its great granite monument donated a century earlier by Father Clarence Walworth, remained; and soon the busloads of pilgrims were resuming their visits from far and wide. I attended mass in the chapel and listened while Kahnawake Catholics prayed for Tekakwitha's canonization. It seemed to me that the faithful band of believers dedicated to the cause of their local saint was rather small and, on average, of advanced years. Most villagers I spoke with outside the church were somewhat dismissive of the Mohawk saint, inclined to treat her story as a myth generated by centuries of religious and cultural imperialism.

Kahnawake attitudes toward Catherine/Kateri Tekakwitha, while shaped no doubt by recent events in that community, seem also to be connected with a general feeling, widespread among First Nations people across Canada, that the Christian churches acted as a prime instrument of oppression and cultural assimilation, especially through the institution of the residential school. Even though residential schools were a modern phenomenon, imposed on Indian children long after the Iroquois-Jesuit encounter, it is easy to imagine why people with painful personal memories of corporal punishment and sexual abuse would respond unfavorably to stories that idealize the suffering and self-punishment of a native who embraced the European's religion.[20] Not that there are no Kateri Tekakwitha devotees within Canada's sizable Christian native population; many Canadian Indians revere her memory, but widespread hostility to the assimilationist associations of the Tekakwitha legend limits their numbers. To find substantial concentrations of Indian devotees, I had to travel thousands of miles, into a western landscape far removed from the rocky hills, the streams, and forest clearings that the Mohawk woman would have recognized.

The car hardly seemed to be moving, though the speedometer registered well above the interstate speed limit as I cruised across the northern plains toward Great Falls. The Rocky Mountains gleamed like saw teeth on the distant horizon, while sagebrush-dotted ranchland stretched out for endless miles. Montana's second city, Great Falls, boasts a university, an air force base, and, in an unobtrusive backstreet office, the national headquarters of the Tekakwitha Conference, my destination. I wanted to learn more about this Indian Catholic organization, with branches across the United States, all dedicated to the canonization of Kateri Tekakwitha.

The two young women working in the office very kindly showed me the group's current publications and the records of annual meetings going back to the 1970s. One of them took time out from her typing and envelope stuffing to tell me about her personal interest in Kateri Tekakwitha and the Tekakwitha Conference. The child of a Plains Cree mother and a white father, this individual had never been active in the mainstream Catholic Church. Yet, as a Native American she was drawn to the Mohawk saint and to the conference. She feels strongly about the need to incorporate indigenous religious styles into church rituals and about the need for more Indian bishops. For her and for other members of the Tekakwitha Conference, as I soon discovered, issues of native identity are the highest priority.

The Tekakwitha Conference had begun in 1939 as a gathering of white missionaries in the western states, but in the 1970s control shifted to an increasingly militant Indian laity. In the post–Vatican II atmosphere of the day, with theologians exploring the concept of "inculturation" as a means of "clothing the Gospel" in non-Western cultures rather than demonizing the latter, the church was receptive to the idea that natives should value both their indigenous and their Christian spirituality. The organization, now fully under the control of Native Americans, expresses its purposes in these terms: "The Tekakwitha Conference strives to unify Native Catholic voice, presence and identity while respecting the diversity. The Conference further strives to empower Native Catholics as Church and to deepen and affirm

Native Catholic identity and pride in their culture, spirituality, and traditions."[21] Annual conferences held at different locations bring together Indian members from across the United States for speeches, prayer sessions, powwow dancing, and other festivities that allow people of all regions and tribal affiliations to meet and mingle.

With chapters on reservations and in major cities across the country, the Tekakwitha Conference is founded on the belief that, notwithstanding tribal diversity, there is an underlying Native American essence. Various symbols meant to evoke generic Indianness—eagles, feathers, tipis—predominate in the organization's iconography. As with other forms of nationalism, the native consciousness of the Tekakwitha Conference stresses "tradition," a set of practices and values located primarily in the past and in need of revival and nourishment by the present generation. Of course, the Conference hardly stands for the preservation of indigenous purity—rather, it seeks to link native traditions and Catholic Christianity—but it does work from the assumption that Native Americans are fundamentally one. Indeed, it strives to foster unity, not least through the practice of assembling Indians from across America at the annual Tekakwitha Conference.[22]

When white Americans such as the Walworths reduced Indian history and culture to instances of an undifferentiated "primitive" essence, there were obvious elements of racism even in their most benign, noble savage portrayals. Yet Native Americans themselves have often participated in the homogenizing process; for example, Iroquois of the early twentieth century would dress up in the buckskin and feathers of Plains Indians in order to "play Indian" for the tourist trade. There was more to this apparent acceptance of stereotypes, however, than cultural victimization or a cynical strategy for extracting a few dollars from a generally contemptuous white society. There were also political motives for cultivating generic symbols of Native American identity, motives that originated in the long struggle to survive in the face of aggressive colonialism.

Since the mid–eighteenth century, there have been repeated efforts to bring together the indigenous nations of America to form a common front against the settler republic that often seemed bent on marginalizing, and even exterminating, all native people. Pan-Indian movements sometimes took military form, as in Pontiac's War; they sometimes focused on political and legal mobilization, as in most contemporary campaigns. Frequently there was also a spiritual dimension to pan-Indianism, such as the religion of the Shawnee prophet in Tecumseh's day, the Ghost Dance movement later in the nineteenth century, and, more recently, the Tekakwitha Conference. Does it seem outlandish to suggest that people affiliated with a hierarchical church headquartered in Rome might be considered in any sense heirs of the Ghost Dance or the anti-European cult of the Delaware prophet Neolin? Though it clearly eschews violence and confrontation generally, the Tekakwitha movement does stand for Native American unity and for the promotion of native interests, especially within the Catholic Church. Indian Catholics took over the organization in the 1970s in a general atmosphere of contestation; the American Indian Movement (AIM), at the time the most visible manifestation of native activism, was very much on the minds of those involved.[23] Obviously, the Tekakwitha Conference was never radical in the way that AIM was, but like other, more overtly political, movements it derived its strength from a long Native American tradition of struggle to bring diverse peoples together in the defense of common interests.

On to New Mexico, the heartland of Native American devotion to Kateri Tekakwitha. Here, in a gorgeous semiarid landscape of mountains and valleys that is even more remote from the lands of the Mohawk, I find images of Tekakwitha almost everywhere. Her image, with dark skin and braided hair and carrying a basket full of multicolored ears of corn, adorns the altar screen of the cathedral at Santa Fe. At the Queen of Angels chapel, a Native American church in Albuquerque, her statue stands in a special shrine where devotees sprinkle themselves with fragments of crushed corn. In Pueblo communities I visit across the state, most of the adobe mission churches contain at least one picture or statue of the Mohawk saint. In this part of the world, in contrast to most parts of Canada, the sense of native identity and the sense of Catholic identity seem to reinforce one another as they serve to distinguish indigenous people from the dominant Anglo-Protestant culture.

New Mexico is also home to dozens of "Kateri Circles," small local groups affiliated with the Tekakwitha Conference. Anthropologist Paula Holmes studied Kateri Circles in pueblo communities, as well as on Navajo and Apache reservations, and discovered that most members were women and that socializing and mutual support formed an important part of their experience as Tekakwitha devotees. Active Catholics all, the women Holmes interviewed were no more prepared than the Iroquois converts of seventeenth-century Kahnawake to surrender their independence to the (largely white) clergy. On one point particularly they expressed open defiance of the church hierarchy: "For me," one woman told Holmes, "I see that she is already a saint. . . . If the Holy Father doesn't see it, well . . ." and here her voice trailed off. Another pueblo devotee made a similar point: "There's this Indian saint, Kateri. She's already a saint to me. Of course, the white people make too much to do with having all this documentation and paperwork. To me, she became a saint the day she died."[24] And as an Indian saint, she is a story to be recounted to the uninitiated; she is a friend and companion whose picture or statue can be included in friendly conversations; and she is a miracle worker.

The Pueblo, Apache, and Navajo women that Holmes interviewed told her, almost without exception, that they were drawn to Tekakwitha as a fellow native: "That is one of the things I could relate to, relate with the Indianness of Kateri, our own Indianness. That's why we feel a lot of closeness with Kateri, because she is Indian and she knows a lot about what's in our hearts." They identified with her as a native and a woman, but also as someone who triumphed over suffering. "Kateri was a very innocent person, very devoted to Jesus," a Jemez woman declared. "She had a hard life, but that makes us strong. Like in my situation, my mom died when I was very small." A member of the Albuquerque Kateri Circle offered a similar observation: "The most important thing about Kateri is her prayerful life and her never giving up, in spite of the hardships she faced. Among us Indians, we have a lot of hardships."[25] These southwestern women felt real sympathy for the trials of a Mohawk woman whose story came down to them from the distant past, and in return they felt she shared in their own miseries and grief.

For three hundred years, believers have been addressing prayers to Tekakwitha in hopes that she might help them, especially in times of illness; native New Mexican devotees are continuing that venerable tradition. Like thousands of nonnatives, they turn to the uncanonized saint when a child breaks a leg, when an ultrasound shows anomalies, or when chemotherapy is ordered. In addition to medical assistance, "white" believers generally request quite practical favors, the sort of help that any magic maker might provide—please get my son into law school; please find a steady job for my husband; my house is on the market, please ensure that I get a good offer[26]—but the requests of Indian supplicants seem less impersonal, on the whole, more reflective of a relationship between two Native Americans, the petitioner with difficulties on earth and the saint in heaven. They ask not only for specific, material advantages but for a fuller kind of personal healing that is at once physical, mental, and spiritual.

The "hardships" that afflict modern Native Americans include all the universal human tragedies, as well as a high incidence of poverty, despair, addiction, and domestic discord—symptoms of the lingering effects of colonialism—and these problems form a conspicuous theme in discussions within many Kateri Circles. Some analysts have suggested that a basic division underlies the anguish of colonized peoples everywhere: souls torn apart by the conflicting identity demands of native "traditions" and the dominant society.[27] If there is any validity to this perhaps overly polarized view of native psychology, then "healing" for those affected would mean integration, or at least a successful negotiation of competing senses of identity. And, indeed, Indian devotees of Kateri Tekakwitha frequently express a yearning for wholeness in their lives. They admire the Mohawk saint partly for her ability to remain fully native while becoming fully Catholic; in other words, Tekakwitha seems inspiring as a woman who could respond creatively to what the Euro-American world had to offer without sacrificing or

betraying her indigenous culture. Perhaps these women see in her an idealized image of the courage and strength they themselves need to avoid being
torn asunder as they try to be effective in the contemporary world while
staying true to their native heritage.

While some Indian devotees of Tekakwitha pray for her canonization,
others demand that the church grant it, or resolutely insist that she is already a saint by popular acclamation regardless of her status in the eyes of
the Vatican. Perhaps their desire to secure official recognition of Kateri's
saintly status is particularly fervent because it carries layers of symbolic
meaning. "Her canonization will allow for the full realization and incorporation of the Church and our ways," a Navajo nun, Sister Jean, declared.
"Her canonization will heal our Native American people."[28] Other issues
may lie beneath this impulse to rehabilitate relations between native people
and the Catholic Church: full "healing" might require a more complete
acceptance of "our ways" within North American society generally. Just as
the smallpox scars miraculously vanished from Tekakwitha's face after her
radiant death, so the native women who pray to her seem to be looking
forward to a day when, freed from the scars and injuries of colonialism,
they can enjoy a sense of wholeness in their lives.

Over the centuries, for diverse and frequently quite strange purposes,
many have laid claim to the image and the story of Catherine Tekakwitha.
She has been carried to France and Mexico, New York and Montreal; in recent
years she has even found followers in Africa, Asia, and South America. She
has been invoked to challenge racial and sexual discrimination, to cure
pneumonia and to help deliver babies, to bolster French nationality and to
Americanize the Catholic Church, to facilitate real estate transactions and to
make white people feel good about nature. Now, at last, Native Americans
are having their turn to fashion a Tekakwitha that matches their needs. And
so she moves to take up residence in the sun-drenched pueblos of the Southwest, hardly the obvious choice of home for this longhouse Iroquois from
the Mohawk Valley. Yet, in spite of the long centuries and the profound
cultural differences that separate the historical Tekakwitha from the Indian
women who venerate her today, they do share a common experience as
survivors of the trauma of colonization; as a consequence, these Apaches,
Pueblos, and Navajos seem able to connect to her life story at a deeper personal level than may be possible for nonnatives. That being the case, then
yes, the native saint has come home.

Abbreviations

ARSI   Archivum Romanum Societatis Iesus (Fondo Gesuitico). Rome.

ASJCF   Archives de la société de Jésus, Canada français. St.-Jérôme, Quebec.

ASQ   Archives du Séminaire de Québec. Quebec City.

JR   Reuben Thwaites, ed. *The Jesuit Relations and Allied Documents*. 73 vols. Cleveland: Burrows Brothers, 1896–1900.

MNF   Lucien Campeau, ed. *Monumenta Novae Franciae*. 7 vols. to date. Quebec: Presses de l'Université Laval, 1967–87; Montreal: Editions Bellarmin, 1989–.

Pos   *The Positio of the Historical Section of the Sacred Congregation of Rites on the Introduction of the Cause for Beatification and Canonization and on the Virtues of the Servant of God, Katharine Tekakwitha, the Lily of the Mohawks.* New York: Fordham University Press, 1940.

Notes

Preface

1. On the broader context in which this instance of colonial hagiography is situated, see Allan Greer, "Colonial Saints: Gender, Race, and Hagiography in New France," *William and Mary Quarterly*, 3rd ser., 57 (April 2000): 323–48; as well as the articles assembled in *Colonial Saints: Discovering the Holy in the Americas, 1500–1800,* ed. Allan Greer and Jodi Bilinkoff (New York: Routledge, 2003).

2. I only hope that any sense of identification with Chauchetière works to reinforce, rather than distract from, the original goal of examining the native experience of colonization. I draw comfort from Jill Lepore's observation that microhistorians frequently tend to identify with an investigator figure in their attempts to retrieve the experience and outlook of the historically inarticulate. Jill Lepore, "Historians Who Love Too Much: Reflections on Microhistory and Biography," *Journal of American History* 88 (June 2001): 129–44.

3. The prime example of this ethnohistorical approach is Bruce G. Trigger, *The Children of Aataentsic: A History of the Huron People to 1660* (Montreal: McGill–Queen's University Press, 1976).

4. The negative view of the Jesuits of New France is prevalent in the current literature in the field. In addition to Trigger, *Children of Aataentsic,* see James P. Ronda, "The Sillery Experiment: A Jesuit-Indian Village in New France, 1637–1663," *American Indian Culture and Research Journal* 3 (1979): 1–18; Denys Delâge, *Bitter Feast: Amerindians and Europeans in Northeast North America, 1600–64* (Vancouver: University of British Columbia Press, 1993); Karen Anderson, *Chain Her by One Foot: The Subjugation of Women in Seventeenth-Century New France* (London: Routledge, 1991); Carole Blackburn, *Harvest of Souls: The Jesuit Missions in North America, 1632–1650* (Montreal: McGill–Queen's University Press, 2000). For a different view, see James Axtell, *The Invasion Within: The Contest of Cultures in Colonial North America* (New York: Oxford University Press, 1985).

5. For bibliographical information, see Carlos Sommervogel et al., *Bibliothèque de la Compagnie de Jésus,* 12 vols. (Paris and Louvain, 1890–1960), passim; Edward-Xavier Evans, "The Literature Relative to Kateri Tekakwitha, the Lily of the Mohawks, 1656–

1680," *Bulletin des recherches historiques* 46 (July 1940): 193–209; (August 1940): 241–55; Allan Greer, "Savage/Saint: The Lives of Kateri Tekakwitha," in *Habitants et marchands, vingt ans après: Lectures de l'histoire des XVIIe et XVIIIe siècles canadiens*, ed. Sylvie Dépatie et al. (Montreal: McGill–Queen's University Press, 1998), 138–59.

6. Nancy Shoemaker, "Kateri Tekakwitha's Tortuous Path to Sainthood," in *Negotiators of Change: Historical Perspectives on Native American Women*, ed. Nancy Shoemaker (New York: Routledge, 1995), 49–71; K. I Koppedrayer, "The Making of the First Iroquois Virgin: Early Jesuit Biographies of the Blessed Kateri Tekakwitha," *Ethnohistory* 40 (Spring 1993): 277–306; Natalie Z. Davis, "Iroquois Women, European Women," in *Women, "Race," and Writing in the Early Modern Period*, ed. Margo Hendricks and Patricia Parker (London: Routledge, 1994), 256; John Demos, *The Unredeemed Captive: A Family Story from Early America* (New York: Random House, 1994), 128–30; Daniel K. Richter, *Facing East from Indian Country: A Native History of Early America* (Cambridge, Mass.: Harvard University Press, 2001).

7. Though she relied heavily on a very imperfectly translated volume of source material (Robert Holland, *The Positio of the Historical Section of the Sacred Congregation of Rites on the Introduction of the Cause for Beatification and Canonization and on the Virtues of the Servant of God, Katherine Tekakwitha, the Lily of the Mohawks*. [New York: Fordham University Press, 1940]) for her reconstruction of Tekakwitha's life narrative, Shoemaker does present a convincing argument to the effect that Iroquois women made use of Christianity in pursuit of their own ends as natives and as women. She is right to point to the influence of the *Life* of Catherine of Siena as a model for the hagiographic texts devoted to Catherine Tekakwitha (Shoemaker, "Tortuous Path," 55). Furthermore, she offers some valuable insights on the resemblances between Catholicism and Iroquoian religion that facilitated conversion, though her analysis here is suggestive rather than exhaustive.

8. My thanks to Brian Deer for his advice on Mohawk pronunciation.

Chapter 1

1. This account of the death of Tekakwitha is based on the written testimony of two Jesuit priests, Claude Chauchetière and Pierre Cholenec, who witnessed the event. The main manuscript sources are "Extraict d'une autre lettre du pere Chonelec [sic] sur le mesme suiet et la mort d'une ste fille, escritte le premier jour de may 1680," ASQ, 374; Claude Chauchetière, "La vie de la B. Catherine Tegakouita, dite à présent La Saincte Sauvagesse," ASJCF, ms 343 (published as *La Vie de la B. Catherine Tegakouita dite à présent la Saincte Sauvagesse par le R.P. Claude Chauchetière pretre missionnaire de la Compagnie de Jésus* [New York: Presse Cramoisy, 1887]) (hereafter "La vie"); Pierre Cholenec, "La vie de Catherine Tegakouita, première vierge Iroquoise," Archives de l'hôtel-dieu de Québec (hereafter "Vie de Catherine Tegakouita"). The quotation is from Cholenec, "Vie de Catherine Tegakouita," 61 (*Pos*, 300).

2. ASQ, 374, "Extraict d'une autre letter."

3. "Notes autobiographiques du P. Claude Chauchetière," nineteenth-century copy of a letter dated August 1695, ASJCF, ms. 390, p. 14.

4. The death of a pious native convert was a staple theme of North American mission-ary writings of the period, Protestant as well as Catholic. See Erik R. Seeman, "Reading Indians' Deathbed Scenes: Ethnohistorical and Representational Approaches," *Journal of American History* 88 (June 2001): 17–47.

5. Jérôme Lalemant, Relation of 1640, JR 19:93 (also Allan Greer, ed., *The Jesuit Relations: Natives and Missionaries in Seventeenth-Century North America* [Boston: Bedford Books, 2000], 91). On the Huron epidemics of the 1630s, see Bruce G. Trigger, *The Children of Aataentsic: A History of the Huron People to 1660* (Montreal: McGill–Queen's University Press, 1976), 499–602; Bruce G. Trigger, *Natives and Newcomers: Canada's "Heroic Age" Reconsidered* (Montreal: McGill–Queen's University Press, 1985), 229–51.

6. In Europe as well as America, the Jesuits gave priority to saving the souls of the dying, sometimes to the neglect of any attempt to relieve the suffering of the living. Lynn Martin tells of Jesuits at the 1577 siege of Avignon exhorting wounded soldiers to repent, while ignoring their pleas for food and water. Lynn Martin, *The Jesuit Mind: The Mentality of an Elite in Early Modern France* (Ithaca, N.Y.: Cornell University Press, 1988), 216.

7. Jean de Brébeuf, Relation of 1635, JR 8:169.

8. JR 58:219. On the baptism of moribund infants, see Denise Lemieux, *Les petits innocents: L'enfance en Nouvelle-France* (Quebec: Institut québécois de recherche sur la culture, 1985), 89–97.

9. Relation of 1679, JR 61:228–29. This same Jean de Lamberville was happy to report his success in rescuing the souls of war captives marked for execution by the Onondaga. He was allowed to instruct and baptize two Gannaouen women just before they were burned alive. Letter of 25 August 1682, JR 62:54–107.

10. Relation of 1679, JR 61:237

11. Paul Le Jeune, Relation of 1633, JR 5:225.

12. Quoted in François du Creux, *The History of Canada or New France*, ed. James B. Conacher trans. Percy J. Robinson, 2 vols. (Toronto: Champlain Society, 1951), 528.

13. Philippe Ariès, *The Hour of Our Death*, trans. H. Weaver (Oxford: Oxford University Press, 1981), 332.

14. See Pascal's *Pensées* for this sense of the nullity of existence without God. Pascal was no friend of the Jesuits, but his writings convey a basic mood shared by learned Catholics of various stripes in this period.

15. Michel Vovelle, *La mort et l'occident de 1300 à nos jours* (Paris: Gallimard, 1983), 247.

16. Marie de l'Incarnation to her son, summer 1647, in *Marie de l'Incarnation, Ursuline (1599–1672): Correspondance*, ed. Dom Guy Oury (Solesmes: Abbaye Saint-Pierre, 1971), 324.

17. On the martyrs of New France, see Guy Laflèche, *Les saints martyrs canadiens*, 5 vols. (Laval, Quebec: Singulier, 1988–95); Allan Greer, "Colonial Saints: Gender, Race, and Hagiography in New France," *William and Mary Quarterly*, 3rd ser., 57 (April 2000): 323–48; Paul Perron, "Isaac Jogues: From Martyrdom to Sainthood," in *Colonial Saints: Discovering the Holy in the Americas, 1500–1800*, ed. Allan Greer and Jodi Bilinkoff (New York: Routledge, 2003), 153–68. For period documents by and about Jean de Brébeuf, see René Latourelle, *Etude sur les écrits de Saint Jean de Brébeuf*, 2 vols. (Montreal:

Les éditions de l'Immaculée-Conception, 1952–53); "Quelques remarques sur les vertus de Père de Brébeuf, par le Père Joseph-Marie Chaumonot," MNF 7:471–72. A modern biography, from a Catholic point of view, is Joseph P. Donnelly, *Jean de Brébeuf, 1593–1649* (Chicago: Loyola University Press, 1975).

18. Kenneth S. Latourette, *A History of the Expansion of Christianity*, 4 vols. (New York: Harper, 1939); S. Delacroix, *Histoire universelle des missions catholiques*, 4 vols. (Paris: Grund, 1956–59); Maxime Haubert, *La vie quotidienne au Paraguay sous les jésuites* (Paris: Hachette, 1967); Philip Caraman, *The Lost Paradise: An Account of the Jesuits in Paraguay 1607–1768* (London: Sidgwick and Jackson, 1975); Stephen Neill, *A History of Christianity in India: The Beginnings to AD 1707* (Cambridge: Cambridge University Press, 1984); J. F. Moran, *The Japanese and the Jesuits: Alessandro Valignano in Sixteeenth-Century Japan* (London: Routledge, 1993); Dauril Alden, *The Making of an Enterpise: The Society of Jesus in Portugal, Its Empire, and Beyond 1540–1750* (Stanford, Calif.: Stanford University Press, 1996).

19. "These Churches were born amid Crosses: they have begotten their children amid sufferings, persecutions, epidemics, anguish." Paul Ragueneau, Relation of 1649–50, JR 35:235. See also Jérôme Lalemant, Relation of 1644–45, JR 28:46–69.

When deadly epidemics struck non-Christian populations or when individual opponents of Christianity fell ill, the Jesuits, predictably, interpreted these events as instances of God's terrible punishment. See Carole Blackburn, *Harvest of Souls: The Jesuit Missions and Colonialism in North America, 1632–1650* (Montreal: McGill–Queen's University Press, 2000), 113–21.

20. For general treatments of this subject, see Alfred Crosby, *The Columbian Exchange: Biological and Cultural Consequences of 1492* (Westport, Conn.: Greenwood, 1972); Alfred Crosby, *Ecological Imperialism: The Biological Expansion of Europe, 900–1900* (Cambridge: Cambridge University Press, 1986); David Stannard, *American Holocaust: Columbus and the Conquest of the New World* (New York: Oxford University Press, 1992); Noble David Cook, *Born to Die: Disease and New World Conquest, 1492–1650* (Cambridge: Cambridge University Press, 1998).

21. Although one school of thought contends that native populations of the Americas were devastated by old-world disease running ahead of human intruders from Europe, with the implication that eastern North America was depopulated in the sixteenth century, the research of Kim Lamphear and Dean Snow demonstrates that infections appeared here at a later stage in the contact process than they did in the densely populated regions of South America and Mesoamerica. It was only after French and English children arrived in Canada and New England that interior natives such as the Iroquois began to fall prey to smallpox. This revisionist view helps to reinforce the notion that the seventeenth century was a time of sudden and unprecedented calamity for the Five Nations. Dean R. Snow and Kim M. Lamphear, "European Contact and Indian Depopulation in the Northeast: The Timing of the First Epidemics," *Ethnohistory* 35 (1988): 15–33. Cf. Henry F. Dobyns, *Their Numbers Become Thinned: Native American Population Dynamics in Eastern North America* (Knoxville: University of Tennessee Press, 1983).

22. *Bradford's History of Plymouth Plantation*, ed. W. T. Davis (New York: Barnes and Noble, 1908), 312–13, as cited in Dean R. Snow, *The Iroquois* (Oxford: Blackwell, 1994), 95.

23. Daniel K. Richter, *The Ordeal of the Longhouse: The Peoples of the Iroquois League in the Era of European Colonization* (Chapel Hill: University of North Carolina Press, 1992), 58–59; William A. Starna, "The Biological Encounter: Disease and the Ideological Domain," *American Indian Quarterly* 16 (Fall 1992): 511–19.

24. Jérôme Lalemant, Relation of 1662–63, JR 48:79 (English translation corrected by the author).

25. Joseph-François Lafitau, *Customs of the American Indians Compared with the Customs of Primitive Times*, ed., and trans. William N. Fenton and Elizabeth L. Moore. 2 vols. (Toronto: Champlain Society, 1974), 2:227.

26. Claude Chauchetière, *Narration de la mission du Sault depuis sa fondation jusqu'en 1686*, ed. Hélène Avisseau (1686; Bordeaux: Archives départementales de la Gironde, 1984), 54.

27. Snow, *The Iroquois*, 105–6.

28. Lafitau, *Customs of the American Indians*, 2:237–38, 2:251–56.

29. The epic of Deganawidah and Hiawatha and the founding of the League of the Five Nations is a part of the living Iroquois oral tradition. Different versions of the story were recorded, in the native languages and in English translation, over the course of the nineteenth and twentieth centuries. It is difficult to know exactly how the tale was told in the seventeenth century. The subplot about Hiawatha is recounted here not because we can be sure that the young Tekakwitha would have heard it in this or in any other form—unfortunately, there is simply no way of attaining that degree of certainty about oral traditions stretching back over three centuries—but because the tale seems to convey something enduring about Iroquois reactions to death.

In summarizing the Hiawatha legend, I have drawn mainly on the version recounted in 1880 by Seth Newhouse of the Six Nations reserve in Ontario and published by the Iroquois ethnographer Arthur C. Parker, but I have taken into account another narrative, told in 1912 by John A. Gibson. Arthur C. Parker, "The Constitution of the Five Nations or the Iroquois Book of the Great Law," in *Parker on the Iroquois*, ed. William Fenton (Syracuse, N.Y.: Syracuse University Press, 1968); John A. Gibson, *Concerning the League: The Iroquois League Tradition as Dictated in Onondaga*, ed. and trans. Hanni Woodbury et al. (Winnipeg: Algonquian and Iroquoian Linguistics, 1992).

The following secondary works discuss the Deganawidah-Hiawatha epic: Paul Wallace, *The White Roots of Peace* (Philadelphia: University of Pennsylvania Press, 1946); Christopher Vecsey, "The Story and Structure of the Iroquois Confederacy," *Journal of the American Academy of Religion* 54 (1986): 79–106; Matthew Dennis, *Cultivating the Landscape of Peace: Iroquois-European Encounters in Seventeenth-Century America* (Ithaca, N.Y.: Cornell University Press, 1993); Snow, *The Iroquois*, 58–60; William N. Fenton, *The Great Law and the Longhouse: A Political History of the Iroquois Confederacy* (Norman: University of Oklahoma Press, 1998), 51–97.

30. Parker, "Constitution of the Five Nations," 19.

31. Ibid., 20.

32. Ibid., 23–24.

33. See Richter, *Ordeal of the Longhouse*, 39–42.

34. Daniel K. Richter, "War and Culture: The Iroquois Experience," *William and Mary Quarterly* 40 (1983): 528–59. See also Anthony F. C. Wallace, *The Death and Rebirth of the Seneca* (New York: Random House, 1969), 93–107; Lafitau, *Customs of the American Indian*, 2:242.

35. Bibliothèque municipal de Poitiers, registres paroissiaux, St. Porchaire; Archives départementales de Vienne, fichier registres paroissiaux de Poitiers.

36. Guy Cabourdin, Jean-Noel Biraben, and Alain Blum, "Les crises démographiques," in *Histoire de la population française*, ed. Jacques Dupâquier, vol. 2, *De la Renaissance à 1789* (Paris: Presses Universitaires de France, 1988), 203–6.

37. Jacques Péret, "De Louis XIV à la Révolution," in *Histoire de Poitiers*, ed. Robert Favreau (Toulouse: Privat, 1988), 241; "Journal d'Antoine Denesde, marchand ferron à Poitiers et de Marie Barré sa femme (1628–1687)," in *Archives historiques du Poitou* (Poitiers: Imprimerie Ouidin, 1885), 194.

38. "Notes autobiographiques," ASJCF, no. 390, p. 3.

39. Ariès, *The Hour of Our Death*, 311; Vovelle, *La mort et l'occident*, 237–364.

40. Chauchetière, "La vie," 50 (*Pos*, 148); Chauchetière, *Narration*, 24.

41. Chauchetière, "La vie," 115 (*Pos*, 204).

42. Cholenec, "Vie de Catherine Tegakouita," 65 (*Pos*, 305).

43. Chauchetière, "La vie," 115 (*Pos*, 204).

44. Chauchetière, "La vie," 115–16 (*Pos*, 204–05).

45. Cholenec, "Vie de Catherine Tegakouita," 66 (*Pos*, 306–7).

46. Chauchetière, "La vie," 117 (*Pos*, 205).

47. "Abbrégé de la vie de Catherine Tegaskouita chrestienne Iroquoise decedée en la meme mission du sault de st Franc. Xavier, le 17 avril 1680," Archives françaises de la Compagnie de Jésus, Fonds Brotier, 162:153 (*Pos*, 86–87).

48. This paragraph draws on Peter Brown's brilliant study, *The Cult of the Saints: Its Rise and Function in Latin Christianity* (Chicago: University of Chicago Press, 1981), quotations at 68, 71.

49. ASJCF, ms 350, [Chauchetière], "Receuil de ce qui s'est passé depuis le decès de Catherine," 1–2. (This is a nineteenth-century copy made by Félix Martin, S.J. The copyist declares that the original was in Claude Chauchetière's hand, but that original document can no longer be located.)

50. Snow, *The Iroquois*, 106.

51. Cholenec, "Vie de Catherine Tegakouita," 68b (*Pos*, 312).

52. ASJCF, ms 350, "Receuil," 1–2; Cholenec, "Vie de Catherine Tegakouita," 68b (*Pos*, 311–12).

53. Chauchetière, *Narration*, 48, 51–52; Cholenec, "Vie de Catherine Tegakouita," 69 (*Pos*, 312–13).

54. Chauchetière, "La vie," 3 (*Pos*, 114).

55. Chauchetière, "La vie," 6 (*Pos*, 116). On the importance of hagiographic texts as material objects, see Julia Boss, "Saints' Lives and Catholic Community: The Uses of Hagiography in Seventeenth-Century New France," in Greer and Bilinkoff, *Colonial Saints*, 209–31.

56. The classic study of "local religion" in this period focuses on a region of Spain, though the general pattern of devotion to religious heroes and healing cults seems

to have extended throughout Catholic Europe. William A. Christian Jr., *Local Religion in Sixteenth-Century Spain* (Princeton, N.J.: Princeton University Press, 1981). Kenneth Woodward notes that, while there were fewer than three hundred canonizations between 1234, when the papacy asserted its exclusive right to name new saints, and 1990, church histories record ten thousand locally venerated "saints" for the same period, Kenneth L. Woodward, *Making Saints: How the Catholic Church Determines Who Becomes a Saint, Who Doesn't and Why* (New York: Simon and Schuster, 1990), 17.

57. ASQ, 374 "Extraict d'une autre lettre."
58. Relations of 1667–68 and 1668–69, JR 52:27–43, 228–33. For additional cases from New France, see Denis Lafrenière, "L'éloge de l'Indien dans les Relations des Jésuites," *Canadian Literature*, no. 131 (Winter 1991): 26–35; Allan Greer, "Colonial Saints: Gender, Race, and Hagiography in New France," *William and Mary Quarterly*, 3rd ser., 57 (April 2000): 323–48. Similar accounts of native piety from colonial Mexico (all of them concerning women) can be found in Carlos de Sigüena y Góngora, *Paraíso Occidental* (Mexico City: Juan de Rivera, 1683; Mexico City: Cien, 1995), libro tercero, cap. XIV–XV.
59. See Greer and Bilinkoff, *Colonial Saints*.
60. Cholenec, "Vie de Catherine Tegakouita," 71–72 (*Pos*, 316).
61. The hagiographic texts are discussed in detail in Allan Greer, "Savage/Saint: The Lives of Kateri Tekakwitha," in *Habitants et marchands, vingt ans après: Lectures de l'histoire des XVIIe et XVIIIe siècles canadiens*, ed. Sylvie Dépatie et al. (Montreal: McGill–Queen's University Press, 1998), 138–59.

Chapter 2

1. Barthélemy Vimont, Relation of 1642, JR 22:246–69, quotations at 252–53, 262–63, 264–65 (modified translations). Although the Jesuit account of the captives' ordeal rings true in most respects, some details—roasting babies?—may well be exaggerations or fabrications. A degree of skepticism is always in order when dealing with wartime atrocity stories reported by the victims' side.
2. Modern studies of the effects of torture indicate that the experience tends to have a corrosive effect on a person's beliefs and sense of self. Elaine Scarry, *The Body in Pain: The Making and Unmaking of the World* (New York: Oxford University Press, 1985).
3. Daniel Richter, *Facing East from Indian Country: A Native History of Early America* (Cambridge, Mass.: Harvard University Press, 2001), 151–88.
4. Daniel K. Richter, *The Ordeal of the Longhouse: The Peoples of the Iroquois League in the Era of European Colonization* (Chapel Hill: University of North Carolina Press, 1992).
5. Archaeologists designate these locations the "Printup Site" and the "Freeman Site," respectively. The same community moved in 1666 to a spot known as "Fox Farm." Dean R. Snow, *Mohawk Valley Archaeology: The Sites* (Albany, N.Y.: Institute for Archaeological Studies, University at Albany, 1995), 8, 365–75; Dean R. Snow, personal communication.
6. On the basis of archaeological evidence, Snow estimates the population of Tekakwitha's birth village ("Printup Site") at 374 and the village occupied after 1666 ("Fox Farm")

at 560. No figures are available for the original Gandaouagué site. Snow, *Mohawk Valley Archaeology*, 370, 418.

7. Ibid., 372.

8. This is the site Snow calls "Fox Farm." Ibid., 415–19.

9. Quoted in ibid., 418.

10. Champlain, 1616, quoted in Dean Snow, *The Iroquois* (Oxford: Blackwell, 1994), 40. Compare Lafitau's description, similar in most respects to Champlain's, of Iroquois longhouses of the early eighteenth century: Joseph-François Lafitau, *Customs of the American Indians Compared with the Customs of Primitive Times*, ed. and trans. William N. Fenton and Elizabeth L. Moore, 2 vols. (Toronto: Champlain Society, 1974), 2:19–22.

11. Snow, *Mohawk Valley Archaeology*, 416. All three of the Mohawk sites where it is presumed that Tekakwitha lived were badly disturbed before archaeologists got to them, and so it is not possible to obtain systematic data about artifacts and buildings. Also, it is only fair to note that there is no way to be certain that these sites correspond to the Gandaouagué of her time, though Dean Snow, the leading expert in this field, believes that they do.

12. The original, rather crudely economic, interpretation of Five Nations war and diplomacy as a single-minded pursuit of fur trade advantage was put forward by George T. Hunt in *Wars of the Iroquois: A Study in Intertribal Trade Relations* (Madison: University of Wisconsin Press, 1940). Much more subtle and qualified treatments of the connections between Iroquois commerce and Iroquois foreign relations have been put forward since Hunt's time in several works, including Bruce G. Trigger, *The Children of Aataentsic: A History of the Huron People to 1660* (Montreal: McGill–Queen's University Press, 1976); Bruce G. Trigger, *Natives and Newcomers: Canada's "Heroic Age" Reconsidered* (Montreal: McGill–Queen's University Press, 1985); Richter, *Ordeal of the Longhouse*. José Brandao, *"Your Fyre Shall Burn No More": Iroquois Policy toward New France and Its Native Allies To 1701* (Lincoln: University of Nebraska Press 1997), an overargued revisionist work, in my opinion, contends that the so-called Beaver Wars had nothing to do with the fur trade.

13. Natalie Zemon Davis, "Polatities, Hybridities: What Strategies for Decentring?" in *Decentring the Renaissance: Canada and Europe in Multidisciplinary Perspective, 1500–1700*, ed. Germaine Warkentin and Carolyn Podruchny (Toronto: University of Toronto Press, 2001), 19–32.

14. Chauchetière, "La vie," 12 (*Pos*, 120–21); Cholenec, "Vie de Catherine Tegakouita," 2 (*Pos*, 242).

15. Chauchetière, "La vie," 13–14 (*Pos*, 121).

16. Bacqueville de la Potherie, *Histoire de l'Amérique septentrionale*, 4 vols. (Paris: Chez Borcas, 1753), 2:32, quoted in Marc Jetten, *Enclaves amérindiennes: Les "réductions" du Canada 1637–1701* (Quebec: Septentrion, 1994), 76 (my translation).

17. Of course Claude Chauchetière was also the product of affiliations and collectivities: he had to view himself in relation to his living brothers and his deceased parents, as a member of the Catholic Church and the French nation, a citizen of Poitiers, and, most immediately, a member of the Society of Jesus. Clichés relying on a simple contrast between European "individualism" and native "communal identities" have

been discredited by recent scholarship on early modern personal identities. (See Natalie Davis, "Boundaries and the Sense of Self in Sixteenth-Century France," in *Reconstructing Individualism: Autonomy, Individuality, and the Self in Western Thought*, ed. Thomas C. Heller et al. [Stanford, Calif.: Stanford University Press, 1986], 53–63.) There were nevertheless ways in which Europeans of this period had become accustomed to thinking of persons as autonomous actors in some particular circumstances. The issue of the boundaries of the self will come up again in chapter 7.

18. Gabriel Sagard, *The Long Journey to the Country of the Hurons*, ed. G. M. Wrong, trans. H. H. Langton (Toronto: Champlain Society, 1939), 133.

19. Chauchetière, "La vie," 14 (*Pos*, 122).

20. Trigger, *Children of Aataentsic*, 37, 40.

21. Chauchetière, "La vie," 77 (*Pos*, 172).

22. For a good description of fuel gathering, though based on observation of the Hurons, see Sagard, *Long Journey*, 94.

23. Chauchetière, "La vie," 17–18 (*Pos*, 123–24).

24. William C. Orchard, *The Technique of Porcupine-Quill Decoration among the North American Indians* (New York: Museum of the American Indian, 1916); Christian F. Feest, *Native Arts of North America* (London: Thames and Hudson, 1992), 138–41.

25. Lewis H. Morgan, *League of the Ho-dé-no-sau-nee, or Iroquois* (Rochester, N.Y.: Sage and Brother, 1851), 365.

26. Feest, *Native Arts*, 106. My thanks to Christian Feest for his patient efforts to teach me about twining and false embroidery.

27. On wampum, ibid., 119–20; J. C. H. King, *First Peoples, First Contacts: Native Peoples of North America* (London: British Museum, 1999), 47–49; Bruce Elliott Johansen and Barbara Alice Mann, eds., *Encyclopedia of the Haudenosaunee (Iroquois Confederacy)* (Westport, Conn.: Greenwood, 2000), 325.

28. See William C. Orchard, *Beads and Beadwork of the American Indians* (New York: Museum of the American Indian, 1929), esp. 107, on the bow loom and its use.

29. Laurier Turgeon, personal communication.

30. Daniel Harmon, quoted in Dorothy K. Burnham, *To Please the Caribou: Painted Caribou-Skin Coats Worn by the Naskapi, Montagnais, and Cree Hunters of the Quebec-Labrador Peninsula* (Toronto: Royal Ontario Museum, 1992), 27.

31. See Morgan, *League of the Iroquois*, 386; Snow, *The Iroquois*, 92.

32. Lafitau, *Customs of the American Indians*, 2:44. Champlain also notes the use of eel-skin hair ribbons among the Hurons: H. P. Biggar, ed., *The Works of Samuel de Champlain*, 6 vols. (Toronto: Champlain Society, 1922–36), 3:134.

33. On Iroquois eel fishing, see the New York State Museum's Web site: www.nysm. mysed.gov/histmonth.html; on red colors, see Lafitau, *Customs of the American Indians*, 2:32; on "sturgeon glue," see Burnham, *To Please the Caribou*, 37. Eel-skin hair ribbons are one of several features of native costume that were adopted by white settlers. Washington Irving, who mentions them in describing a festive gathering of farmers in the Hudson Valley, suggests that they were valued for more than just their appearance: "The sons, in short square-skirted coats, with rows of stupendous brass buttons, and their hair generally queued in the fashion of the times, especially if they could procure an eelskin for the purpose, it being esteemed throughout the

country as a potent nourisher and strengthener of the hair." Washington Irving, "The Legend of Sleepy Hollow" (electronic version: http://www.bri-dge.com/short_takes/short24.html). My thanks to Laura Peers of the Pitt-Rivers Museum, Oxford, for her advice on this topic in general and for the Irving reference in particular.

34. Lafitau, *Customs of the American Indians*, 2:21; Morgan, *League of the Iroquois*, 366.

35. See Feest, *Native Arts*, 58–60. Examples of such "bark sgraffito" come from later centuries; we have no definite information on the use of such techniques in Tekakwitha's day.

36. Lafitau, *Customs of the American Indians*, 2:97. On mats, see also ibid., 2:21; Sagard, *Long Journey*, 102.

37. Morgan, *League of the Iroquois*, 370–72; Arthur C. Parker, "Iroquois Uses of Maize and Other Food Plants," in *Parker on the Iroquois*, ed. William Fenton (Syracuse, N.Y.: Syracuse University Press, 1968), 46–49; Lafitau, *Customs of the American Indians*, 2:59. On the similar culinary practices of the Hurons, see Champlain, *Works*, 3:125–30; Trigger, *Children of Aataentsic*, 37.

38. Carolyn Niethammer, *Daughters of the Earth: The Lives and Legends of American Indian Women* (New York: Macmillan, 1977), 108.

39. Parker, "Iroquois Uses of Maize," 36–37, 44.

40. James W. Herrick, *Iroquois Medical Botany*, ed. Dean Snow (Syracuse, N.Y.: Syracuse University Press, 1995), 85.

41. Chauchetière, "La vie," 31 (*Pos*, 137).

42. Parker, "Iroquois Uses of Maize," 23–27

43. Snow, *The Iroquois*, 69.

44. Ibid., 70.

45. Johansen and Mann, *Encyclopedia of the Haudenosaunee*, 314. Note that much of what has been published about "Iroquois culture" follows the conventions of traditional anthropology, which tended to ignore history and describe native customs as though they existed in a timeless past. It is clear that ritual practices changed a great deal in the centuries following Tekakwitha's lifetime, partly, but not entirely, through contact with Christianity and other European influences. However, there is no way of knowing with any certainty whether or not invocations of "the Creator"—mentioned in nineteenth- and twentieth-century descriptions of the Planting Ceremony—reflect the foreign influence of monotheism.

46. Inga Clendinnen, *Aztecs: An Interpretation* (Cambridge: Cambridge University Press, 1991), 29–30; Ramon A. Gutiérrez, *When Jesus Came, the Corn Mothers Went Away: Marriage, Sexuality, and Power in New Mexico, 1500–1846* (Stanford, Calif.: Stanford University Press, 1991), 27–30.

47. Chauchetière, "La vie," 75 (*Pos*, 170).

48. Chauchetière, "La vie," 13 (*Pos*, 121).

49. Chauchetière, "La vie," 75 (*Pos*, 170).

50. Chauchetière, "La vie," 20 (*Pos*, 125).

51. On Iroquoian marriage customs, see Snow, *The Iroquois*, 129; Trigger, *Children of Aataentsic*, 49–50; Lafitau, *Customs of the American Indians*, 1:340.

52. Presumably it was at this point that she became "Tekakwitha." Prior to the initiation she must have had a different name, one never revealed in any of the documents. For want of an alternative, I have referred to her as "Tekakwitha" throughout.

53. Lafitau, *Customs of the American Indians*, 1:217. On menstrual seclusion, see ibid., 1:178; Anthony F. C. Wallace, *The Death and Rebirth of the Seneca* (New York: Random House, 1969), 38.

54. Chauchetière, "La vie," 18 (*Pos*, 124).

55. Archives de la ville de Poitiers, cassier 48, 1661; "Journal d'Antoine Denesde, marchand ferron à Poitiers et de Marie Barré sa femme (1628–1687)," in *Archives historiques du Poitou* (Poitiers: Imprimerie Oudin, 1885), 59, 79–80, 134, 143–44, 188–90, 193.

56. Donald Crawford, ed., *Journals of Sir John Lauder Lord Fountainhall with His Observations on Public Affairs and Other Memoranda 1665–1676* (Edinburgh: Scottish Historical Society, 1900), 119.

57. François LeMercier, Relation of 1669–70, JR 53:136–59.

58. The journey from Montreal to the Mohawk country is related in François Le Mercier, Relation of 1667–68, JR 51:178–219 (an updated English translation of this document can be found in Allan Greer, ed., *The Jesuit Relations: Natives and Missionaries in Seventeenth-Century North America* [Boston: Bedford Books, 2000], 137–40; quotation at 138–39). See also Trigger, *Natives and Newcomers*, 289–96.

59. Jean Pierron, Relation of 1669–70, JR 53:200–37 (Greer, *Jesuit Relations*, 142–46).

60. Jean Pierron, Relation of 1669–70, JR 53:201 (Greer, *Jesuit Relations*, 141).

61. Chauchetière, La vie, 39 (*Pos*, 135).

62. Daniel Richter's work on this subject is of fundamental importance, and I have relied heavily in what follows on his interpretations of Iroquois history. Daniel K. Richter, "Iroquois versus Iroquois: Jesuit Mission and Christianity in Village Politics, 1642–1686," *Ethnohistory* 32 (1985): 1–16; Richter, *Ordeal of the Longhouse*, 105–28.

63. Relation of 1672–73, JR 57:89.

64. Chauchetière, "La vie," 31–32 (*Pos*, 136).

65. Chauchetière, "La vie," 32 (*Pos*, 136) (emphasis added).

66. Chauchetière, "La vie," 32–33 (*Pos*, 136). Cholenec says the priest spent "the entire winter in teaching her thoroughly," but he provides no indication as to the nature and content of that teaching. Cholenec, "Vie de Catherine Tegakouita," 6 (*Pos*, 245).

67. Chauchetière, "La vie," 33 (*Pos*, 136–37).

68. Chauchetière has her meeting Lamberville in "the spring" and then proceeding to baptism on Easter Sunday 1675. Cholenec says she met the missionary in the autumn of 1676 and was baptized on "Easter," presumably Easter 1677, except that Cholenec later has her leaving for Kahnawake in the autumn of 1677, one and a half years after her baptism. The church authorities who prepared the brief for her beatification in the 1930s decided, quite reasonably, that she must have received baptism in the spring of 1676, but there seems no way of determining the duration of her instruction. Chauchetière, "La vie," 30–34; Cholenec, "Vie de Catherine Tegakouita," 5–7 (*Pos*, 20, 135–37, 244–46).

69. Cholenec, "Vie de Catherine Tegakouita," 6 (*Pos*, 245).

70. Chauchetière, "La vie," 58 (*Pos*, 154).

71. On names and personal identities, see Richard White, "'Although I am dead, I am not entirely dead, I have left a second of myself': Constructing Self and Persons on the Middle Ground of Early America," in *Through a Glass Darkly: Reflections on Personal Identity in Early America*, ed. Ronald Hoffman, Mechal Sobel, and Frerika J. Teute (Chapel Hill: University of North Carolina Press, 1997), 404–18.

72. Chauchetière, "La vie," 73 (*Pos*, 169).

73. Chauchetière, "La vie," 35 (*Pos*, 138).

74. Chauchetière, "La vie," 35–36 (*Pos*, 138).

75. Lafitau, *Customs of the American Indians*, 1:234.

76. Wallace, *Death and Rebirth*, 59–75. On analogous Huron customs and beliefs, see Greer, *Jesuit Relations*, 48–49, 77. On the Mohawk midwinter ceremony as celebrated in more recent times, see Johansen and Mann, *Encyclopedia of the Haudenosaunee*, 52–53, 203; Snow, *The Iroquois*, 7.

77. Jérôme Lalemant, Relation of 1639, JR 17:147 (Greer, *Jesuit Relations*, 76).

78. Claude Dablon, Relation of 1672–73, JR 57:68–75.

79. Trigger, *Natives and Newcomers*, 101; Richter, *Ordeal of the Longhouse*, 119.

80. Chauchetière, "La vie," 37–40; Archives françaises de la Compagnie de Jésus, Fonds Brotier, A6–2, vol. 162:152, "Abbrégé de la vie de Catherine Tegaskouita chretienne iroquoise" (*Pos*, 78–90, 139–41, 246–48).

81. See, for example, the story of Saint Margaret as recounted in Jacobus de Voraigne, *The Golden Legend: Readings on the Saints*, trans. W. G. Ryan, 2 vols. (Princeton, N.J.: Princeton University Press, 1993), 1:368–70.

82. Chauchetière, "La vie," 56–58 (*Pos*, 152–54); Cholenec, "Vie de Catherine Tegakouita," 9–10 (*Pos*, 246–48).

Chapter 3

1. ASJCF, ms. 390, "Notes autobiographiques du P. Claude Chauchetière," 7 August 1695 (hereafter Chauchetière autobiography). The original version of this document has never been found. I used the manuscript copy made by Father Felix Martin in 1881 and held at the Canadian Jesuit archives at St.-Jérôme, Quebec.

2. ARSI, Catalogi breves, Aquitania 7, 1670–99.

3. On seventeenth-century Montreal, see Louise Dechêne, *Habitants and Merchants in Seventeenth-Century Montreal*, trans. L. Vardi (Montreal: McGill–Queen's University Press, 1992); Yves Landry, ed., *Pour le Christ et le Roi: La vie au temps des premiers Montréalais* (Montreal: Editions Libre Expression, 1992).

4. ASJCF, A20, Claude Chauchetière to Jean Chauchetière, 7 August 1694 (JR 64:116–41); ASJCF, A12, Claude Chauchetière to Jacques Jouheneau, 20 September 1694 (JR 64:142–57).

5. Donald Crawford, ed., *Journals of Sir John Lauder Lord Fountainhall with His Observations on Public Affairs and Other Memoranda 1665–1676* (Edinburgh: Scottish Historical Society, 1900), 101.

6. Bibliothèque municipal de Poitiers, registres paroissiaux, St-Porchaire; Charles

Babinet, "Le présidal de Poitiers: Son personel de 1551 à 1790," *Bulletin et mémoires de la société des antiquaires de l'ouest* 25 (1901):151–340.

7. H. Beauchet-Filleau and Charles de Chergé, *Dictionnaire historique et généalogique des familles du Poitou*, 6 vols. (Poitiers: Oudin, 1895), 2:340–41. The records give no definite information about the social background of Claude's mother, Elizabeth de la Noue; the parish registers refer to her as "Dame Elizabeth de la Noue," suggesting aristocratic connections, but it is hard to be sure of her social status, since priests and notaries tended to award such honorifics very freely. After Elizabeth's death, Jehan Chauchetière married Dame Susanne Brunet (1655), who came from a high echelon of the local elite, her father being "avocat au parlement" and seigneur of a rural fief.

8. Jacques Péret, "De la Renaissance à Louis XIV," in *Histoire de Poitiers*, ed. Robert Favreau (Toulouse: Privat, 1985), 203–9. On the establishment of the Jesuits at Poitiers, see Pierre Delattre, *Les établissements des Jésuites en France*, 5 vols. (Enghien, Belgium: Institut supérieur de théologie, 1949–57), 4:3–43.

9. For a recent survey of the subject and of its literature, see R. Po-Chia Hsia, *The World of Catholic Renewal 1540–1770* (Cambridge: Cambridge University Press, 1998). See also Marvin R. O'Connell, *The Counter Reformation, 1559–1610* (New York: Harper and Row, 1974); Jean Delumeau, *Catholicism between Luther and Voltaire: A New View of the Catholic Reform* (London: Burns and Oates, 1977); A. D. Wright, *The Counter-Reformation: Catholic Europe and the Non-Christian World* (New York: St. Martin's Press, 1982). This last work, like Po-Chia Hsia's textbook, helpfully takes a global approach to a topic that is usually considered as a purely European phenomenon.

10. Claude says almost nothing about his schooling in the autobiography. The basic program took five years, and Chauchetière entered his novitiate at eighteen, and so it is inferred that he came to the Jesuits at age thirteen.

11. Delattre, *Les établissements des Jésuites*, 4:3–43; Joseph Delfour, *Les Jesuites à Poitiers (1604–1762)* (Paris: Hachette, 1902).

12. John W. O'Malley, *The First Jesuits* (Cambridge, Mass.: Harvard University Press, 1993), 200–241; J. C. H. Aveling, *The Jesuits* (London: Blond and Briggs, 1981), 214. On the *Ratio Studiorum* as taught in French Jesuit colleges of the period, see also Delfour, *Les Jesuites à Poitiers*, 262–70; G. Dupont-Ferrier, *Du Collège de Clermont au lycée Louis-le-Grand: La vie quotidienne d'un collège parisien (1563–1920)*, 3 vols. (Paris: E. de Boccard, 1922–25), vol. 1, passim. See also Christopher Chapple, ed., *The Jesuit Tradition in Education and Missions: A 450-Year Perspective* (Scranton, Pa.: University of Scranton Press, 1993).

13. François Dainville, "L'évolution de l'enseignement de la rhétorique au dix-septième siècle," in *L'éducation des Jésuites XVIIe–XVIIIe siècles* (Paris: Minuit, 1978), 185–208; Marc Fumaroli, *L'age de l'éloquence: Rhétorique et "res literaria" de la Renaissance au seuil de l'époque classique* (Geneva: Librairie Droz, 1980).

14. On the program at the Poitiers Jesuit college, see Delfour, *Les Jésuites à Poitiers*, 262–70.

15. Lynn Martin, *The Jesuit Mind: The Mentality of an Elite in Early Modern France* (Ithaca, N.Y.: Cornell University Press, 1988), 62.

16. *The Constitutions of the Society of Jesus* (London: J. G. and F. Rivington, 1838).

17. Pedro de Ribadeneira, quoted in François Dainville, *La naissance de l'humanisme moderne* (Paris: Beauchesne, 1940), 37 (my translation). See also Philippe Ariès, *L'enfant et la vie familial sous l'ancien régime* (Paris: Plon, 1960); Georges Snyders, *La pédagogie en France aux XVIIe et XVIIIe siècles* (Paris: P.U.F., 1964).

18. The literature on the early modern Jesuits is immense, though there is no satisfactory survey. John O'Malley's authoritative study, *The First Jesuits*, covers only the sixteenth century. In addition to O'Malley, I found the following general works useful: Aveling, *The Jesuits*; Luce Giard and Louis de Vaucelles, eds., *Les Jésuites à l'âge baroque 1540–1640* (Grenoble: Jérôme Millon, 1996); Jean Lacouture, *Jesuits: A Multibiography*, trans. Jeremy Leggatt (London: Harvill Press, 1996); and Anthony Grafton, "The Soul's Entrepreneurs," *New York Review of Books*, 3 March 1994, 33–37.

19. Quoted in O'Malley, *The First Jesuits*, 68

20. O'Malley, *The First Jesuits*, 239.

21. Ignatius of Loyola, *The Spiritual Exercises*, trans. T. Corbishley (London: Burns and Oates, 1963); Adrien Demoustier, "L'originalité des 'Exercises spirituels,'" in Giard and Vaucelles, *Les Jésuites à l'âge baroque*, 23–35.

22. *Constitutions of the Society of Jesus*, 22.

23. ARSI, Aquitania 10, Catalogi triennales, 1651–65.

24. Chauchetière autobiography, 6, 8. A modern guidebook comes to a similar verdict on Tulle: "a strange, unattractive-looking place . . . grey, run-down." Kate Baillie and Tim Salmon, *The Rough Guide to France* (London: Rough Guides, 2001), 656.

25. Javier Melloni, *The Exercises of St. Ignatius of Loyola in the Western Tradition* (Leominster: Gracewing, 2000).

26. Chauchetière autobiography, 5–6.

27. The classic work on the subject is William James, *The Varieties of Religious Experience: A Study in Human Nature* (London: Longmans, Green, 1902), 189–258.

28. Chauchetière autobiography, 6–7.

29. Ibid., 6.

30. See Grace M. Jantzen, *Power, Gender and Christian Mysticism* (Cambridge: Cambridge University Press, 1995).

31. Mino Bergamo, *La science des saints: Le discours mystique au XVIIe siècle en France* (Grenoble: Jérôme Millon, 1992), 11. See also Jacques LeGoff and René Rémond, eds., *Histoire de la France Religieuse*, vol. 2, *Du Christianism flamboyant à l'aube des Lumières* (Paris: Seuil, 1988), 342–60; and, on the literary aspects of the "mystic invasion" of France, Henri Brémond, *Histoire littéraire du sentiment religieux en France depuis la fin des guerres de religion jusqu'à nos jours*, 11 vols. (Paris: Bloud et Gay, 1929–33), vol. 1.

32. Michel de Certeau, *The Mystic Fable*, vol. 1, *The Sixteenth and Seventeenth Centuries* (Chicago: University of Chicago Press, 1992), 241–70.

33. In what follows, I rely mainly on Certeau, *Mystic Fable*, and Bergamo, *La science des saints*.

34. François du Creux, *The History of Canada or New France*, ed. James B. Conacher, trans. Percy J. Robinson, 2 vols. (Toronto: Champlain Society, 1951), 2:551–55.

35. Certeau, *Mystic Fable*, 26.

36. Michel de Certeau, "L'illettré éclairé dans l'histoire de la lettre de Surin sur le Jeune

Homme du coche (1630)," *Revue d'ascétique et de mystique* 44 (1968): 369–412; Certeau, *Mystic Fable*, 206–40.

37. Bergamo, *La science des saints*, 123–60.

38. "Je veux paraître en ce monde un sauvage, / En méprisant ses plus sévères lois. / Ce m'est tout un, que je vive ou je meure, / Il me suffit, que l'Amour me demeure." Jean-Joseph Surin, "De l'abandon intérieure, pour se disposer à la perfection de l'Amour Divin," quoted in ibid., 45.

39. Bergamo, *La science des saints*, 123–60. It has been said that exoticism was a French specialty in the early modern centuries. From Montaigne and Jean de Léry to Montesquieu and Diderot, French intellectuals, secular as well as religious, displayed a sympathetic interest in distant lands with strange people and unfamiliar customs, evoking them as a device for critiquing European civilization or as a medium for reflecting on human nature. Critics of exoticism emphasize the basic ethnocentrism that generally lay concealed beneath the apparent interest in the Other. The feathered headdress was only regarded as significant, they suggest, when displayed in a European museum, and the native village only took on meaning when imagined with a European observer placed in its midst. No doubt it is true that travel writings of the period, like Surin's accounts of his spiritual and metaphoric voyages, were predominantly projections outward from an observing position that was assumed to be central. Only exceptionally and to a limited degree could this sort of discourse on the inspired illiterate or the noble savage lead to a shifting of the center and an opening to the possibility that peasants or natives might possess a full human reality worthy of respect even if it did not simply represent the antithesis of civilization's ills. See Roger Célestin, *From Cannibals to Radicals: Figures and Limits of Exoticism* (Minneapolis: University of Minnesota, Press 1996); Peter Mason, *Infelicities: Representations of the Exotic* (Baltimore: Johns Hopkins University Press, 1998).

40. Chauchetière autobiography, 8.

41. Ibid., 9–11 (emphasis in original).

42. Francis Xavier to his companions in Rome, 15 January 1544, *The Letters and Instructions of Francis Xavier* (St. Louis, Mo.: Institute of Jesuit Sources, 1992), 67–68 (emphasis in original).

43. Joseph de Guibert, *The Jesuits: Their Spiritual Doctrine and Practice: A Historical Study*, trans. W. J. Young (Chicago: Institute of Jesuit Sources, 1964), 288n.

44. On devotional confraternities (sodalities), see Louis Chatellier, *L'Europe des dévôts* (Paris: Flammarion, 1987). On rural missions, see Alain Croix, *La Bretagne aux 16e et 17e siècles: La vie, la mort, la foi*, 2 vols. (Paris: Maloine, 1981), esp. 1211–40; Bernard Dompnier, "La Compagnie de Jésus et la mission de l'intérieur," in Giard and Vaucelles, *Les Jésuites à l'âge baroque*, 155–79. On the connections linking internal missions in France and overseas missions to New France, see Dominique Deslandres, "Le modèle français d'intégration socio-religieuse, 1600–1650: Missions intérieures et premières missions canadiennes" (Ph.D. diss., University of Montreal, 1990).

45. Some older works provide good global overviews of Jesuit missionary activities in the period: Kenneth S. Latourette, *A History of the Expansion of Christianity*, 4 vols. (New York: Harper, 1939); Mgr. S. Delacroix, *Histoire universelle des missions catholiques*, 4 vols.

(Paris: Grund, 1956–59); G. de Vaumas, *L'Eveil missionnaire de la France au XVIIe siècle* (Paris: Bloud and Gay, 1959). On the Jesuits in Asia, see Jonathan Spence, *The Memory Palace of Matteo Ricci* (New York: Penguin, 1984); Stephen Neill, *A History of Christianity in India: The Beginnings to AD 1707* (Cambridge: Cambridge University Press, 1984); J. F. Moran, *The Japanese and the Jesuits: Alessandro Valignano in Sixteenth-Century Japan* (London: Routledge, 1993); Ines G. Zupanov, *Disputed Mission: Jesuit Experiments and Brahmanical Knowledge in Seventeenth-Century South India* (New Delhi: Oxford University Press, 1999). The Jesuit missions in colonial Latin America are covered in the following works: Maxime Haubert, *La vie quotidienne au Paraguay sous les jésuites* (Paris: Hachette, 1967); Philip Caraman, *The Lost Paradise: An Account of the Jesuits in Paraguay 1607–1768* (London: Sidgwick and Jackson, 1975); Dauril Alden, *The Making of an Enterprise: The Society of Jesus in Portugal, Its Empire, and Beyond 1540–1750* (Stanford, Calif.: Stanford University Press, 1996). Important primary works on the Jesuit missions of colonial Latin America include Antonio Ruiz de Montoya, *The Spiritual Conquest Accomplished by the Religious of the Society of Jesus in the Provinces of Paraguay, Parana, Uruguay, and Tape*, ed. and trans. C. J. McNaspy (St. Louis, Mo.: Institute of Jesuit Sources, 1993); Andrés Pérez de Ribas, *History of the Triumphs of Our Holy Faith amongst the Most Barbarous and Fierce Peoples of the New World* [1645], trans. Daniel Reff, Maureen Ahern, and Richard Danford (Tucson: University of Arizona Press, 1999).

46. Chauchetière autobiography, 12. Louis Lallement, an influential French Jesuit, judged the Canadian mission field to be "plus féconde en travaux & en croix, elle est moins éclatante, & contribue plus que les autres à la sanctification de ces missionnaires." Lallement, *La doctrine spirituelle de Louis Lallement*, ed. Champion (1685), 10, cited in Peter Goddard, "The Devil in New France: Jesuit Demonology, 1611–1650," *Canadian Historical Review* 78 (1997): 50n51.

47. Deslandres, "Le modèle français d'intégration socio-religieuse," 203–6; Giovanni Pizzorusso, "Le choix indifférent: Mentalités et attentes des jésuites aspirants missionnaires dans l'Amérique française au XVIIe siècle," *Mélanges de l'école française de Rome—Italie et Méditerranée* 109 (1997): 881–94.

48. See Peter N. Moogk, "Reluctant Exiles: Emigrants from France in Canada before 1760," *William and Mary Quarterly*, 3rd ser., 46 (1989): 463–505.

49. Guy Laflèche, *Les saints martyrs canadiens*, 5 vols. (Laval, Quebec: Singulier, 1988–95); Allan Greer, "Colonial Saints: Gender, Race, and Hagiography in New France," *William and Mary Quarterly*, 3rd ser, 57 (2000): 323–48.

50. James P. Ronda, "The Sillery Experiment: A Jesuit-Indian Village in New France, 1637–1663," *American Indian Culture and Research Journal* 3 (1979): 1–18; Marc Jetten, *Enclaves amérindiennes: Les "réductions" du Canada 1637–1701* (Quebec: Septentrion, 1994), 30–56.

51. See, for example, Jérôme Lalement's bitter reflections on the disappointing progress of the faith among the Hurons. Those Indians, he explained, remained perfectly free, while the missionaries had no help, either from God, who had so far withheld miracles of the sort that had aided Francis Xavier, or from the colonial state. "We cannot here have force at hand, and the support of that sharp sword which serves the Church in so holy a manner to give authority to her Decrees, to maintain Justice, and curb the insolence of those who trample under foot the holiness of her

Mysteries." Relation of 1644–45, JR 28:55. See Carole Blackburn, *Harvest of Souls: The Jesuit Missions and Colonialism in North America, 1632–1650* (Montreal: McGill–Queen's University Press, 2000), 105–28.

52. Marie de l'Incarnation to Mère Marie-Gillette Roland, 4 September 1640, in *Word from New France: The Selected Letters of Marie de l'Incarnation*, ed. and trans. Joyce Marshall, (Toronto: Oxford University Press, 1967), 81. On Marie de l'Incarnation, see Natalie Z. Davis, *Women on the Margins: Three Seventeenth-Century Lives* (Cambridge, Mass.: Harvard University Press, 1995), 63–139.

53. Chauchetière autobiography, 13.

54. Ibid.

55. Claude Chauchetière, *Narration de la mission du Sault depuis sa fondation jusqu'en 1686*, ed. Hélène Avisseau (1686; Bordeaux: Archives dèpartementales de la Gironde, 1984), 20; Chauchetière autobiography, 13.

56. This paragraph is inspired by Caroline Walker Bynum's discussion of gender reversals in *Holy Feast and Holy Fast: The Religious Significance of Food to Medieval Women* (Berkeley: University of California Press, 1987), 295. On a different version of colonial cross-dressing, see Anne McClintock, *Imperial Leather: Race, Gender and Sexuality in the Colonial Contest* (New York: Routledge, 1995), 65–71.

57. ARSI, Aquitania 11, Catalogi triennales, 1669–81.

58. Chauchetière autobiography, 13.

59. ARSI, Francia 16, Catalogi triennales, folio 385v. Note that Claude took the "tertiary vows," becoming thereby a "spiritual coadjutor." Men who had completed their theology and secured a university degree (Pierre Cholenec was in this situation) took a fourth vow and entered the order in an elite category as "professed" fathers "of the four vows," but Claude would remain at the lower rank. The distinction was a technical one, largely invisible to the outside world; he performed the same functions as any other Jesuit, though his lack of a degree probably prevented him being appointed to supervisory positions. De Certeau says that the difference between spiritual coadjutors and "professed of the four vows" was purely a matter of educational, rather than spiritual, attainments. He suggests that the majority of French Jesuits were in the former category. The Jesuit *Constitutions*, out of a concern to curtail "ambition," prohibited coadjutors from advancing into the professed rank. De Certeau, *Mystic Fable*, 353n5; *Constitutions of the Society of Jesus*, 6.

60. *Dictionary of Canadian Biography* (Toronto: University of Toronto Press, 1966–), 2:144; ARSI, Catalogi triennales, Francia 13, folio 357v, folio 407v; Francia 14, folio 26, f.82; Francia 15, folio 60v, 108v.

61. Chauchetière refers to the correspondence in his autobiography: "Il y a 17 ans que vous m'éscrivites une lettre dans laquelle je vous voyois fort en doute sur ma vocation au Canada." (1).

62. Chauchetière autobiography, 1, 14.

63. ASJCF, A20, Chauchetière to Jean Chauchetière, 7 August 1694 (my translation). See also JR 64:131.

64. Chauchetière autobiography, 15.

65. Ibid., 14; National Archives of Canada, MG17, A6-2, Compagnie de Jésus, province de Paris, fonds Canada, box 16, number 3, death notice of Claude Chauchetière.

Chapter 4

1. On the early history of Montreal, see Gustave Lanctot, *Montreal under Maisonneuve, 1642–1665*, trans. Alta Lind Cook (Toronto: Clarke Irwin, 1969); Louise Dechêne, *Habitants and Merchants in Seventeenth-Century Montreal*, trans. L. Vardi (Montreal: McGill–Queen's University Press, 1992); Yves Landry, ed., *Pour le Christ et le Roi: La vie au temps des premiers Montréalais* (Montreal: Editions Libre Expression, 1992).

2. Bruce G. Trigger, *The Children of Aataentsic: A History of the Huron People to 1660* (Montreal: McGill–Queen's University Press, 1976), 218–24.

3. Pierre Cholenec, "Of the Mission of St. François Xavier du Sault near Montreal," 2 January 1677, JR 60:276–77 (original, ASQ, manuscript 216); Claude Chauchetière, *Narration de la mission du Sault depuis sa fondation jusqu'en 1686*, ed. Hélène Avisseau (1686; Bordeaux: Archives départementales de la Gironde, 1984), 38–40. Note that the site of Kahnawake has shifted over the years; now located above the Lachine rapids (Sault St. Louis), it stood just below them in 1680. On the history of Kahnawake, see Edward James Devine, *Historic Caughnawaga* (Montreal: Messenger Press, 1922); Henri Béchard, *The Original Caughnawaga Indians* (Montreal: International Publishers, 1976); Cole Harris, ed. *Historical Atlas of Canada*, vol. 1, *From the Beginning to 1800* (Toronto: University of Toronto Press, 1987), plate 47; Marc Jetten, *Enclaves amérindiennes: Les "réductions" du Canada 1637–1701* (Quebec: Septentrion, 1994); Gretchen Green, "A New People in an Age of War: The Kahnawake Iroquois, 1667–1760" (Ph.D. diss., College of William and Mary, 1991); Denys Delâge, "Les Iroquois chrétiens des 'réductions,' 1667–1770: I—Migration et rapports avec les Français," *Recherches amérindiennes au Québec* 21 nos., 1–2 (1991): 59–70; Denys Delâge, "Les Iroquois chrétiens des 'réductions,' 1667–1770: II—Rapports avec la Ligue iroquoise, les Britanniques et les autres nations autochtones," *Recherches amérindiennes au Québec* 21, no. 3 (1991): 39–50; Archives nationales du Québec, Documents concernant les concessions de terre, 1676–1762, Sault St-Louis.

4. Letter of R. P. Jacques Bruyas, 21 January 1668, JR 51:119–43. The account that follows is based on Bruyas's letter, supplemented by two documents by Claude Chauchetière: "La vie," 343, 58–68 (*Pos*, 154–62); Chauchetière, *Narration*, 20–24.

5. "Letter from Reverend Father Jacques Bruyas," JR 51:118–43, quotation at 123.

6. Such a possibility is suggested by Bruce Trigger's discussion of Joseph Chiouatenhoua, the leading Huron convert in the early years of the first Huron mission. Chiouatenhoua was almost the only baptized adult in Huronia during the late 1630s, and though the Jesuits portrayed him as a religious hero, Trigger thinks he was more likely an opportunist seeking to enhance his influence in Huron society by controlling access to French goods. Trigger, *Children of Aataentsic*, 600. See also Denis Lafrenière, "L'éloge de l'Indien dans les Relations des Jésuites," *Canadian Literature*, no. 131 (Winter 1991): 26–35.

7. Gandeacteua died before Chauchetière arrived in Canada. In writing of her, he appears to have drawn on the recollections of fellow Jesuits and of native residents of Kahnawake.

8. For the general context of this northward migration, see Daniel K. Richter, "Iroquois versus Iroquois: Jesuit Mission and Christianity in Village Politics, 1642–1686,"

Ethnohistory 32 (1985): 1–16; and Daniel K. Richter, *The Ordeal of the Longhouse: The Peoples of the Iroquois League in the Era of European Colonization* (Chapel Hill: University of North Carolina Press, 1992), 105–32. On its western branch, see Victor Konrad, "An Iroquois Frontier: The North Shore of Lake Ontario during the Late Seventeenth Century," *Journal of Historical Geography* 7 (1981): 129–44. The missionary bias of the Jesuit sources has led scholars to treat the movement to the St. Lawrence settlement as an isolated phenomenon, mainly the product of evangelization. The Iroquois settlements near Montreal did develop unique characteristics as a consequence of their Catholic character and close proximity to the French, but these developed only after the migration took place. Through the late 1660s and early 1670s, people moved back and forth between the Montreal area and the new settlements north of Lake Ontario.

9. On the early history of La Prairie, see, in addition to Claude Chauchetière's primary accounts, John Demos, *The Unredeemed Captive: A Family Story from Early America* (New York: Random House, 1994), 122–31.

10. Louis Lavallée, *La Prairie en Nouvelle-France 1647–1760: Etude d'histoire sociale* (Montreal: McGill–Queen's University Press, 1992).

11. Jennifer S. H. Brown, *Strangers in Blood: Fur Trade Company Families in Indian Country* (Vancouver: University of British Columbia Press, 1980); Cornelius J. Jaenen, *Friend and Foe: Aspects of French-Amerindian Cultural Contact in the Sixteenth and Seventeenth Centuries* (Toronto: McClelland and Stewart, 1976), 161–65.

12. Dean Snow, *The Iroquois* (Oxford: Blackwell, 1994), 120–21.

13. In various documents from the early 1670s, Jesuits refer to the La Prairie/Kentake settlement as a "Huron colony," a "church composed entirely of different nations," and the "Iroquois Mission of St. François Xavier." Relation of 1672–73, JR 57:75, 145; Relation of 1675, JR 59:289.

14. Louise Tremblay, "La politique missionaire des Sulpiciens au XVIIe et début XVIIIe siècle, 1668–1735" (master's thesis, University of Montréal, 1981), 49–57; Lucien Campeau, "Roman Catholic Missions in New France," in *Handbook of North American Indians*, vol. 4, *History of Indian-White Relations*, ed. Wilcomb E. Washburn (Washington, D.C.: Smithsonian Institution, 1988), 468; Green, "A New People in an Age of War," 42–44.

15. Chauchetière, *Narration*, 26–27; Relation of 1672–73, JR 58:77; "Of the Mission of St. Francis-Xavier du Sault near Montreal," JR 60:275–93.

16. Chauchetière, *Narration*, 27.

17. Bacqueville de la Potherie, *Histoire de l'Amérique septentrionale*, 4 vols. (Paris: Chez Borcas 1753), 1:360–64. See also Joseph-François Lafitau, *Customs of the American Indians Compared with the Customs of Primitive Times*, ed. and trans. William N. Fenton and Elizabeth L. Moore, 2 vols. (Toronto: Champlain Society, 1974), passim.

18. "Lettre du père Nau au père Bonin [2 October 1735]," *Rapport de l'Archiviste de la Province de Québec*, 1926–27, p. 283

19. See James Axtell, *The Invasion Within: The Contest of Cultures in Colonial North America* (New York: Oxford University Press, 1985), 68–70; Jaenen, *Friend and Foe*, 180; Jetten, *Enclaves amérindiennes*, 123–28.

20. Jan Grabowski, "The Common Ground: Settled Natives and French in Montréal,

1667–1760" (Ph.D. diss., University of Montreal, 1993), 155. In another murder case, this one dating from 1722, the relatives of the accused, a Kahnawake Iroquois, gave presents to the family of the French-Canadian victim, "covering" the blood-shed and compensating the mourners as required by native custom. The government released the murderer, and the conflict between French and Iroquoian justice concluded with the triumph of the latter. W. J. Eccles, "Sovereignty Association, 1500–1783," in *Essays on New France* (Toronto: Oxford University Press, 1987), 214n58.

21. Richard White, *The Middle Ground: Indians, Empires, and Republics in the Great Lakes Region, 1650–1815* (Cambridge: Cambridge University Press, 1991).

22. On the broader dimensions of the conflict, see Francis Jennings, *The Ambiguous Iroquois Empire: The Covenant Chain Confederation of Indian Tribes with English Colonies from Its Beginnings to the Lancaster Treaty of 1744* (New York: Norton, 1984), 172–85; Richter, *Ordeal of the Longhouse*, 133–61. The difficulties of the Kahnawake Iroquois are detailed in Green, "A New People in an Age of War," 68–103.

23. Chauchetière, *Narration*, 28. The Jesuits claimed, quite plausibly, that the prohibition of alcohol served to attract many Iroquois to Kentake/La Prairie. See, for example, Relation of 1679, JR 61:238–41.

24. On the linguistic obstacles to the communication of Christian doctrine, see John Steckley, "The Warrior and the Lineage: Jesuit Use of Iroquoian Images to Communicate Christianity," *Ethnohistory* 39 (fall 1992): 478–509; Allan Greer, "Conversion and Identity: Iroquois Christianity in Seventeenth-Century New France," in *Conversions: Old Worlds and New*, ed. Kenneth Mills and Anthony Grafton (Rochester, N.Y.: University of Rochester Press, 2003), 175–98.

25. See, for example, Chauchetière, "La vie," 47 (*Pos*, 146).

26. Chauchetière, *Narration*, 51.

27. "Of the Mission of St. François Xavier du Sault near Montreal, 2 January 1677," JR 60:290.

28. Alternating male and female choral singing is a feature of the Iroquois Feast of the Dead as celebrated in present-day Kahnawake. Brian Deer, personal communication.

29. "Letter of Claude Chauchetière, respecting the Iroquois Mission of Sault St. François Xavier, near Montreal [14 October 1682]," JR 62:166–87, quotation at 189.

30. Kenneth Morrison makes a similar point in relation to the Montagnais converted to Christianity by the Jesuits earlier in the seventeenth century: "Baptism and Alliance: The Symbolic Mediations of Religious Syncretism," *Ethnohistory* 37 (Fall 1990): 416–37. Iroquoian approaches to alliance are examined in Trigger, *Children of Aataentsic*, passim.

31. Axtell, *Invasion Within*, 220.

32. Of the Maya of Yucatan, Nancy Farriss writes: "Acknowledging the political sovereignty of the Spanish king and acknowledging the spiritual sovereignty of the Christian God must have appeared at first as familiar and related acts of vassalage from a defeated people." Nancy M. Farriss, *Maya Society under Colonial Rule: The Collective Enterprise of Survival* (Princeton, N.J.: Princeton University Press, 1984), 286.

33. Chauchetière, *Narration*, 32.

34. Relation of 1675, JR 59:265; Chauchetière, *Narration*, 34–35.

35. Relation of 1675, JR 60:31–41.

36. In their study of conversion to Christianity in nineteenth-century southern Africa, Jean Comaroff and John Comaroff write:

> Through such reactions "native peoples" seek to plumb the depths of the colonizing process. They search for the coherence—and, sometimes, the *deus ex machina*—that lies behind its visible face. For the recently colonized, or those who feel the vibrations of the imperial presence just over the horizon, generally believe that there is something invisible, something profound, happening to them—and that their future may well depend on gaining control over its "magic." Thus, for instance, many "Christianized" peoples the world over are, or once were, convinced that whites have a second, secret bible or set of rites (cricket? telegraphs? tea parties?) on which their power depends. The whimsical 'unreason' of such movements as cargo cults stems from precisely this conviction. These movements, as is now well known, are early efforts to capture and redeploy the colonialist's ability to produce value. And they are often seen as enough of a threat to elicit a punitive response.

Their basic insight—Christianization as a positive act of appropriation on the part of natives—seems broadly applicable and a valuable antidote to the common tendency to see converts as victims of assimilation, but their analysis cannot be transposed holus-bolus into seventeenth-century North America. For one thing, the "whites" in this case cut an altogether less impressive figure and the empire they represented was less overwhelming than that erected in the late Victorian period by the British in Africa. Jean Comaroff and John Comaroff, *Of Revelation and Revolution: Christianity, Colonialism, and Consciousness in South Africa*, 2 vols. (Chicago: University of Chicago Press, 1991), 1:31–32.

37. Relation of 1672–73, JR 58:76, 84; "Iroquois Mission of Saint François du Sault, during the Year 1677," JR 61:52.

38. Translated in 1974 as *Customs of the American Indians Compared with the Customs of Primitive Times.* William N. Fenton's ample introduction to this edition (1:xxix–cxix) provides exhaustive background on the author and the text.

39. According to Fenton, Lafitau was a rigorous ethnographer as well as a master of erudition. Fenton, "Introduction," in Lafitau, *Customs of the American Indians,* 1:lxxx.

40. Lafitau, *Customs of the American Indians,* 1:246, 1:243, 1:133.

41. Louis Hennepin, *A New Discovery of a Vast Country in America* [1698], ed. R. G. Thwaites (Chicago: A. C. McClurg, 1903), 587. See also the Recollet work sometimes attributed to Chretien Le Clercq, *First Establishment of the Faith in New France*, trans. J. G. Shea, 2 vols. (New York: J. G. Shea, 1881), 2:24–25.

42. Jesuits called the herdsmen of the Eboli region of southern Italy "men who had nothing human about them except their form . . . totally ignorant not only of prayers, or of the other special mysteries of the holy faith, but also of the very knowledge of God." Quoted in Carlo Ginzburg, *The Cheese and the Worms: The Cosmos of a Sixteenth-Century Miller,* trans. John Tedeschi and Anne Tedeschi (Harmondsworth: Penguin, 1982), 112.

43. William A. Christian Jr., *Local Religion in Sixteenth-Century Spain* (Princeton, N.J.: Princeton University Press, 1981).

Chapter 5

1. In addition to the works on Iroquois culture cited in this chapter and in chapter 2, see Elisabeth Tooker, ed., *Native North American Spirituality of the Eastern Woodlands: Sacred Myths, Dreams, Visions, Speeches, Healing Formulas, Rituals and Ceremonials* (New York: Paulist Press, 1979), 33–68, 268–81; Horatio Hale, ed., *The Iroquois Book of Rites* [1883], reprinted with an introduction by W. N. Fenton (Toronto: University of Toronto Press, 1963); Christopher Vecsey, "The Story and Structure of the Iroquois Confederacy," *Journal of the American Academy of Religion* 54 (1986): 79–106; James W. Herrick, *Iroquois Medical Botany*, ed. Dean Snow (Syracuse, N.Y.: Syracuse University Press, 1995).

2. In this respect, too, there were some basic similarities with the attitude of European laypeople of the period, especially peasants. The difference is that anticlerical feeling in Europe was fueled by the tithe and other clerical exactions, whereas the church in New France imposed no economic burdens on Indian converts.

3. See "Lettre du père Nau au père Bonin [2 October 1735]," *Rapport de l'Archiviste de la Province de Québec*, 1926–27, p. 283.

4. For the case of New Spain, see Robert Ricard, *The Spiritual Conquest of Mexico: An Essay on the Apostolate and the Evangelizing Methods of the Mendicant Orders in New Spain: 1523–1572*, trans. L. B. Simpson (Berkeley: University of California Press, 1966); Francisco Morales, *Ethnic and Social Background of the Franciscan Friars in Seventeenth-Century Mexico* (Washington, D.C.: Academy of American Franciscan History, 1973); Stafford Poole, "The Declining Image of the Indian among Churchmen in Sixteenth-Century New Spain," in *Indian-Religious Relations in Colonial Spanish America*, ed. Susan E. Ramirez (Syracuse, N.Y.: Syracuse University Press, 1989), 11–19; Stafford Poole, "Church Law on the Ordination of Indians and Castas in New Spain," *Hispanic American Historical Review* 61 (November 1981): 637–50.

5. Cornelius J. Jaenen, *Friend and Foe: Aspects of French-Amerindian Cultural Contact in the Sixteenth and Seventeenth Centuries* (Toronto: McClelland and Stewart, 1976), 165–75; James Axtell, *The Invasion Within: The Contest of Cultures in Colonial North America* (New York: Oxford University Press, 1985), 56–58.

6. There are a few exceptions to this rule: among the handful of girls raised in convents, inevitably some wanted to become nuns. One of them was, in fact, admitted, but it was a symbolic gesture on the part of the Quebec Hôtel-Dieu sisters: they only accepted her on the point of death. Lynn Berry, "Nuns and Natives: The Hôtels-Dieu of Quebec and Montreal and the Indians of New France" (master's thesis, York University, 1994), 27–28.

7. Insofar as Indians in the Spanish empire manifested an interest in joining the Catholic clergy, the demand came mainly from urban and Hispanicized elements of the native population.

8. Claude Chauchetière, *Narration de la mission du Sault depuis sa fondation jusqu'en 1686*, ed. Hélène Avisseau (1686; Bordeaux: Archives départementales de la Gironde, 1984), 35; Chauchetière, "La vie," 65 (*Pos*, 160).

9. On the Marian congregations and on European confraternities generally, see Louis Chatellier, *The Europe of the Devout: The Catholic Reformation and the Formation of a New Society*, trans. Jean Birrell (Cambridge: Cambridge University Press, 1989). On the confraternity of the Holy Family in New France, see Marie-Aimée Cliché, *Les Pratiques de*

dévotion en Nouvelle-France: Comportements populaires et encadrement ecclésial dans le gouvernement de Québec (Quebec: Les Presses de l'Université Laval, 1988), 158–65; Pierre Chaumonot, *Autobiographie du père Chaumonot et son complément par le R. P. Félix Martin* (Paris: H. Oudin, 1885), 58–66.

10. Nancy Shoemaker, "Kateri Tekakwitha's Tortuous Path to Sainthood," in *Negotiators of Change: Historical Perspectives on Native American Women*, ed. Nancy Shoemaker (New York: Routledge, 1995), 59, 61.

11. Snow, *The Iroquois* (Oxford: Blackwell, 1994), 101. See also Arthur C. Parker, "Secret Medicine Societies of the Seneca," *American Anthropologist* 11 (1909): 161-85.

12. James A. Tuck, "Northern Iroquoian Prehistory," in *Handbook of North American Indians*, vol. 15, Northeast, ed. Bruce G. Trigger (Washington, D.C.: Smithsonian Institution, 1978), 332. For a different view on the subject, see William N. Fenton, "Northern Iroquoian Culture Patterns," in ibid., 318.

13. Chauchetière, *Narration*, 42 (my translation).

14. "Letter of Father Claude Chauchetière, 14 October 1682," in *The Jesuit Relations: Natives and Missionaries in Seventeenth-Century North America*, ed. Allan Greer (Boston: Bedford Books, 2000), 150-51. For similar reports, see Chauchetière, *Narration*, 41–42; Relation of 1672–73, JR 58:74–89.

15. Cholenec, "Vie de Catherine Tegakouita," 45 (*Pos*, 282).

16. On ascetic practices at other Jesuit missions, see Marc Jetten, *Enclaves amérindiennes: Les "réductions" du Canada 1637-1701* (Quebec: Septentrion, 1994), 103–7; Relation of 1644–45 (Tadoussac), JR 27:190–201; Relation of 1645–46 (Huron), JR 30:38–41; Relation of 1663–64 (Lorette), JR 49:74–87; Relation of 1677–78 (Lorette), JR 61:34–55; letter of Jacques Bigot, Sillery, 24 June 1681, JR 62:43–45,

17. John W. O'Malley, *The First Jesuits* (Cambridge, Mass.: Harvard University Press, 1993), 342-43.

18. A. D. Wright, *The Counter-Reformation: Catholic Europe and the Non-Christian World* (New York: St. Martin's Press, 1982), 144. In South America, there was flagellant behavior among the Mocobies but not among the neighboring Guarani, even though the latter had been subject to Jesuit missions for longer than the former. This contrast seems to reinforce the point that penitential self-mortification arose through the interaction of indigenous culture and Jesuit influence. See Maxime Haubert, *La vie quotidienne au Paraguay sous les jésuites* (Paris: Hachette, 1967), 337-38.

19. Inga Clendinnen, *Aztecs: An Interpretation* (Cambridge: Cambridge University Press, 1991); J. Jorge Klor de Alva, "'Telling Lives': Confessional Autobiography and the Reconstruction of the Nahua Self," in *Spiritual Encounters: Interactions between Christianity and Native Religions in Colonial America*, ed. Nicholas Griffiths and Fernando Cervantes (Lincoln: University of Nebraska Press, 1999), 136–62.

20. Relation of 1655–56, JR 42:152–53.

21. Ibid., 156–57.

22. William N. Fenton, *The False Faces of the Iroquois* (Norman: University of Oklahoma Press, 1987), 73. On Huron use of fire and coals in healing rituals, see Gabriel Sagard, *The Long Journey to the Country of the Hurons*, ed. G. M. Wrong, trans. H. H. Langton (Toronto: Champlain Society, 1939), 200–201.

23. Relation of 1655–56, JR 42:171.

24. P. F. X. de Charlevoix, *Journal of a Voyage to North-America Undertaken by Order of the French King*, 2 vols. (London: R. and J. Dodsley, 1761), 2:84–85. See also Joseph-François Lafitau, *Customs of the American Indians Compared with the Customs of Primitive Times*, ed. and trans. William N. Fenton and Elizabeth L. Moore, 2 vols. (Toronto: Champlain Society, 1974), 2:158, 2:160–61; Relation of 1633, JR 5:130–33.

25. See P. F. X. de Charlevoix, "Catherine Tegahkouita: An Iroquois Virgin," in Greer, *Jesuit Relations*, 181–82. The Jesuits themselves, for all their desire to place a strictly Christian construction on the penitents' activity, were not entirely unaware of the indigenous roots of native asceticism. See "Lettre du père Cholenec," in *Lettres édifiantes et curieuses écrites des mission étrangères par quelques missionnaires de la Compagnie de Jésus*, 30 vols. (Paris: N. LeClerc, 1708-73), 12 (1717): 119–212 (*Pos*, 368).

26. Though the Jesuits did report something along these lines among Huron converts struggling to overcome sexual impulses. "I know more than one of them who have applied upon their bodies coals and burning brands, in order to stifle that same fire of hell,—saying to themselves, to overcome the temptation: 'And how couldst thou, wretched man, bear an eternal fire, if thou canst not accustom thyself to this one, which is but a feeble painting of that?'" Relation of 1645–46, JR 30:38–41.

27. Michel Foucault, *The History of Sexuality*, vol. 3, *The Care of the Self*, trans. R. Hurley (New York: Random House, 1986), 59; Charles Taylor, *Sources of the Self: The Making of the Modern Identity* (Cambridge, Mass.: Harvard University Press, 1989), 219.

28. A. C. Parker, "Iroquois Uses of Maize and Other Plant Foods," in *Parker on the Iroquois*, ed. William Fenton (Syracuse, N.Y.: Syracuse University Press, 1968), 64. See also Dean Snow, *Iroquois*, 127; Relation of 1636, JR 10:206–7; Relation of 1637, JR 12:65; Lafitau, *Customs of the American Indians*, 2:113.

29. Raymond of Capua, *Life of St. Catherine of Siena*, trans. G. Lamb (London: Harvill Press, 1960), 53–57; Pedro de Ribandeira, *Les Fleurs de la Vie des Saints et des festes de toute l'année suivant le calendrier & martyrologue romain*, trans. René Gautier, 2 vols. (Paris: Christophe Jounel, 1687), 1:425–31.

30. For a critical examination of the psychoanalytic concept of masochism, see Ariel Glucklich, *Sacred Pain: Hurting the Body for the Sake of the Soul* (Oxford: Oxford University Press, 2001), 85–89.

31. Friedrich Nietzsche, "The Genealogy of Morals," in *The Philosophy of Nietzsche* (New York: Modern Library, 1927), 717–93, quotation at 792. Emphasis in original.

32. Caroline Walker Bynum, *Holy Feast and Holy Fast: The Religious Significance of Food to Medieval Women* (Berkeley: University of California Press, 1987); Peter Brown, *The Body and Society: Men, Women and Sexual Renunciation in Early Christianity* (New York: Columbia University Press, 1988).

33. Glucklich, *Sacred Pain*, quotation at 59. Of interest also on the question of pain and the self is Elaine Scarry, *The Body in Pain: The Making and Unmaking of the World* (New York: Oxford University Press, 1985), which concentrates almost exclusively on the political use of torture in the modern world. Though lacking in historical depth and in any interest in religious self-torture, Scarry's study nevertheless offers penetrating insight into the power of pain to destroy language-based reality and undermine the sufferer's self.

34. Bynum, *Holy Feast and Holy Fast*, 34.

35. See Brown, *The Body and Society*, 331.

36. Bynum, *Holy Feast and Holy Fast*, 243, 84–85.

37. Chauchetière, *Narration*, 47.

38. Chauchetière, "La vie," 95–96 (*Pos*, 185–86); Archives du séminaire de Québec, Manuscrit 216, "Extraict d'une lettre du père Chonelec [sic] contenant le récit de la ste vie et penitences extraordinaires de quelques femmes sauvagesses, escrittes de St françois xavier du Sault proche de montreal au mois de febvrier 1680."

39. Cholenec, "Vie de Catherine Tegakouita," 47 (*Pos*, 284).

40. Some scholars have been so taken with the image of native women staunchly resisting the patriarchal church that they have ignored the religious creativity of Christian converts, leaving the impression that missionaries so dominated the consciousness of native women that the latter could conceive of no options other than stubborn resistance and abject surrender. See Karen Anderson, *Chain Her by One Foot: The Subjugation of Women in Seventeenth-Century New France* (London: Routledge, 1991); Carol Devens, *Countering Colonization: Native American Women and Great Lakes Missions, 1630-1900* (Berkeley: University of California Press, 1992).

Chapter 6

1. Chauchetière, "La vie," 74 (*Pos*, 169–70).

2. Chauchetière, "La vie," 80 (*Pos*, 174).

3. Cholenec, "Vie de Catherine Tegakouita," 14–15 (*Pos*, 252–53).

4. Chauchetière, "La vie," 87 (*Pos*, 179–80).

5. Claude Chauchetière, "Letter of October 14, 1682," in *The Jesuit Relations: Natives and Missionaries in Seventeenth-Century North America*, ed. Allan Greer (Boston: Bedford Books, 2000), 153.

6. These are details Tekakwitha related to her best friend, who later passed on the information to Father Chauchetière when he was preparing his biography. Chauchetière, "La vie," 86–88 (*Pos*, 179–80); Cholenec "Vie de Catherine Tegakouita," 20 (*Pos*, 257).

7. Cholenec, "Vie de Catherine Tegakouita," 22 (*Pos*, 259). On the early modern Christian, and especially Jesuit, view of wilderness as a spiritually desolate environment, see Carole Blackburn, *Harvest of Souls: The Jesuit Missions and Colonialism in North America, 1632–1650* (Montreal: McGill–Queen's University Press, 2000), 42–55.

8. Chauchetière, "La vie," 105–8 (*Pos*, 192–95); Cholenec, "Vie de Catherine Tegakouita," 24–26 (*Pos*, 260–62).

9. Chauchetière, "La vie," 92 (*Pos*, 183).

10. Cholenec, "Vie de Catherine Tegakouita," 30 (*Pos*, 266).

11. Archives françaises de la Compagnie de Jésus, Fonds Brotier, A6-2, vol. 162:152, "Abbrégé de la vie de Catherine Tegaskouita chretienne iroquoise" (*Pos*, 83).

12. On the importance of *athenrosera*, special friendships between individuals of the same sex, see Joseph-François Lafitau, *Customs of the American Indians Compared with the Customs of Primitive Times*, ed. and trans. William N. Fenton and Elizabeth L. Moore, 2 vols. (Toronto: Champlain Society, 1974), 1:361–65.

13. Chauchetière, "La vie," 81 (*Pos*, 175).

14. On the Quebec hospital, see [Mère St-Ignace and Mère Ste-Hélène], *Histoire de l'Hôtel-Dieu de Québec* (Montauban: Jérosme Legier, 1751). On Catherine de Saint Augustin,

see *Dictionary of Canadian Biography* (Toronto: University of Toronto Press, 1966), 1:607–10; Paul Ragueneau, *La Vie de la mère Catherine de Saint Augustin, religieuse hospitalière de la miséricorde de Québec en la Nouvelle-France* (Paris: Florentin Lambert, 1671); JR 52:56–97.

15. "Letter of Father Claude Chauchetière, 14 October 1682," in Greer, *Jesuit Relations*, 150. Another text, the *Life* of Tekakwitha prepared for publication by Pierre Cholenec in 1715, has Catherine herself encountering nuns on a visit to Montreal and determining to take them as her model. In this case, the emphasis is on their vow of chastity rather than their ascetic devotions. None of the other texts gives any hint of direct contact between Tekakwitha and any nuns, and it must be said that Cholenec's late version of her biography is the one that shows the most signs of a tendency to rework the raw data to form an edifying story. "Lettre du Père Cholenec . . . au Père Augustin LeBlanc . . . le 27 août 1715," in *Lettres édifiantes et curieuses écrites des missions étrangères*, 30 vols. (Paris: N. Leclerc, 1708–71), 12 (1717): 119–211.

16. Chauchetière, *Narration*, 33–34.

17. Chauchetière, "La vie," 95 (*Pos*, 185).

18. Chauchetière, "La vie," 82 (*Pos*, 176).

19. Ibid.

20. R. Po-Chia Hsia, *The World of Catholic Renewal 1540–1770* (Cambridge: Cambridge University Press, 1998), 33–41; Elisja Schulte van Kessel, "Virgins and Mothers between Heaven and Earth," in *A History of Women in the West*, vol. 3, *Renaissance and Enlightenment Paradoxes*, ed. N. Z. Davis and A. Farge (Cambridge, Mass.: Harvard University Press, 1993), 137–38; Elizabeth Rapley, *The Dévotes: Women and Church in Seventeenth-Century France* (Montreal: McGill–Queen's University Press, 1990).

21. Cholenec, "Vie de Catherine Tegakouita," 38 (*Pos*, 276).

22. Lafitau, *Customs of the American Indians*, 2:242.

23. Chauchetière, "La vie," 84 (*Pos*, 177–78).

24. Chauchetière, "La vie," 73 (*Pos*, 169).

25. Cholenec, "Vie de Catherine Tegakouita," 37 (*Pos*, 276); ibid., 41 (*Pos*, 279).

26. Cholenec, "Vie de Catherine Tegakouita," 55 (*Pos*, 293); Chauchetière, "La vie," 91 (*Pos*, 182–83).

27. Chauchetière, "La vie," 90–91 (*Pos*, 182). According to Cholenec, Tekakwitha's ability to withstand the torment was doubly "miraculous" in that there were no burn marks to be seen on her foot the next day! Cholenec, "Vie de Catherine Tegakouita," 56 (*Pos*, 294).

28. Cholenec, "Vie de Catherine Tegakouita," 49–57 (*Pos*, 286–96), quotation at 57 (*Pos*, 295).

29. ASQ, manuscrit 216, "Extraict d'une lettre du père Chonelec [sic] contenant le récit de la ste vie et penitences extraordinaires de quelques femmes sauvagesses, escrittes de St. françois xavier du Sault proche le montreal au mois de febvrier 1680."

30. ASQ, manuscrit 374, "Extraict d'une autre lettre du pere Chonelec [sic] sur le mesme suiet et la mort d'une ste fille, escritte le premier jour de may 1680." This manuscript, contained within a larger work entitled "Des Missions Iroquoises en l'année 1676 [sic]," purports to be a copy of part of a letter by Pierre Cholenec

dated 1 May 1680. Henri Béchard published the text as an appendix to *L'héroique indienne Kateri Tekakwitha* (Montreal: Fides, 1967), 189–94. The original letter has never been located.

31. Chauchetière, "La vie," 115 (*Pos*, 204).

32. ASQ, manuscrit 374, "Extraict d'une autre lettre."

33. Cholenec, "Vie de Catherine Tegakouita," 54, 60–61 (*Pos*, 291–92, 299); Chauchetière, "La vie," 114 (*Pos*, 203).

34. J. N. B. Hewitt, "Iroquoian Cosmology," Smithsonian Institution, Bureau of American Ethnology, *Annual Report*, 1899–1900 (Washington, D.C.: Smithsonian Institution, 1903), 255; Dean Snow, *The Iroquois* (Oxford: Blackwell, 1994), 73.

Chapter 7

1. Joseph Kellogg narrative, Historical Society of Pennsylvania, Gratz Collection, Case 8, Box 28, "Papers relating to the attack on Deerfield." My thanks to Evan Haefli for bringing this document to my attention and for providing me with a copy. On Joseph Kellogg, see John Demos, *The Unredeemed Captive: A Family Story from Early America* (New York: Random House, 1994), 78, 144, 151.

2. R. Po-Chia Hsia, *The World of Catholic Renewal 1540–1770* (Cambridge: Cambridge University Press, 1998), 136.

3. Allan Greer and Jodi Bilinkoff, eds., *Colonial Saints: Discovering the Holy in the Americas, 1500–1800* (New York: Routledge, 2003).

4. Marie-Aimée Cliche, *Les Pratiques de dévotion en Nouvelle-France: Comportements populaires et encadrement ecclésial dans le gouvernement de Québec* (Quebec: Les presses de l'Université Laval, 1988), 27–50.

5. Joseph Kellogg narrative.

6. François Lebrun, *Se soigner autrefois: Médecins, saints et sorceriers aux 17e et 18e siècles* (Paris: Temps actuels, 1983), 113.

7. Hippolyte Delehaye, *The Legends of the Saints: An Introduction to Hagiography*, trans. V. M. Crawford (London: G. Chapman, 1962); Michel de Certeau, "A Variant: Hagio-Graphical Edification," in his *The Writing of History*, trans. Tom Conley (New York: Columbia University Press, 1988), 269–83; Alain Boureau, "Franciscan Piety and Voracity: Uses and Strategems in the Hagiographic Pamphlet," in *The Culture of Print: Power and the Use of Print in Early Modern Europe*, ed. Roger Chartier, trans. Lydia G. Cochrane (Princeton, N.J.: Princeton University Press, 1989), 15–18.

8. Edith Wyschogrod, *Saints and Postmodernism: Revisioning Moral Philosophy* (Chicago: University of Chicago Press, 1990), 3–30.

9. Pierre Delooz, "Towards a Sociological Study of Canonized Sainthood in the Catholic Church," in *Saints and Their Cults: Studies in Religious Sociology, Folklore and History*, ed. Stephen Wilson (Cambridge: Cambridge University Press, 1983), 199.

10. The Caron incident is recounted, with some embellishments, in Cholenec "Vie de Catherine Tegakouita," 74 (*Pos*, 316–17). More immediate accounts can be found in ASJCF, ms 350, "Receuil de ce qui s'est passé depuis le decès de Catherine," 2–3; and Archives françaises de la Compagnie de Jésus, Fonds Brotier, 162: 153v-54, "Abbrégé

de la vie de Catherine Tegaskouita chrestienne Iroquoise decedée en la meme mission du sault de st Franc. Xavier, le 17 avril 1680" (*Pos*, 78–90).

11. Cholenec, "Vie de Catherine Tegakouita," 76 (*Pos*, 322). Cf. André Vauchez, *La sainteté en occident aux derniers siècles du moyen âge d'après les procès de canonisation et les documents hagiographiques* (Rome: Ecole française de Rome, 1988), 530.

12. Cholenec, "Vie de Catherine Tegakouita," 76 (*Pos*, 321).

13. ASJCF, ms 344, Pierre Rémy to Pierre Cholenec, 12 March 1696 (*Pos*, 215–35).

14. Ibid., 11 (*Pos*, 226–27).

15. The standard work on the settlement of this region is Louise Dechêne, *Habitants and Merchants in Seventeenth-Century Montreal*, trans. L. Vardi (Montreal: McGill–Queen's University Press, 1992). See also Louis Lavallée, *La Prairie en Nouvelle-France 1647–1760: Etude d'histoire sociale* (Montreal: McGill–Queen's University Press, 1992).

16. Daniel K. Richter, *The Ordeal of the Longhouse: The Peoples of the Iroquois League in the Era of European Colonization* (Chapel Hill: University of North Carolina Press, 1992), 160.

17. Jan Grabowski, "The Common Ground: Settled Natives and French in Montréal, 1667–1760" (Ph.D. diss., University of Montreal, 1993), 278.

18. ASJCF, manuscript 344, 6, Pierre Rémy to Pierre Cholenec, 12 March 1696 (*Pos*, 229). See also ibid., 12 (*Pos*, 227).

19. Mary Lindemann, *Medicine and Society in Early Modern Europe* (Cambridge: Cambridge University Press, 1999), 199.

20. On European and colonial medical therapies in the seventeenth century, see Lebrun, *Se soigner autrefois*; Lindemann, *Medicine and Society*; Laurence Brockliss and Colin Jones, *The Medical World of Early Modern France* (Oxford: Clarendon Press, 1997); Rénald Lessard, "Pratique et praticiens en contexte colonial: Le corps médical canadien aux 17e et 18e siècles" (Ph.D. thesis, Laval University, 1994). Lessard states (149–50) that bleeding was by far the most common treatment for the widest range of ailments, in both France and New France.

21. Lessard, "Pratique et praticiens," 242–47.

22. ASJCF, manuscript 344, 3, Pierre Rémy to Pierre Cholenec, 12 March 1696 (*Pos*, 217–18).

23. Cholenec, "Vie de Catherine Tegakouita," 75 (*Pos*, 320).

24. Relation of 1676–77, "On the Mission of St. François Xavier du Sault Near Montreal," *JR* 60:286–87.

25. Cholenec, "Vie de Catherine Tegakouita," 76 (*Pos*, 320–21).

26. Chauchetière, "La vie," 102 (*Pos*, 191).

27. "Abbrégé," 154.

28. Joseph-François Lafitau, *Customs of the American Indians Compared with the Customs of Primitive Times*, ed. and trans. William N. Fenton and Elizabeth L. Moore, 2 vols. (Toronto: Champlain Society, 1974), 2:202; P. F. X. de Charlevoix, *Journal of a Voyage to North-America Undertaken by Order of the French King*, 2 vols. (London: R. and J. Dodsley, 1761), 2:173.

29. Rénald Lessard discusses the French assimilation of native pharmaceutical knowledge in "Pratique et praticiens," 180–89. The distribution of sugar and raisins to Hurons struck by deadly influenza is described in Relation of 1637–38, *JR* 15:69. On Jesuit treatment of Indians with theriac, see Relation of 1663–64, *JR* 49:56–59.

The quotation describing the composition of that drug comes from Brockliss and Jones, *The Medical World of Early Modern France*, 160.

30. Some medicinal herbs, François Lebrun reports, had to be gathered during the night of Saint John the Baptist. Lebrun, *Se soigner autrefois*, 69.

31. Anthony F. C. Wallace, *The Death and Rebirth of the Seneca* (New York: Random House, 1969), 59–75.

32. Herbert Benson, *Timeless Healing: The Power and Biology of Belief* (New York: Scribner, 1996).

33. On the long resistance to Cartesian dualism in European conceptions of the self, see Charles Taylor, *Sources of the Self: The Making of the Modern Identity* (Cambridge, Mass.: Harvard University Press, 1989), 188–89. The "Hippocratic/Galenic tradition" is succinctly outlined in Lindemann, *Medicine and Society*, 8–21.

34. Lindemann, *Medicine and Society*, 17.

35. Relation of 1668–69, JR 52:125.

36. Though the point may not apply to seventeenth-century Iroquois medicine, a contemporary account of shamanistic curing among the Oglala Sioux stresses this preliminary stage of extended consultation. See Thomas H. Lewis, *The Medicine Men: Oglala Sioux Ceremony and Healing* (Lincoln: University of Nebraska Press, 1990), 169–89.

37. Harmen Meyndertz van den Bogaert, "A Journey into Mohawk and Oneida Country 1634–1635," in *In Mohawk Country: Early Narratives about a Native People*, ed. Dean Snow, Charles Gehring, and William Starna (Syracuse, N.Y.: Syracuse University Press, 1996), 6. For another early account, this one related by French Jesuits who visited the Onondaga, see Relation of 1655–56, JR 42:147–49.

38. Curing ceremonies of these kinds among the Hurons, whose medical culture resembled that of the Iroquois, are described in Greer, *Jesuit Relations*, 70–93. Modern explanations of the curative powers of gambling are set out in Harold Blau, "Notes on the Onondaga Bowl Game," in *Iroquois Culture, History and Prehistory*, ed. Elisabeth Tooker (Albany: University of the State of New York, 1967), 37.

39. Claude Lévi-Strauss, *Structural Anthropology*, trans. Claire Jacobson (Harmondsworth: Penguin, 1963), 179.

40. To be sure, the church sometimes staged public prayers and processions in response to epidemics and other great collective emergencies. Moreover, there was a theatrical dimension to European healing at the time, particularly if we include "charlatans" promoting their special potions in the marketplace. One such performer visited Poitiers when Claude Chauchetière was a boy and boasted of having the antidote to every poison. After gathering a crowd, he would offer to ingest any toxic substance offered by the audience; then, staggering and gasping, he would rush to mix up a curative elixir that always seemed to revive him just as he was sinking to the floor. These were, however, special cases: a community response to a general catastrophe in one case, advertising for a commercial product in the other. See Donald Crawford, ed., *Journals of Sir John Lauder Lord Fountainhall with His Observations on Public Affairs and Other Memoranda 1665–1676* (Edinburgh: Scottish Historical Society, 1900).

41. See, for example, Relation of 1637, JR 13:99.

42. There were indeed collective measures as well—public health precautions and public prayers—especially in times of real and threatened epidemic. Such approaches had

their analogue in various Iroquoian responses to pestilence, but they represent a different order of phenomenon from the therapies, shamanistic and medical/religious, that focused on curing sick individuals.

43. For a discussion of issues connected with "the boundaries of the self" in the context of indigenous Mexican responses to Christian notions of sin and confession, see J. Jorge Klor de Alva, "'Telling Lives': Confessional Autobiography and the Reconstruction of the Nahua Self," in *Spiritual Encounters: Interactions between Christianity and Native Religions in Colonial America*, ed. Nicholas Griffiths and Fernando Cervantes (Lincoln: University of Nebraska Press, 1999), 136–62.

44. Recall Lafitau's observation, noted on page 108, that all but the most "heroic" Iroquois Catholics turned to shamans in time of illness. Lafitau, *Customs of the American Indians*, 1:246.

45. Claude Chauchetière, *Narration de la mission du Sault depuis sa fondation jusqu'en 1686*, ed. Hélène Avisseau (1686; Bordeaux: Archives départementales de la Gironde, 1984), 55.

46. "Letter of Claude Chauchetière, respecting the Iroquois Mission of Sault St. François Xavier, near Montreal, October 14, 1682," JR 62:166–89, quotation at 189; Chauchetière, *Narration*.

47. De Certeau, "A Variant," 277–79.

48. Chauchetière, "La vie." In the original French even more than in my English translation, the phrase "dite à present la saincte sauvagesse" seems to have been carefully worded to suggest saintly status that has not for the moment been ratified by the Vatican. Chauchetière seems to have begun writing it in 1685, though it long remained a work in progress. He revised the text in 1695 when a new round of miracle cures reanimated his excitement. It was only published two centuries later. Chauchetière autobiography, 15.

49. D. Karl Uitti, as quoted in D. R. Woolf, "The Rhetoric of Martyrdom: Generic Contradictions and Narrative Strategy in John Foxe's Acts and Monuments," in *The Rhetorics of Life-Writing in Early Modern Europe: Forms of Biography from Fedele to Louis XIV*, ed. Thomas F. Mayer and D. R. Woolf (Ann Arbor: University of Michigan Press, 1995), 276n10.

50. Chauchetière, "La vie," 1–3.

51. De Certeau, "A Variant," 276–77.

52. Chauchetière autobiography, 14.

53. Statement signed Duluth, Fort Frontenac, 15 August 1696 in "Lettre du Père Cholenec . . . au Père Augustin LeBlanc . . . le 27 août 1715," in *Lettres édifiantes et curieuses écrites des missions étrangères*, 30 vols. (Paris: N. Leclerc, 1708–71), vol. 12 (1717): 210. Just for the record, Duluth's biography reveals that his chronic gout was only temporarily relieved; six years later he was completely incapacitated. Yves Zoltvany, "Daniel Greysolon Dulhut," in *Dictionary of Canadian Biography* (Toronto: University of Toronto Press, 1966–), 2:261–64.

54. Cholenec, "Vie de Catherine Tegakouita," 79–83 (*Pos*, 326–30). On river travel in New France, see Louise Dechêne, *Le partage des subsistances au Canada sous le régime français* (Montreal: Boréal, 1994), 63.

55. Cholenec, "Vie de Catherine Tegakouita," 80–81 (*Pos*, 327). The La Colombière cure seems to have been widely discussed, as witness this excerpt from a letter written at

the time: "Je ne donnerais pas aisément croiance à la pensée que vous me dites qu'on a eu qu'il pourait y avoir de la diablerie dans la maladie de M. de la Colombière. Je suis un peu incrédule en matière de sortilège. Je serais plus disposé à croire qu'il y a eu du miraculeux dans sa guérison, et que Dieu pour relever la vie humble de cette bonne Vierge Sauvagesse rendrait son tombeau glorieux par des guérisons merveilleuses." ASQ, Lettres O, no. 12, Tremblay to Glandelet, 8 April 1696 (a copy of this document was kindly provided by Marie-Aimée Cliché).

56. Transformed into martyr narratives, the deaths of Etienne te Ganonakoa, Françoise Gouannhatenha, and Margueritte Garongouas were later recounted for publication by Pierre Cholenec. "Lettre du Père Cholenec, Missionaire de la Compagnie de Jesus en la Nouvelle France, au Père Jean-Baptiste Du Halde, de la même Compagnie," in *Lettres édifiantes et curieuses*, 6:100–127.

57. Cholenec, "Vie de Catherine Tegakouita," 84 (*Pos*, 331–32).

58. Cholenec, "Vie de Catherine Tegakouita," 86–88 (*Pos*, 331–34). On Kahnawake's situation in the French-Iroquois war, see Richter, *Ordeal of the Longhouse*, 162–89; Gretchen Green, "A New People in an Age of War: The Kahnawake Iroquois, 1667–1760" (Ph.D. diss., College of William and Mary, 1991), 68–168.

59. Claude Chauchetière, *Vie de la Bienheureuse Catherine Tegakouita, dite à présent la saincte Iroquoise* (New York: Presse Cramoisy, 1887).

Chapter 8

1. Cholenec, "Vie de Catherine Tegakouita," 87–88 (*Pos*, 334–35).

2. Archives départementales, Finistère, registres paroissiaux de St-Thomas de Landerneau, baptême, 30 June 1641; Archives de la ville de Landerneau, délibérations des assemblées de communauté, 1648–63. Landerneau was a linen-manufacturing center in the seventeenth century; quite likely Le Cholenec was involved in that trade as a merchant.

3. Alain Croix, *La Bretagne aux 16e et 17e siècles: La vie, la mort, la foi*, 2 vols. (Paris: Maloine, 1981), 2:1211–40; Alain Croix, *L'age d'or de la Bretagne 1532–1675* (Rennes: Editions Ouest-France, 1993), 503.

4. On Cholenec's Jesuit career, see *Dictionary of Canadian Biography* (Toronto: University of Toronto Press, 1966–), 2:144; ARSI, Francia 13–19, Catalogi triennales, 1651–1730, passim.

5. R. Po-Chia Hsia, *The World of Catholic Renewal 1540–1770* (Cambridge: Cambridge University Press, 1998), 41.

6. Mary Douglas, *Purity and Danger: An Analysis of the Concepts of Pollution and Taboo* (London: Routledge and Kegan Paul, 1966), 157–58.

7. Joseph-François Lafitau, *Customs of the American Indians Compared with the Customs of Primitive Times*, ed. and trans. William N. Fenton and Elizabeth L. Moore, 2 vols. (Toronto: Champlain Society, 1974), 1:218.

8. Elaine Pagels, *Adam, Eve, and the Serpent* (New York: Random House, 1988).

9. Jean Delumeau, *Sin and Fear: The Emergence of a Western Guilt Culture, 13th–18th Centuries* (New York: St. Martin's Press, 1990), 431–45.

10. 1 Corinthians 7:32, 33, 35. For discussions of early Christian celibacy, see Pagels, *Adam, Eve, and the Serpent*, 78–97; Peter Brown, *The Body and Society: Men, Women, and*

Sexual Renunciation in Early Christianity (New York: Columbia University Press, 1988), passim.

11. Claude Chauchetière, *Narration de la mission du Sault depuis sa fondation jusqu'en 1686*, ed. Hélène Avisseau (1686; Bordeaux: Archives départementales de la Gironde, 1984), 51. The renunciation of sex within marriage was not unknown in Europe: see Dyan Elliott, *Spiritual Marriage: Sexual Abstinence in Medieval Wedlock* (Princeton, N.J.: Princeton University Press, 1993).

12. Cholenec, "Vie de Catherine Tegakouita," 35 (*Pos*, 273).

13. Douglas, *Purity and Danger*, 158.

14. Lafitau, *Customs of the American Indians*, 1:129.

15. Brown, *The Body and Society*, 263.

16. Chauchetière, *Narration*, 41.

17. Cholenec, "Vie de Catherine Tegakouita," 49–50 (*Pos*, 286–87).

18. Thomas Aquinas, *Summa Theologica*, Supplement to the Third Part, Question 96, article 5, "Whether an aureole is due on account of virginity" (on-line edition: http://www.newadvent.org/summa/).

19. Cholenec, "Vie de Catherine Tegakouita," 50–51 (*Pos*, 288).

20. Chauchetière, "La vie," 126 (*Pos*, 211).

21. Cholenec, "Vie de Catherine Tegakouita," 71–72 (*Pos*, 316).

22. Bacqueville de la Potherie, *Histoire de l'Amérique septentrionale*, 4 vols. (Paris: Brocas, 1753), 1:355.

23. Anthony Pagden, *The Fall of Natural Man: The American Indian and the Origins of Comparative Ethnology* (Cambridge: Cambridge University Press, 1982); Olive P. Dickason, *The Myth of the Savage and the Beginnings of French Colonialism in the Americas* (Edmonton: University of Alberta Press, 1984); Francis Jennings, *The Invasion of America: Indians, Colonialism, and the Cant of Conquest* (Chapel Hill: University of North Carolina Press, 1975).

24. Anne McClintock, *Imperial Leather: Race, Gender and Sexuality in the Colonial Contest* (New York: Routledge, 1995), 21–25.

25. Louis Montrose, "The Work of Gender in the Discourse of Discovery," in *New World Encounters*, ed. Stephen Greenblatt (Berkeley: University of California Press, 1993), 177–217; Peter Mason, *Infelicities: Representations of the Exotic* (Baltimore: Johns Hopkins University Press, 1998), 61–63.

26. See Paul Lejeune's account of a perilous winter hunt with the Montagnais (Innu/Naskapi) of Quebec in Relation of 1634, JR 7:106–15.

27. Cholenec, "Vie de Catherine Tegakouita," 31–35 (*Pos*, 267–71). This passage appears, almost word for word, in the published 1717 *Life*. "Lettre du P. Cholenec, missionnaire de la compagnie de Jésus, au P. Augustin le Blanc, de la même compagnie, procureur des missions du Canada," in *Lettres édifiantes et curieuses écrites des missions étrangères*, 30 vols. (Paris: N. Leclerc, 1708–71), vol. 12 (1717):119–211 (*Pos*, 361–62).

28. The tenuous nature of food supplies in the forests of the Canadian Shield and the consequent sense that survival cannibalism, though rare in practice, is always a possibility would seem to underlie the windigo syndrome found among many Algonquian peoples of the north. In these societies, it is believed that individuals can be transformed into antisocial monsters, often as a result of tasting human flesh.

Once individuals have become windigos, they turn on those closest to them, killing them and eating their bodies. Robert A. Brightman, "The Windigo in the Material World," Ethnohistory 35 (Fall 1988): 337–79.

29. Michel de Montaigne, "On Cannibals," in Essays, trans. J. M. Cohen (Harmondsworth: Penguin, 1958), 105–19; Jean de Léry, History of a Voyage to the Land of Brazil, Otherwise Called America, ed. and trans. Janet Whatley (Berkeley: University of California Press, 1990), 132. On cannibalism as a colonialist ideology, see William Arens, The Man-Eating Myth: Anthropology and Anthropophagy (New York: Oxford University Press, 1979); Pagden, Fall of Natural Man, 80–89; Peter Hulme, Colonial Encounters: Europe and the Native Caribbean (London: Methuen, 1986); Frank Lestringant, Cannibals: The Discovery and Representation of the Cannibal from Columbus to Jules Verne, trans. Rosemary Morris (Cambridge: Polity Press, 1997).

30. Pagden, Fall of Natural Man, 83.

31. Bernadette Bucher, Icon and Conquest: A Structural Analysis of the Illustrations of de Bry's "Great Voyages" (Chicago: University of Chicago Press, 1981), 46–64.

32. JR 64:126, Claude Chauchetière to Jean Chauchetière, 7 August 1694; Cholenec, "Vie de Catherine Tegakouita," 69, 80 (Pos, 313, 327).

33. "Lettre du P. Cholenec," in Lettres édifiantes et curieuses, 12 (1717): 119–211. See Allan Greer, "Savage/Saint: The Lives of Kateri Tekakwitha," in Habitants et marchands, vingt ans après: Lectures de l'histoire des XVIIe et XVIIIe siècles canadiens, ed. Sylvie Dépatie, Catherine Desbarats, and Thomas Wien (Montreal: McGill–Queen's University Press, 1998), 147–50.

34. Catherine M. Northeast, The Parisian Jesuits and the Enlightenment 1700–1762 (Oxford: Voltaire Foundation, 1991).

35. In addition to Northeast, Parisian Jesuits, see Andreas Motsch, Lafitau et l'émergence du discours ethnographique (Sillery, Quebec: Septentrion; Paris: Presses de l'Université de Paris-Sorbonne, 2001).

36. La gracia triunfante en la vida de Catharina Tegakovita, india iroquesa, y en las de otras, Assi de su Nacion, como de esta Nueva-España (Mexico City: Joseph Bernardo de Hogal, 1724).

37. Ibid., 4.

38. Ascunción Lavrin, "Women in Convents: Their Economic and Social Role in Colonial Mexico," in Liberating Women's History: Theoretical and Critical Essays, ed. Bernice A. Carroll (Urbana: University of Illinois Press, 1976), 257.

39. For a more detailed account of the circumstances surrounding the Mexican edition of 1724, see Allan Greer, "Iroquois Virgin: The Story of Catherine Tekakwitha in New France and New Spain," in Colonial Saints: Discovering the Holy in the Americas, 1500–1800, ed. Allan Greer and Jodi Bilinkoff (New York: Routledge, 2003), 233–48.

40. Anthony Pagden, European Encounters with the New World: From Renaissance to Romanticism (New Haven, Conn.: Yale University Press, 1993).

41. P.-F.-X. de Charlevoix, History and General Description of New France, 6 vols., trans. J. G. Shea (New York: Francis P. Harper, 1900), 4:283–96. (This text can also be found in Allan Greer, ed., The Jesuit Relations: Natives and Missionaries in Seventeenth-Century North America [Boston: Bedford Books, 2000], 172–85.)

42. François-René de Chateaubriand, Les Natchez, ed. Gilbert Chinard (Baltimore: Johns Hopkins Press, 1932), 167–68.

43. Hulme, *Colonial Encounters*, 137–73, 225–63; quotations at 141. In a similar vein, see Mary Louise Pratt, *Imperial Eyes: Travel Writing and Transculturation* (London: Routledge, 1992), 90–102.

44. Harry Liebersohn, *Aristocratic Encounters: European Travelers and North American Indians* (Cambridge: Cambridge University Press, 1998), 39–60.

45. Leonard Cohen, *Beautiful Losers* (New York: Viking, 1966). (A personal note: In spite of the obscenity, the only passage in *Beautiful Losers* that makes me squirm is this one: "Catherine Tekakwitha, I have come to rescue you from the Jesuits. Yes, an old scholar dares to think big.")

46. Linda Hutcheon, *The Canadian Postmodern: A Study of Contemporary English-Canadian Fiction* (Toronto: Oxford University Press, 1988), 26–30, 109.

Chapter 9

1. R. Po-Chia Hsia, *The World of Catholic Renewal 1540–1770* (Cambridge: Cambridge University Press, 1998), 122–30.

2. Robert H. Wiebe, *The Search for Order 1877–1920* (New York: Hill and Wang, 1967); John Higham, *Strangers in the Land: Patterns of American Nativism, 1860–1925* (New York: Atheneum, 1963).

3. Anne McClintock, *Imperial Leather: Race, Gender and Sexuality in the Colonial Contest* (New York: Routledge, 1995), 352–89.

4. Philip J. Deloria, *Playing Indian* (New Haven, Conn.: Yale Univerity Press, 1998). See also Robert F. Berkhofer, *The White Man's Indian: Images of the American Indian from Columbus to the Present* (New York: Vintage Books, 1979); Sherry L. Smith, *Reimagining Indians: Native Americans through Anglo Eyes 1880–1940* (New York: Oxford University Press, 2000).

5. Claude Chauchetière, *Vie de la Bienheureuse Catherine Tegakouita, dite à présent la saincte Iroquoise* (New York: Presse Cramoisy, 1887). Walworth's contribution is not mentioned anywhere in the book, but it is noted in another hagiographic work: Nicholas Burtin, *Vie de Catherine Tekakwitha, vierge iroquoise, décédée en odeur de sainteté à l'ancien village du Sault Saint-Louis Le 17 avril 1680* (Quebec: L. Brousseau, 1894), vii.

6. Ellen Hardin Walworth, *The Life and Times of Kateri Tekakwitha, the Lily of the Mohawks, 1656–1680* (Buffalo, N.Y.: Peter Paul and Brother, 1891).

7. Ibid., 131, 185, 253.

8. See Charles Taylor, *The Malaise of Modernity* (Concord, Ont.: House of Anansi, 1991).

9. Ibid., 239.

10. See Simon Schama, *Landscape and Memory* (New York: Knopf, 1995).

11. Walworth, *Life and Times*, 1.

12. Burtin, *Vie de Catherine Tekakwitha*.

13. Ibid., xix.

14. See, for example, Henri Béchard, *L'héroique Indienne Kateri Tekakwitha* (Montreal: Fides, 1960); and Pierre Théoret, *Kateri, 1656–1680: Vièrge iroquoise* (Lyon: Emmanuel Vitte, 1960). However, note the adoption of Ellen Walworth's invented name.

15. There is no up-to-date bibliography, but for the period before 1940, see Edward-Xavier Evans, "The Literature Relative to Kateri Tekakwitha, the Lily of the Mohawks, 1656–1680," *Bulletin des recherches historiques* 46 (July 1940): 193–209;

(August 1940): 241–55. The World Wide Web provides an excellent window on the current profusion of images, texts, and devotional groups; "Kateri Online" (www.tekakwitha.org) is a good point of entry.

16. Juliette Lavergne, *La vie gracieuse de Kateri Tekakwitha* (Montreal: Editions Albert Lévesque, 1934).

17. Fernando Bea, *Catarina Tekakwitha, prima Vergine Irochese* (Turin: Marietti, 1962).

18. Margaret Bunson and Matthew Bunson, *Kateri Tekakwitha* (Huntington, Ind.: Our Sunday Visitor Publishing, 1993), 8. On Tekakwitha as the patroness of the environment, see the "Catholic Online" Web site, www.catholic.org/saints/.

19. Christopher Vecsey, *The Paths of Kateri's Kin* (Notre Dame, Ind.: University of Notre Dame Press, 1997), 107–8.

20. See K. I. Koppedrayer, "The Making of the First Iroquois Virgin: Early Jesuit Biographies of the Blessed Kateri Tekakwitha," *Ethnohistory* 40 (Spring 1993): 278.

21. The quotation is from "Kateri's Miracle: Completing the Circle," program of the Fifty-ninth Annual Tekakwitha Conference, Memphis, Tennessee, August 1998. On the history of the Tekakwitha Conference, see Carl F. Starkloff, "Native Americans and the Catholic Church," in *The Encyclopedia of American Catholic History*, ed. Michael Glazier and Thomas J. Shelley (Collegeville, Minn.: Liturgical Press, 1997), 1018–19. On inculturation, see Paula Holmes, "'We Are Native Catholics': Inculturation and the Tekakwitha Conference," *Studies in Religion/Sciences Religieuses* 28 (1999): 153–74.

22. Paula Holmes, "Symbol Tales: Paths towards the Creation of a Saint" (Ph.D. diss., McMaster University, 2000), 190–202. My discussion of the native Tekakwitha movement is heavily dependent on Holmes's fine research and penetrating analysis.

23. Ibid., 192–94. On AIM, see also "Tekakwitha Conference 39th Annual Conference Proceedings," at the Tekakwitha Conference National Center, Great Falls, Montana.

24. Paula Holmes, "The Narrative Repatriation of Blessed Kateri Tekakwitha," *Anthropologica* 43 (2001): 95.

25. Holmes, "Symbol Tales," 232, 237–38.

26. See the "Testimonies of Favors Obtained" section in each issue of the quarterly magazine *Kateri: Lily of the Mohawks* (Kahnawake, Quebec).

27. Julia Kristeva, *Strangers to Ourselves*, trans. Leon Roudiez (New York: Columbia University Press, 1991).

28. Holmes, "Symbol Tales," 320.

Index

Abenakis, 27, 155
Albany (New York). *See* Fort Orange
Algonquins
  assimilated into Iroquois, 27
  enemy of Mohawks, 25, 29, 184
  Jesuit mission among, 82, 117
  in fur trade, 95–96, 98–99
Americans, Native
  cultivation of generic identity, 202–3
Apaches, 203, 205
Auriesville (New York)
  shrine to Tekakwitha at, 194

baptism
  Iroquois views of, 7, 52–53
  Jesuit practice of, 6–7, 8–9, 51–52,
    82, 107, 209nn6
Bordeaux
  Jesuit college of, 64, 67, 69
Brébeuf, Jean de, 6, 8, 23–24, 81–82,
  149, 191, 209n17
Bruyas, Jacques, 48, 50, 85, 91–93
Burtin, Nicholas, 197
  hagiography of Tekakwitha, 197–98

Canada
  contemporary, 200–1, 203
  French, 89, 92–93, 98–99, 109,
    114, 156, 180, 193, 198 (*see also*
    New France)

as place of self-sacrificing mission,
  59, 61, 82–86, 172
cannibalism
  in European colonial imagination,
    184–86 survival, 182–84,
    238n28
Caron, Claude, 151, 167
Catherine of Siena
  namesake of Tekakwitha, xi, 52–53,
    102, 197
  mysticism and self-denial of, 73,
    120, 122, 166
  struggle to preserve virginity, 46,
    175
Catholic. *See* Catholicism, European
Catholicism, European
  Counter-Reformation, 63–64, 109,
    139, 172–73, 227n42
  cult and culture of saints, 18, 22,
    148–50, 193
  in France, 64, 75, 110, 115, 142, 156
  sexuality in, 173–78, 189
Catholics, Native, 201–5
Cayugas, 11–12, 33, 93, 96, 118
celibacy, among women at
  Kahnawake, 140–42, 144, 174,
  181
Champigny, Madame de, 168
Charlevoix, Pierre-François-Xavier de,
  190